COACHING BASEBALL SUCCESSFULLY

Mike Curran

Ross Newhan

Human Kinetics

Library of Congress Cataloging-in-Publication Data

Curran, Mike, 1950-
  Coaching baseball successfully / Mike Curran, Ross Newhan.
    p. cm.
  Includes index.
  Rev. ed. of: Coaching baseball successfully / Andy Lopez with John Kirkgard. 1996.
  ISBN-13: 978-0-7360-6520-7 (soft cover)
  ISBN-10: 0-7360-6520-2 (soft cover)
  1. Baseball–Coaching. I. Newhan, Ross. II. Lopez, Andy, 1953- Coaching baseball successfully. III. Title.
  GV875.5.L67 2007
  796.35707–dc22
                        2006034295

ISBN-10: 0-7360-6520-2
ISBN-13: 978-0-7360-6520-7

Acquisitions Editor: Jason Muzinic; **Developmental Editor:** Kevin Matz; **Assistant Editor:** Laura Koritz; **Copyeditor:** Bob Replinger; **Proofreader:** Jim Burns; **Indexer:** Bobbi Swanson ; **Graphic Designer:** Nancy Rasmus; **Graphic Artist:** Francine Hamerski; **Photo Manager:** Laura Fitch; **Cover Designer:** Keith Blomberg; **Photographer (cover and interior):** Neil Burnstein, except for photos on pages 8, 160, 166, and 172 © Human Kinetics; **Art Manager:** Kelly Hendren; **Illustrator:** Denise Lowry; **Printer:** United Graphics

Human Kinetics books are available at special discounts for bulk purchase. Special editions or book excerpts can also be created to specification. For details, contact the Special Sales Manager at Human Kinetics.

Printed in the United States of America

10 9 8 7 6 5 4 3 2 1

Human Kinetics
Web site: www.HumanKinetics.com

United States: Human Kinetics
P.O. Box 5076
Champaign, IL 61825-5076
800-747-4457
e-mail: humank@hkusa.com

Canada: Human Kinetics
475 Devonshire Road Unit 100
Windsor, ON N8Y 2L5
800-465-7301 (in Canada only)
e-mail: orders@hkcanada.com

Europe: Human Kinetics
107 Bradford Road
Stanningley
Leeds LS28 6AT, United Kingdom
+44 (0) 113 255 5665
e-mail: hk@hkeurope.com

Australia: Human Kinetics
57A Price Avenue
Lower Mitcham, South Australia 5062
08 8372 0999
e-mail: liaw@hkaustralia.com

New Zealand: Human Kinetics
Division of Sports Distributors NZ Ltd.
P.O. Box 300 226 Albany
North Shore City
Auckland
0064 9 448 1207
e-mail: info@humankinetics.co.nz

COACHING BASEBALL
SUCCESSFULLY

CONTENTS

Part IV   Coaching Defense

Part V   Coaching Games

Part VI   Coaching Evaluation

FOREWORD

I have spent more than 45 years in baseball as a player, coach, and instructor, most recently traveling the world on behalf of Major League Baseball to teach the game to youngsters and help expand its global reach. I was fortunate as a player to collect more than 3,000 hits at the big league level, win seven American League batting titles, and be elected to the Hall of Fame. It's been a great ride, as they say, and the last 15 or so years have been enhanced by my friendship and working respect for Coach Curran.

I met Coach Curran while operating a hitting school for both amateur and professional players in the area of Esperanza High School, where he has produced one of the nation's most successful high school programs. I have since worked with him at his clinics and camps and developed a strong admiration for what he brings to coaching and how he imparts his knowledge.

While working with many coaches at various levels over the years I have seen many young players turned off to the game because of a lack of patience by their coaches and a tendency to punish mistakes rather than correct them through patience and encouragement. Sadly, too many coaches want to discourage rather than encourage. Too many coaches are set in their ways, even if those ways are proven to be unsuccessful.

Coach Curran knows what he is doing. His record documents it, and I have seen him at work. As a good teacher he brings the patience of the classroom to the ball field. He knows the game inside out, but he's not afraid to take advice. Despite his success he's always looking for more information, an important approach that he discusses in *Coaching Baseball Successfully*.

When I heard that Coach Curran was writing a book, I looked forward to the opportunity to read it, and it's all here, a valuable primer for coaches of all ages.

In *Coaching Baseball Successfully* Coach Curran lays out a championship foundation based on the teaching of skills and strategies, good philosophy, good practice and game coaching, the art of motivation, selecting staff, working with community leaders and school administrators, and making the right evaluations. Any serious and enthusiastic coach who respects the game, treats the ballpark as his office, and knows how to encourage players, while showing patience and making practice a fun event, should benefit even if he incorporates only three or four of the concepts recommended by Coach Curran.

This is a book designed to enlighten coaches at all levels, and that's what coaching is all about—the constant search to better understand a game that shows us something new every day and the constant search for better ways to pass that understanding on to players of all ages. In *Coaching Baseball Successfully* it's gift wrapped by a coach who understands.

Rod Carew
Hall of Fame hitter and batting instructor

PREFACE

I am writing this book to provide information about coaching the great game of baseball. This book is a working manual to help coaches increase their knowledge of the skills, strategies, and thought processes that are an integral part of the game.

Coaching Baseball Successfully will focus on three primary objectives. First, it will demonstrate how to build a successful baseball program by establishing a coaching philosophy, setting goals, and establishing team rules with players and assistants. Second, to teach the skills that are necessary to play each position, it will provide drills to develop the skills, and instruction for coordinating an efficient practice plan. Third, it will provide insight on how to strategically coach the game from offensive and defensive perspectives.

One of the responsibilities of coaching is teaching the fundamental skills of the game. Fundamental skills are essential to winning and the more your players practice, the better prepared they will be to react in game situations. This book will illustrate these principles with drills, photos, and diagrams to help the reader easily visualize the exact technique. Along with charts, tables, and checklists, you'll have the tools to easily put this information to use.

I have coached baseball for over 30 years at the high school level. I have been lucky enough to have coached some great teams, and even luckier to have taught some wonderful players. My goal with this book is to pass on some of the knowledge that has contributed to my success. My hope is that this information not only makes you a better coach but also increases your love for the great game of baseball.

Mike Curran

I became aware of Mike Curran and the success of his program at Esperanza High School when my daughter, Sara, was attending Esperanza in the mid- to late 80s and my son, David, was moving through Little League levels with a goal of playing for him. In the competitive environment of Southern California, Curran consistently took his teams deep into the playoffs, often winning league and sectional championships in the process. When David arrived and ultimately became a two year varsity starter in Mike Curran's program, I watched Curran mold a team that would be ranked number one in the country by USA Today by emphasizing fundamentals, discipline and aggressive play–often to a greater extent than many of the managers I have followed during 45 years of major league baseball coverage. Curran also recognizes the importance of strong parental and community involvement and spends considerable time building support on both levels. David came out of the Esperanza program to receive Division I scholarship offers, has since played at the major league level for San Diego, Philadelphia and Baltimore, and he credits the fundamentals he learned from Curran for providing a foundation on which he has since built. What young player wouldn't want to be schooled in that environment? What coach wouldn't want to study the technique? I'm glad to have worked with Mike on this book to help other coaches learn those techniques and use them to build successful baseball programs of their own.

Ross Newhan

KEY TO DIAGRAMS

P	Pitcher
C	Catcher
CO	Coach
1B	1st base player
2B	2nd base player
3B	3rd base player
SS	Shortstop
LF	Left fielder
CF	Center fielder
RF	Right fielder
B	Batter
R	Runner
U	Umpire
X	Any player, if position isn't applicable
⟶	Path of runner/fielder (solid line)
- - - - - - ▸	Path of hit/tossed ball (dashed line)
⋯⋯⋯⋯▸	Path of throw (dotted line)

Part I

COACHING FOUNDATION

CHAPTER 1
DEVELOPING A BASEBALL COACHING PHILOSOPHY

The first question that coaches usually ask when developing a program is, "Where do I start?" As a coach, you need to come up with a philosophy that conveys the style with which you want your teams to play. The philosophy that you implement can come from a number of sources, including, of course, your own experience and the programs and coaches whom you admire. After you have decided on a philosophy, you must then ask yourself, "How do I implement it? How do I translate my experiences into a message that my players can relate to? How do I get them to perform like the teams whose coaches I admire?" You do this by building a philosophy and consistently accomplishing established goals. You want to develop a personality your team can interact with. You need to have your players buy into your philosophy and understand what they can accomplish by following it.

DEFINING YOUR PHILOSOPHY

When I started coaching I had to develop my own philosophy. I was hired as a varsity baseball coach at St. Paul High School in Santa Fe Springs, California. I had never coached a sport in my life and, at 23 years old, I was taking over a baseball program that had a losing record the year before

and no direction. I would spend six years teaching and coaching at St. Paul, and during that time we won four league championships, three in my first three years of coaching. We qualified for the playoffs all six years. My philosophy was not developed from any coaching experience I had, because I had none. I looked back at all the coaches I had been exposed to and the ones for whom I really enjoyed playing. Why did I like playing for them? What style did I like to play?

After contemplating these two questions, I began to develop a philosophy in my first season. I was not afraid or intimidated by this seemingly daunting task; rather, I was excited by the challenge. At the time I didn't know that 30 years later I would still be coaching baseball and would have compiled a record that included a national championship, three California Interscholastic Federation (CIF) Championships, six final-game appearances in the CIF playoffs, and 14 league championships.

The coach who is starting to develop his own philosophy must remember that baseball is not always the number one priority with today's players—and it shouldn't be. Family, church, and school are three things that should always come before any sport. When the player takes care of each of these properly, then baseball can help complete the picture. A sound philosophy will help your high school athletes understand where baseball fits into their lives.

That philosophy, of course, should start with a commitment of time and energy—by the players when they are in uniform and by the coach and his staff, in and out of uniform. The commitment of time and energy by coaches and players should be reflected in the attitude and pride that they exhibit at practice and at games, and in the quality of their daily work ethic.

Your players and assistant coaches must accept these concepts at every level, and you must make sure that they do this without exception.

The philosophy that you implement should come from the programs or coaches you respect, from your personal experiences, and from what motivated you to become a coach in the first place. How do I get my players to perform in the manner of the coaches I admire? You take the approach, ideas, and personality that you want your teams to play with and you incorporate them into a philosophy that should coincide with how you want to accomplish your goals. You need to have your players buy into your philosophy and understand why you are using it and what can be accomplished by using it.

Successful companies in our country develop a philosophy by identifying the qualities that they want to display. Southwest Airlines is a successful company in an extremely competitive field. Their company philosophy focuses on low fares, being on time, and making flying fun. The first two traits are obviously important to success in business. The third relates to the amusing way in which their flight attendants read their rules before takeoff. By having fun at their jobs, they help customers relax. This philosophy defines Southwest Airlines.

A coach should consider the following points when developing a philosophy:

1. A coach wants his players to be ready to commit both time and energy.
2. A coach should have the attitude that he can continually learn something about this game and then put that mind-set into action.
3. A coach wants his players always to play to the best of their ability in both practice and games.
4. A coach's philosophy should come from the programs or coaches he respects.

Why Coach?

Before you are able to develop a philosophy you need to ask yourself, "Why am I getting involved in this game?" The answer should never be for the money. People want to coach and want to be successful at it for a number of reasons. We should all start with a sincere love for the game. A good coach is addicted to the game of baseball. He watches it, analyzes it, dissects each play. He takes that information and passes it on to his players as a motivational tool or learning drill. Watch the College World Series and document how those teams execute a squeeze, a hit-and-run, a double steal. Note how they come up with the game-winning hit. In time you will find a way to interpret those actions for your own players, no matter the level.

An inexperienced 23-year-old teaching and coaching at a high school, can be in for a tough time, as I was when I first started. I'm not sure why I did not feel any personal pressure that first year; perhaps I was preoccupied with the pressure of turning my baseball program into a success. I was only five years older than my senior players, but I never had a problem with any of them because they embraced the concept and philosophy that I introduced. They finally had a coach who was teaching them baseball skills and had a specific approach to how they could improve. Their buying into my program was a subtle but tremendous boost in my development as a coach, although I don't think I realized it at the time.

Many good players become good coaches, but you do not need to be a great player to be a great coach. To be a great coach, you must be a good teacher.

Use Your Experiences

When I look back on my playing career, I recognize that I was never a great player. On some of the teams that I played on, I wasn't even able to make the starting lineup.

I grew up in Whittier, California, and went to grade school in the city of Pico Rivera, which had a large Hispanic population. Baseball was popular and competitive. The city had some tough kids, but that didn't bother me. I think that this environment worked for me. I was able to get street smart and tough skinned at the same time. When you played Little League baseball, you signed up and tried out for a specific team. If you didn't make that team, you would be placed on another. I found out about competition in fifth grade. I tried out for the Termites, a new team that included some of the best players in the city, many of them my close friends. The last day before they gave out uniforms, the coach called me over and told me that I hadn't made the team. He was as nice as he could be, but I knew that the bottom line was that he didn't think I was good enough. Of course, I felt I was as good as a couple of the guys they were keeping, but that didn't matter.

Whenever a player gets cut from a team, it's a shock, and my being cut had a big effect on me later in life. As a high school coach I have to cut players from my program every year. Personally, because of my experiences, this is a painful part of coaching. Having had the experience of being cut, I feel for these players. I know how much they want to play, but we have to get down to the desired number. Still, a coach can make those cuts compassionately.

The interesting part of my story is that after being cut by the Termites, I was put on a team of players I didn't know at all. I made some great friendships and was an all-star in each of the next two years. This turned out to be a positive experience for me as I continued to play baseball in Pico Rivera before attending St. Paul, the school that would later hire me for that first coaching job. I found out, as any athlete does, that the competition in high school is much more intense than it is in grade school or junior high. The class that I came in with and graduated with was talented in both football and baseball—the two sports that I played in high school. As a senior we were voted the number one team in California in football, and in baseball, where I generally played, we lost a 2-1 game in the California Division Championship game.

The experience and success that I enjoyed while being part of those teams made me want to stay in the game, and later I realized that I could continue to have all those positive experiences in the coaching field.

People ask, "When did you decide you wanted to coach, what made you want to get into coaching, and what was it that made you feel this was the right profession?" Thirty years later, still coaching, I have no easy answers. I stepped back

and concluded that coaching was in my blood. It was just something that I've always done.

When we would pick captains for our playground games when I was in grade school, I always wanted to be the captain. I wanted to be the one who directed the action, the one in control. I wanted to be able to use the strategy to say, here's the lineup, here's the things we're going to do—all the things that later would become part of coaching. And this sort of organizing was something that was fun for me even then. I would take just two bites out of my sandwich and run out at lunch so that I had the full time to play and organize the teams. On holidays I would invite everyone over to my house, and my brother Pat would do the same. We'd try to get 15 to 18 guys over, beg my mom to pack a lunch, and go down to school and play baseball all day. I was always pleading to be the captain.

Before I got my first coaching job, I played in an adult football league, and I would organize the offense. I never thought of myself as a football coach in those days. I was just trying to draw things up, to organize things. I'd call all the guys and tell them that we've got a game in this adult league and be sure that you're there. If we had a guy who was a flake, I'd go by and pick him up at his house to make sure that he got there. We ended up winning the championship. We won because we got all our guys together. I felt good about the fact that I was organizing it, and it was fun to direct the guys, to have them listen when I talked. I thought, this is cool, this is what I'd like to do. That experience was one of my first tastes of coaching, without my being declared the coach, and it was something that stayed with me.

When I reflect and put all those experiences together, when I look at them in that way, I can understand how I was led in the direction of a coaching career and why I've stayed with it. I know that everyone doesn't have the same story that I have. So you come back to the question, "Why coach?" The answer lies in each person and what motivated him. For everyone it starts with the love of the game of baseball. From there, it usually involves a positive experience that happened in relation to the game—playing on a championship team or just playing with a great group of guys. The influence of someone special related to baseball can also be the motivating force that gets a person into coaching. Still another could be the reason that I coach: Without realizing it, I just always wanted to be a coach.

Learn From Others

The coaching profession, of course, has many different personalities working at every level. Some coaches have had tremendous success in their sport. All good coaches have borrowed drills, techniques, plays, and other parts of the game to put together their own programs. Good coaches want to hear and talk to others to increase their knowledge of the game. The inspiration to coach and the desire to improve as a coach come from those in the field who have had success and, perhaps, those who have had a personal influence.

Following high school I went to Rio Hondo Community College. I played baseball there for two years before transferring to Cal Poly Pomona. I was never a regular starter at Rio Hondo, and I played at Cal Poly for only one quarter before I realized that my career was over and that I needed to concentrate on getting my degree. My coach at Rio Hondo, Al Verdun, was an inspiration. He broke the game down and covered each technique. Having no assistant coaches, he put in long hours both on and off the field. We practiced seven days a week. Al had a great work ethic, a desire to help us succeed. That was my first exposure to what I would call a baseball man, someone who was all about baseball. All my previous coaches were basically football coaches who coached baseball or they were parents who helped out as coaches.

I entered Cal Poly Pomona as a junior in class standing and a second baseman. I was slow, had a weak arm, and couldn't hit—a bad combination. The coach was John Scolinos, an outstanding teacher and mentor, a legend among Southern California college coaches, and now in the college coaches' Hall of Fame. I knew that I could not compete with the players around me and would not be part of that team, but I continued playing in the fall to learn from this man.

Coach Scolinos would coach technique by making sure that his players were always aware of the possibilities on each play and were always looking for that one possibility, or more, to occur. On a ground ball, for instance, he would make sure that his players were aware of the various potential hops, knowledge that made it easier to field the ball with confidence. When we hit, depending on the count and the score, he schooled us on what our approach should be. His pitchers attacked hitters from the same basis. Offensively, he continually talked about putting pressure on the defense.

Coach Scolinos explained this approach well, with a style of his own. He had numerous stories to back up his points, and this method made him a great teacher. I have heard him speak at many clinics and have had him speak at my own clinics. This man could teach and get his point across better than anyone. Crossing paths with him was a major boost in my subsequent coaching career because I was not exposed to as many coaches as a person who plays all four years of major college ball, signs a pro contract, and then moves up through several seasons in the minor leagues, possibly reaching the majors. At each level that player is exposed to a variety of coaches who can have an influence on him.

I did not have that advantage. But I was able to take from my youth league, high school, and two college coaches some outstanding qualities that I have incorporated into my coaching philosophy. I am not exactly like any of my coaches, but I have a little bit of each of them in me. And as I've progressed through the years I've made it a point to study the top coaches in my profession at the high school, college, and professional levels. I wanted to learn from the best.

When I finished my first year of coaching, I asked people in the business who they thought had the best baseball program at the high school level. Everyone I talked to pointed to Lakewood High School and their successful coach, John Herbold. I began to make the 30-mile drive to Lakewood to watch Coach Herbold's team play. They played quite a few night games, which made it easy for me to get there after my games. I stood behind his dugout and watched his style and the play of his team. His teams were not only talented but also well coached and fundamentally sound. Coach Herbold was extremely vocal and many times critical of his players. I did not use that part of his often innovative approach, but I did try to get my players to display the confidence and aggressiveness that his teams did. His teams at Lakewood took the field ready to play the game in all aspects. Fundamentally, they were excellent in every way—fielding, hitting, pitching, and running the bases. His players' confidence was evident. They knew that they were going to win. To defeat his teams, the opponent would have to be both fundamentally sharp and mentally tough. John Herbold always had his teams ready to play. I had seen what I needed to see to get my program to a winning level. My philosophy and goal from then on was to get to the level of those Lakewood High teams of the 1970s. Because I made those drives to Lakewood, I knew how my teams needed to improve and the areas in which my philosophy needed to change.

By this time, whenever I talked with a college coach, I was thinking of questions that I could ask to help me improve my teams. My school, Esperanza High School in Anaheim, California, is close to Cal State Fullerton University, which has one of the nation's top baseball programs. When Augie Garrido, now at the University of Texas, was the Fullerton coach, I would take my staff to one of his practices to see what he was doing and what I needed to change or improve. George Horton followed Garrido at Fullerton, and he has maintained the program. Horton is an outstanding coach. I try to get to his practices and games to improve my program. I noticed how both of these great coaches spent a lot of time on detail and the fundamentals. They also conducted their practices and drills at full speed. This attention to detail was evident in the success that their teams enjoyed, but I feel that a coach gets inspired and educated from all the positive coaches he is exposed to—whether their teams are always winning or simply playing the game right.

What Do You Want To Accomplish?

I have certain absolutes that I am trying to accomplish with my team every year. The main goal of that philosophy is to get each player to perform to the best of his ability. I want my players to know that if they play as a team to the best of their ability and we lose, that's not a problem. We did the best that we could do. I enjoy winning as much as anyone, but I learned

early in my career at Esperanza that the game of baseball is only that—a game. In 1983, my third year as a varsity coach at Esperanza, the school had never won a championship in baseball and had never been to the playoffs. We had the best year in the history of the school that year, finished third in league, and qualified for the playoffs. We drew Garden Grove High School, a league champion, in the first round. We played an excellent game and shut them out 6-0, to advance to the second round. As we got off the bus I reminded our players that we would practice the next morning, Saturday, at 9:00 a.m. My center fielder and second baseman were twins, and they approached to tell me that their sister was going to make her first communion the next day and asked whether they could miss practice to attend. Because this event was all about family and religion, I had no problem allowing them to skip.

"I'll see you Monday," I told them. The next day one of our players showed up at practice and told me that the twins' older brother had been killed the night before in a car accident. This tragedy, of course, was a major shock to everyone and devastating to the two young men and their family. The funeral was scheduled for the day of our next playoff game. With a tragedy of this kind I had no rules to go by. Here I was with a team that had won the first playoff game in school history and was scheduled to play the next round against another league champion on the day that two of my starting players would be attending a funeral for their brother. Neither of these players had practiced for almost a week. All my players would attend the funeral. I had always had a rule that if you didn't show to practice the day before a game, you didn't start at your position on game day. But for me this particular situation was a no-brainer. I told the twins that if they wanted to sit out the game or not attend, that was fine with me. What they were dealing with made baseball trivial in comparison. But I also told them that if they showed up, dressed out, and wanted to play, they would be in the starting lineup. Both played, and we lost to a team that advanced to the finals. It was a tough loss, but, like my players, I wasn't thinking about myself or baseball. We were all thinking about the twins and their brother. This story shows that coaches must be able to bend their philosophy, change their rules, and adjust for situations that make the game seem unimportant by comparison. It's not life or death. A coach who shows his compassion and understanding in difficult personal matters can provide a positive influence for his players.

A coach always wants to have his players focus on team goals, but when a personal issue involving family intervenes, especially the loss of a loved one, a coach needs to be the leader and understand that family always comes first.

I think this story illustrates what we as coaches are trying to accomplish. We want our players to improve and become successful in baseball. All our energy, drills, tasks, and games are geared to this goal, but we must remember it's a game. Treat it as a game.

DEVELOPING A TEAM PHILOSOPHY

You as a coach need to establish the team philosophy—the way that you want your team to think and perform. Naturally, the team philosophy will arise directly from the coach's philosophy. You should direct your players' attitude in your talks with the team and in their practice and play.

Now what do you want your team's identity to be? You must identify the important attributes. I like an up-tempo style in which the players and coaches are enthusiastic and perform with energy. The games are the stage on which you illustrate your style. Your team should do everything at full speed, and the players should continually encourage one another throughout the game. This is a fun way to play the game, and at the same time it can be intimidating to an opponent. An up-tempo game brings out a positive attitude in your players and an aggressive approach.

What do I mean by up-tempo? Your players practice and play the game at maximum speed. They run 90 feet at full speed, whether they hit a ground ball back to the pitcher or a clean single to the outfield. They sprint to their positions on the field and come off the field in the same way. They play the game hard because they practice hard. You as the coach must make sure that they perform in that way.

Hustle in, hustle out. An up-tempo game keeps players motivated and enthusiastic

You also need to identify your philosophy in relation to how you want your players to act during a game. I tell my players to be vocal and positive in rooting for their teammates. I do not want them to say anything to the opposition—good or bad. They focus on themselves and do not let their opponents affect them—either by mouth or performance.

We have a strong policy with our players that their language must always be under control. We do not allow the use of cussing or foul language in practice or games. If a player breaks that policy in a game, we pull him immediately. If it happens in practice, we send him to the clubhouse and he is done for the day. I don't tolerate foul language because it represents a breakdown in poise and class and shows an opponent that the player has lost his grip. As a player, you need to be able to control the things that you have control over. We constantly communicate that message, emphasizing to our players the importance of maintaining class and poise. Self-control is a key component of our philosophy, and hustle is a key component of our up-tempo game.

We talk to our players about situations that involve poise and pride—in themselves and in the program. We cover many aspects, including pride in their equipment and pride in the home field. Our pitchers rake the mound, our infielders rake their respective areas, and our outfielders check before every game to make sure that the playing surface contains no rocks or divots. It's no different from players' making their beds at home. They keep their areas neat, showing pride.

We do not let our guys break bats, throw gloves around, or leave equipment on the field when practice ends. We count our baseballs every day before and after practice. We hit with certain balls during batting practice, and we count them before and after hitting to make sure that we still have them all. If a ball is missing, having been fouled out of the field area, the player who hit it goes after it. The player knows who he is and what his obligation is because we consistently remind the players about the policy. Communication is important. We seldom leave the field with balls having been lost.

Ultimately the head coach alone decides what objectives his team will have, and it is his responsibility to make sure those objectives are achieved.

ESTABLISHING OBJECTIVES FOR COACHES AND PLAYERS

You need to establish and reinforce your objectives and those that you would like your team to have. A coach usually has a list of objectives that he would like his team to strive for or that he himself wants to achieve. The objectives of his players may be more immediate and not as far into the future, but the coach should still have his players understand and work for his goals.

The coach's objectives might start with what he would like to see in the improvement of his team and their record. The coach may have an objective to turn his program around. He may have inherited a losing program and want to get the team back on track with a winning record. Other coaches may have the objective of keeping a winning program on the same course. Some coaches have a goal of moving to a higher

level of coaching in a set number of years. A high school coach may give himself three to five years to move to a college or community college job. An assistant coach may have the goal to become a head coach after a certain amount of time. These are common objectives that coaches set for themselves.

A coach may have a range of objectives for his team. The goal could be to change the behavior of an undisciplined team or improve the fundamentals of a team that executes poorly. A coach may challenge his team to improve their record from the previous year, to win a championship, or to make the playoffs. A coach can set daily objectives for his team by calling the players together every day of practice and telling them what their goals are for that day. The preceding are some of the objectives and ideas that a coach can have for himself and his players. The coach must decide which of them work best into his philosophy.

Coaches' Keys

1. Select a philosophy that fits your personality. But whether you are low key or high energy, you want your team to play up-tempo.

2. Observe and learn from coaches whose programs and style you respect and would like to incorporate into your own. Read about coaches you respect and enjoy. Go to practices and games to see the coaches you would like to emulate. Combine the qualities of coaches who have always been successful.

3. Be willing to change or adjust your philosophy if needed. You must be ready to change some rules and actions if they apply to personal or life-changing events. Baseball should not be the most important thing in a player's life, but it should be the most important thing when he steps on the field.

4. Follow your passion. You must be able to direct your players as their coach. Know that coaching is what you want to do, that it's your profession and love. Then jump in with both feet. Your players will feel your enthusiasm and dedication.

CHAPTER 2 COMMUNICATING YOUR APPROACH

Communication is the key to everything in life—baseball and otherwise. For a coach, communication is essential. After developing a philosophy, you must ask yourself three questions:

1. How am I going to approach my team?
2. How do I want my team to play?
3. What attitude do I want my team to have when they play?

The obvious step after establishing your philosophy is to communicate it to your team so that everyone is on the same page—players, assistant coaches, and parents.

The first people to discuss your philosophy with are your assistant coaches. Then, of course, you must make sure that your players understand it. Besides reaching these two important groups, you want to be sure that parents understand your philosophy and, if you are coaching at a high school or college, that your fellow teachers and administrators comprehend your direction so that you have their support, which can only benefit the program. You should continually talk about your philosophy with all these groups, making it clear what you are trying to accomplish and why you believe that you must do things in a certain way to achieve success for your program. If you blindside your parents and school administrators, it can only spell trouble.

COMMUNICATING WITH YOUR ASSISTANT COACHES

The first people you need to communicate your philosophy to are your assistant coaches. You have personally hired these people. They will control your team if you are not present, and you will delegate a measure of authority to them. If you are coaching a travel ball team or Little League team, you may only have one assistant coach. If you are coaching at the high school level or in a situation where you have control over multiple teams (varsity, junior varsity, freshman), then you have a number of coaches who not only need to understand your philosophy but also need to be able to communicate it and implement it at those multiple levels. Consistency is important because players at the lower levels who may eventually work their way up to varsity need to understand how the program functions. Your lower-level coaches must be adept at communicating with players. Coaches should talk about the philosophy every day after practice and before their teams take the field. As the head coach you should discuss your philosophy with your assistant coaches when you interview them for an opening. They need to know what kind of game you like, how you work with players, and your overall ethic and philosophy. They must know before you hire them what you are trying to do with your program, and they must understand and believe in the philosophy.

It's important to communicate with your assistant coaches to ensure that your goals are consistent.

Meetings

I meet with my assistants on the varsity level every day after practice to go over the practice plan for the next day. In these meetings we discuss how our players did that day and note who is getting better and who is getting worse. We have many coaches' meetings at Esperanza. Some are formal; others are informal. After a game we all go out to eat and talk about our performance that day. If a kid is not hustling at the level we want or not performing with a positive attitude, we discuss what we need to do to

change that behavior, perhaps by changing the lineup or making some other alteration.

Delegating Responsibility to Assistant Coaches

I also ask each of my coaches to take initiative with the guys they are coaching at their positions. For instance, my outfield coach often talks with the outfielders about their technique and approach at practice instead of having me talk to them. Because he is the one working with the outfielders every day, he is the person who should talk to them if they're not hustling or not using proper technique. Sometimes as a coach you will have a player who thinks he's better than everyone else and doesn't need to work as hard. As the head coach I can easily tell them that they need to start working harder to get better. But I want my assistant coaches to be able to do that as well. I want them to be able to talk with their guys and let them know what they need to do. I also want them to have some sense of responsibility for their players and a feeling of ownership in the program. They should feel as if they are in charge of their area of expertise. By giving them the authority to communicate your philosophy, you enhance your assistants' prestige and give them a bigger role in the success of the program.

As they watch games or practices, my assistant coaches should be thinking about how they would handle situations that develop. The last thing I want are assistant coaches who are not focused, not thinking a step ahead, capable only of running drills. I want them to be able to take on additional responsibilities.

Over the years I have lost a number of coaches to head coaching or scouting jobs because they are assertive and have become good at communicating as a coach. As a result, they are ready to move on to the next level as a head coach or college assistant. I don't have any problems with my assistant coaches leaving my program to take a head coaching job elsewhere. I am happy for them when they reach a point where they want to take on a new challenge. In addition, when they move into a head coaching position or a higher level of play, they take a part of my philosophy with them to their new teams, and seeing that occur is rewarding.

This Is How We Do It

As I wrote earlier, I like an up-tempo philosophy, and I have my coaches implement that philosophy. One of the drills that we use in practice to reinforce our philosophy is to have our players play catch at an up-beat tempo. When a player misses a ball and it goes by him, he does not go to get it. Instead, the player across from him, the player who threw the ball, runs to get it and the two players switch places. This little bit of running sharpens the players' focus on making accurate throws and catches. One year we had a freshman coach who did not implement this drill, deciding simply that he didn't like it. I pulled him aside and said, "We use this drill at every level, and I want all my players to know how to use it when they get to varsity." I also told him, "Not only do I want you to use this drill, but I also want you to watch your players closely to make sure they're using it correctly." I wanted to be certain that this lower-level coach used the drills that promoted better skills and maintained the continuity of the program at his level.

You should also be aware of the fact that your assistant coaches are the sounding board for your players. Because your assistants are constantly working with a certain group of players, the players will often approach them with their concerns rather than speak with you. But before your players talk with your assistant coaches, you want to be certain that you and your assistant coaches are on the same page in terms of the approach to take with players. When assistant coaches have to deal with problems or handle situations, they should handle them in the same way that the head coach would. Your assistants may not completely agree with your philosophy and may communicate it to your players in a negative manner. As a result, practices may not be run exactly to your liking. If this happens, you must step in, sit the coach down, and talk through it. You may at times have to convince them that the way you want things done is the right way. If a coach continues to resist implementing your philosophy and you have continual disagreements, you will eventually have to let him go. You may find yourself in a situation in which you have a conflict with a coach that you can't

deal with right away, and you will have to let him finish the season instead of asking him to leave on the spot. Naturally, I would always rather resolve a disagreement amiably. I always want to head off problems before they mushroom into something major. My thinking has always been to find good assistants who can communicate my philosophy, and then give them space and let them coach.

Being based in California, we can't do much physically on a rainy day. Many high schools in the Midwest and East have facilities that accommodate their baseball teams during inclement weather. At schools where indoor facilities are not readily available, rainy days provide an excellent opportunity for coaches to talk with their players about their philosophy on an individual level. Usually we do not get more than 10 rainy days a year, so this strategy may not work as well in regions that get more precipitation. But on rainy days at Esperanza, we break our team into groups and our coaches talk with them about goals that they want them to accomplish that season or other topics related to their positions.

We often bring up our philosophy in relation to these goals and techniques. For example, the pitching coach will talk to his pitchers about the way that we want them to pitch and the way that we want them to approach their position. Everything from technique to attitude is discussed. I often have each coach take his group to a different room to eliminate distractions. For example, my pitching coach may talk to the pitchers in our clubhouse, and my hitting coach may take the hitters to my classroom. I walk through each room throughout the period and listen to each coach, making sure that he is prepared and communicative. By doing this, I can make sure that the coaches are effectively relaying our philosophy. If they can communicate it, talk about it, and explain it, then they're the type of assistants we want.

The day before every league game we have our pitching coach go over the scouting report of our opponent with our pitchers. During this time he will either have them look at a video of the team that we're going to play or talk about their lineup. At this time we form a plan about how we are going to pitch. We talk not only about how we are going to pitch to certain players but also about which hitter or hitters we don't want to beat us. Our pitching coach needs to make sure that the pitchers know who these key players are, and he must effectively communicate the philosophy that we are going to use in the game. Over the years my pitching coaches have done a good job of getting this point across.

You should always encourage your coaches to have pride in their roles and to be possessive of their responsibilities. But you do not want to encourage them to the point that you, as the head coach, are not able to make a final decision. You always must be in control of the program, and your assistant coaches should be helping you implement your standards. They should not be working against you or trying to gain control of your players by turning them against you.

Coaches' Clinics

Besides having meetings, we also attend a number of coaching clinics as a staff. We won't always listen to every speaker at a convention, but I want my coaches to hear certain talks. Many times these talks have to do with philosophy or with their particular coaching assignments.

The two national coaching associations are the BCA (National High School Baseball Coaches Association) for high school baseball coaches and the ABCA (American Baseball Coaches Association), which is the association for high school and college coaches. Both associations welcome any Little League or amateur coach. At these clinics, high school, college, and major league coaches speak on various topics related to coaching baseball.

I have my staff attend the meetings and clinics that we feel are valuable. For instance, my pitching coach listens to talks on pitching, my hitting coach listens to hitting talks, and my infield coach listens to talks on infield play.

When you find assistant coaches who understand and accept your philosophy, you will find them essential in helping reinforce the team and program philosophy.

COMMUNICATING WITH YOUR PLAYERS

After programming your assistant coaches, you must ensure that your players understand what you are trying to accomplish. After all, they are the ones who play the game. Again, communication is critical. The players must understand how you want then to play the game and how you expect them to act on the field.

When watching teams play, I always notice whether guys are walking on and off the field. If most of the team is hustling and one guy is walking, that one guy definitely stands out. You do not want your players to develop a reputation for being lazy, pouting, or throwing their bats and helmets when they strike out. To prevent it, you need to make sure that you have communicated your philosophy to your players, and you must continually reinforce your rules and disciplines. At Esperanza we communicate our philosophy through several avenues, such

Talk to your players frequently to let them know what your expectations are.

as having meetings, telling stories, and posting sayings on our clubhouse bulletin board.

Using Motivational Quotes

One of my favorite sayings involves a Ted Williams quote. A reporter asked him, "What would you do differently if you could play the game again?" He replied, "I'd hit more." We ask our guys, "What does this mean?" It means that the last .400 hitter, one of the greatest hitters in baseball history, wasn't satisfied. If Ted Williams, a Hall of Fame hitter, believes that he could have enhanced his career and accomplished more than he did by working even harder, then a high school or college player has no excuse not to give a similar effort. We try to put up a new quote on the bulletin board every week. Some of them are not by baseball players. For example, we use this quote from Hall of Fame football coach Vince Lombardi: "Fatigue makes cowards of us all."

Using Handouts

We also use handouts to get our philosophy across. I'm a big fan of John Wooden, the great UCLA basketball coach, and all that he accomplished. At an early point in my coaching career I bought a book he wrote titled *They Call Me Coach*. The book centers on his philosophy, which he calls the pyramid of success (figure 2.1). The qualities composing the pyramid are all easily incorporated into any coaching program—dedication, determination, and hard work.

At Esperanza we spend a day or two discussing the pyramid with our players. Each receives a copy of it, and I tell them to post it in their room at home or locker at school, and to review it before practices and games. Some have told me that they put it on the door of their bedroom where they can see it several times a day. That kind of thing really makes you feel good as a coach because you know then that you're getting your point across, that your communication is running deep.

Team Meetings

The team meeting is another tool that we have found useful in communicating our philosophy. During these meetings we communicate both good and bad examples of observed behavior and reinforce how we want them to act. You want to be sure that your players perform in accordance with your philosophy.

Baseball is a sport in which even the best hitters fail 7 times out of 10. As part of our communication program we frequently talk to the players about learning to deal with the negatives and developing a bulldog personality. Over time we've learned that the only players who survive and find a way to go on with baseball after high school and college are those who have learned to cope with failure. No other sport holds you more accountable.

Individual Meetings

We also have individual meetings with our players before the season to discuss philosophy, concepts, where they stand, and what we expect from them. We might ask a player who looks as if he fits a backup role whether he can be comfortable and positive in that situation or whether he is going to become frustrated. Does he think that it might be better to walk away from the game if that is his role?

When the player comes into the meeting he is seated so that he is facing all the varsity coaches. He sits down, and I usually direct his immediate coach to start by telling us what he has done well and poorly and what he needs to work on. The other coach or coaches can add to that. I then address how we would like him to improve his game, attitude, approach, or whatever needs to change. We also reinforce the positive things that the player does.

We have interviews after the season as well to meet with the players who will be returning to discuss the areas in which they need to improve. The whole idea is basic reinforcement, and it can happen only with a consistent, multifaceted program of communication. Ultimately, when we see our players going hard or acting in accordance with our philosophy, we like to reward them, building a foundation at the lower levels of our program. At our postseason banquets we do not give an award for most valuable player on the frosh or junior varsity teams. Instead, we give coach's awards for the players who best executed our philosophy or demonstrated the best attitude over the course of the year. These players are the ultimate team

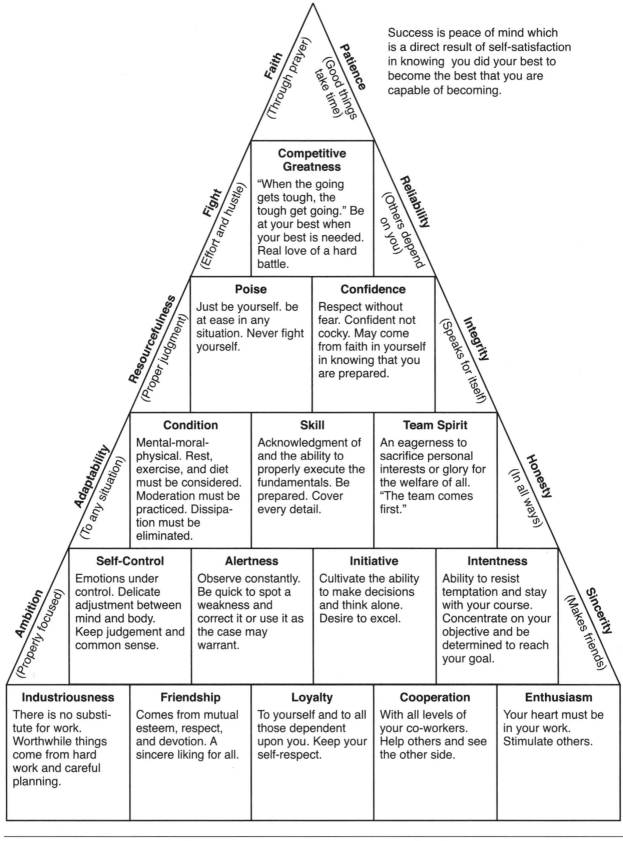

Success is peace of mind which is a direct result of self-satisfaction in knowing you did your best to become the best that you are capable of becoming.

Faith (Through prayer)
Patience (Good things take time)
Fight (Effort and hustle)
Reliability (Others depend on you)
Resourcefulness (Proper judgment)
Integrity (Speaks for itself)
Adaptability (To any situation)
Honesty (In all ways)
Ambition (Properly focused)
Sincerity (Makes friends)

Competitive Greatness
"When the going gets tough, the tough get going." Be at your best when your best is needed. Real love of a hard battle.

Poise
Just be yourself. be at ease in any situation. Never fight yourself.

Confidence
Respect without fear. Confident not cocky. May come from faith in yourself in knowing that you are prepared.

Condition
Mental-moral-physical. Rest, exercise, and diet must be considered. Moderation must be practiced. Dissipation must be eliminated.

Skill
Acknowledgment of and the ability to properly execute the fundamentals. Be prepared. Cover every detail.

Team Spirit
An eagerness to sacrifice personal interests or glory for the welfare of all. "The team comes first."

Self-Control
Emotions under control. Delicate adjustment between mind and body. Keep judgement and common sense.

Alertness
Observe constantly. Be quick to spot a weakness and correct it or use it as the case may warrant.

Initiative
Cultivate the ability to make decisions and think alone. Desire to excel.

Intentness
Ability to resist temptation and stay with your course. Concentrate on your objective and be determined to reach your goal.

Industriousness
There is no substitute for work. Worthwhile things come from hard work and careful planning.

Friendship
Comes from mutual esteem, respect, and devotion. A sincere liking for all.

Loyalty
To yourself and to all those dependent upon you. Keep your self-respect.

Cooperation
With all levels of your co-workers. Help others and see the other side.

Enthusiasm
Your heart must be in your work. Stimulate others.

Figure 2.1 The pyramid of success.

Reprinted courtesy of John Wooden and CoachJohnWooden.com.

players, and we make sure to recognize them. We do the same at the varsity level with an award for most improved and what we call the Bulldog award for the player who best typifies that personality.

Get That Hair Cut!

During my first year coaching, I always had an eye out for potential players and was directed to a sophomore basketball player named Andy Rincon, who I was told had been a dominant pitcher in Little League. I asked him if he would come out for baseball. He asked if he would have to get his hair cut, and I told him that he would—off the ears and off the collar. He reported that first week with his hair borderline but I gave him a little leeway until the weekend. He was a cocky kid, and I started him on Friday against a team that had dominated us in the past, figuring that he'd get knocked down to size. All he did was throw five shutout innings, and we won 7-0. I knew I had something special, but I reminded him that he needed to get a haircut over the weekend.

Naturally, on Monday he showed up without one, and I immediately instructed him to bring me his uniform. I told him that he wouldn't get it back until his hair had been cut. He left in a foul mood but was back 10 minutes later with a terrible trim, but one that satisfied our rules. A football coach who had overheard our discussion told Rincon that he wouldn't let him quit and provided the trim. Rincon ultimately became a three-time league MVP and area Player of the Year as a senior. I probably wouldn't have won a league title in my first three years at St. Paul if it hadn't been for a kid on the verge of quitting, but I had a rule and my players had to observe it.

Rincon later pitched for the St. Louis Cardinals. This story illustrates how important communication and the reinforcement of it are. You function as a unit—no exceptions and no matter what is at stake. Ultimately, I've found that players understand the commitment in time, energy, and emotion that a coach makes to them and his program and they rally behind it.

You are out there alone, but you are also part of a team, and we like to end every practice by talking about those components of our philosophy. We talk to our players about how to deal with each of their teammates, about their conduct with each other, emphasizing the team aspect. We discuss the problems created by "locker room lawyers," players who are always complaining. If our players see this happening we tell them that they need to put a stop to it and not allow negative behavior to destroy the culture. They need to back the team philosophy. Nor do we tolerate double standards. We have rules regarding appearance and hair length because we believe that uniformity reinforces the team concept.

COMMUNICATING WITH OTHERS

As the head coach, most of your communications will be with your staff and players. Sometimes, however, you will find it necessary to communicate with people outside of your team, like parents, teachers and administrators, umpires, and the media. Learning to communicate smoothly with everyone ensures support for your team.

Communicating With Parents

One last thing that has become increasingly important in communicating with the players is the need to talk to them about handling their parents. Obviously, parents don't have the same understanding of our philosophy as the players do, and we want our players to be able to explain to their parents what our expectations are and why we are handling situations the way we do. Parents can be negative, thinking only of their sons. Naturally, they just want what they think is best for their children, but situations can fester at home, spilling into the clubhouse. The dinner table can become the sounding board for parents to discuss their frustrations and opinions of their son, and we try to prepare our players to cope with it, hopeful that they are willing to explain our philosophy and the drive behind it. How do we do that? As with other issues, we use handouts, team meetings, and individual sessions with players—and not just at the beginning and end of the season. Communication is an ongoing process.

Aside from preparing players to deal with their parents, the coach himself must be prepared to communicate with parents. I have been coaching for more than 30 years. Over that time, dealing with parents has become tougher. We still have some outstanding parents who display class in every situation, but too many parents now react to their son's not playing by showing disrespect for the program and the coaches. In what ways should a coach approach potential problems with parents? How can a coach make sure that his players' parents understand the philosophy and priorities?

First of all, as mentioned previously, you can help your players prepare to cope with their parents. Second, you need to communicate with parents as well. They need to know where you're coming from and what the goals are.

We start the year with a mandatory parent meeting. At this meeting we talk about many things, including our baseball booster club. All our parents are members, but we tell them that if they would like to help the program, they can fill offices and positions. If they don't want to volunteer, that's fine, but I require at least one parent of every player to attend the mandatory meeting, where I provide guidelines about how parents should behave when interacting with our baseball program. I tell them that if their son is having a problem at home, church, or school, they can come to me. If they are concerned because their son isn't performing in the classroom, I can help by putting pressure on him to improve, even to the extent of taking away playing time. I want them to know what I can and will do for them, that I will support them in helping their sons do the things that they need them to do. I do not need players in the lineup if their parents feel that they are violating rules and showing disrespect to their families. I can work with parents on that issue. But one point I stress at this meeting is that they should never talk to me about playing time. I will not discuss it.

We tell parents that their sons are always welcome to approach us about playing time. We want them to know what their status is and what they can do to change it. We tell parents to ask their sons why they are not playing more. That's the way we communicate. For this reason I do not allow parents to call and say, "Don't tell my son that I called you." The first thing

I do if I get a phone call of that nature is talk with the player. I don't want misunderstandings—between the player and his parents or between the player and myself. I want to know from the player why he hasn't been communicating with his parents. We also stress at this initial meeting that we don't want parents trying to communicate with their sons on game day. If a parent talks to her or his son during the game, I will pull the player.

Focus on the Game

We had a game in 1986, when we were ranked number one in the nation, that we were winning 11-1. In midgame I pulled all my starters, putting in my second-string guys so that they could get some playing time. After I made those substitutions, without my knowledge, a couple of the players who had been pulled walked out of the dugout to talk to their parents. The other team rallied, closing to 11-10, at which point I put all my starters back in except the three guys who had been talking to their parents. I said to them, "If you want to talk to your parents, go sit with them because you're not going to be playing here." I told them that they should never have left the dugout in the first place because they are always part of the team, whether in the game or not. We ended up winning the game, and one of the second-string guys made the crucial play in the last inning to save it for us.

Again, the idea is not to ostracize parents. We just want them involved in the right way. Parents help by hosting team dinners at their homes the night before our home games. Parents take turns with this event. This routine is a tremendously positive thing, and I salute the parents for doing it. We also have a field maintenance day, and each kid brings a parent to help work on the field with him. This activity is in line with our philosophy of underscoring the importance of equipment and field. Our school is located in a fairly affluent area. Some of the kids, and their parents, have never done much yard work. In my first year at Esperanza, a player reacted to my announcement that we would be working on the field on Saturday for three hours by asking whether he could bring the family gardener. In general, the parents have been extremely generous with offering their time and service, and this work day almost always ends up being extremely positive.

I also tell parents that I'm available if they need help picking a college for their son. My staff and I try to place as many of our players as possible in situations that fit their skills. We want them to be thinking of going on while they're playing for us. We think that this future orientation fosters a stronger focus on trying to improve. My familiarity with college coaches and the recruiting process has been extremely beneficial to parents over the years. On a personal level, seeing my players go on to play at the next level has been one of the most satisfying parts of the game

In the current era, coaches need to be aware of some of the distracting things that parents do. Many parents cannot just let their son go without any contact with him. They need to give him his sports drink or water before the game or they want to give him advice or openly coach him during the game. I tell my parents, "Give your son three hours away from you. Let me have him for three hours." Once they put that uniform on and step onto the field, they're mine. That's the way we do it in our program. Here are some things to consider when dealing with parents:

- Explain your philosophy in a stern but positive way.
- Don't deal with problems with parents before the game.
- Tell parents to leave their sons alone for the time when they are playing the game. The coach, not the parents, should be instructing the players.
- Don't talk to a parent who is out of control.
- Don't feed the complaining parents. Ignore them or confront them.
- Remember that the goals of the team are different from the goals of the parents.

Of course, not all parents cause problems. Most are supportive and can do great things to help develop your program. In extreme cases, though, remember parents just want what they think is best for their sons. The conflict arises when they think you don't. Remind them of the ways you are willing to help their children, but be clear that you also have a responsibility to the school and to the program and must also keep that in mind when dealing with their kids.

Communicating With Teachers and Administrators

In any school-related environment, whether it's junior high, high school, or college, coaches need to deal with and communicate with teachers and administrators, and vice versa. To get them on your side, you need to cultivate their understanding of your philosophy and promote a positive image of you and your program. Players at the high school and college level have to perform in the classroom to be eligible. Sometimes you need to coach your players on how to deal with their teachers or administrators.

To start, of course, the administrators—principals, assistant principals, and counselors—must respect you and the things involved in your program. Sometimes it doesn't hurt to take a simple step like providing administrators with a T-shirt or hat with your logo on it, something that makes them feel a part of your program and promotes it. To you as a head coach, the two most important people in the administration are the principal and the athletic director. These two people can determine your fate if your job is on the line. They were probably the most influential people in hiring you, and they would be the most influential in firing you. We want them wearing our colors, attending our games, meeting our parents. At Esperanza we ask them both to write a welcome message to fans, parents, and players for our yearbook, further making them feel a part of the program. We make sure to invite them to our end-of-the-year awards banquet, where we make a point of recognizing them and thanking them for their support and involvement. These two people are critical, and we never overlook them.

Nor should you ignore your fellow teachers. We give every teacher a yearbook that identifies the players. I also send a letter to all teachers, asking them to notify me if they are having problems with any player so that I can address it immediately. Players cannot take shortcuts. Our players have to perform in the classroom, as well as on the field, and our teachers know that I will go to bat for them when a problem arises with a player. Any other approach would threaten the image of our program with the teaching staff, and we work hard to maintain a positive internal image. We tell our players continuously that if they are good enough on the baseball field to get a scholarship, then they must have good grades to close the deal. A player can be among the best in the country, but if he doesn't have good grades he cannot go to a four-year college. Players need to excel in the classroom.

Communicating With Umpires

Dealing with umpires is a touchy subject with coaches. The first thing that a coach must judge is what type of personality the umpire has. You should determine right away whether one of the umpires has a short fuse that may cause him to toss you out of a game. Next, when a disputed call arises, don't charge the umpire. Make sure that you call time and then go out and voice your opinion. Never use profanity; doing so only embarrasses you and your program. Know the rules and their interpretations.

Communicating With the Media

A coach should try to use the media to boost his program whenever possible. This process starts with answering preseason questionnaires and returning all phone calls from reporters. The coach needs to appoint someone to call the local newspapers with the score after every game, win or lose. You should promote your players whenever you have an opportunity after a win or when a player has a good week or receives an award. Never give the name of a player who made an error or bad pitch or poor play to lose a game. Be as friendly as possible with reporters. If they like you, you are more likely to receive positive press coverage.

Coaches' Keys

1. An essential element of your program is good communication with all parties involved—assistant coaches, players, parents, and administrators and teachers.

2. All those groups need to be plugged into your philosophy and goals. They need to understand your rules and disciplines. You should prevent them from being blindsided by any development.

3. Although communication is the bottom line, you can get there in various ways—team meetings, individual meetings, handouts, appropriate sayings, stories.

4. Involving parents and school staff can help create a base of support, but you must be consistent in reinforcing your philosophy through communication.

5. One set of rules should apply to all.

CHAPTER 3

MOTIVATING YOUR PLAYERS

If communication is a key to coaching success, motivation is not far behind. Motivating players and recognizing specific personalities are essential. What may work for one player may not work for another. Ultimately, a coach must find the one key that puts it all together.

Communicating your philosophy provides the foundation. Motivation helps players put your philosophy to work. When we talk about all the various parts of the game, failure plays a big role. In coping with failure, players have to know that they are required to keep hustling, to play hard with poise and class. As their coach, you play a crucial role in motivating your players. You need to create an environment in which players trust the program, understand the goals, and see the value in motivating themselves to take extra hitting, extra fielding, and extra speed and strength work—the elements that breed success as individuals and as a team.

WHAT MOTIVATES YOUR PLAYERS?

One of the first things you need to establish is that hustle and good attitude take no skill at all. When players integrate those ingredients into their approach and personality, you have a good start. In that regard you must also be part psychologist. Who are your players? How do they go about things? What are their personality traits? Are they passive or aggressive, positive or negative, lazy or self-motivated, selfish or team oriented? As a coach you want to evaluate the type of team that you have. Put them through competitive drills and games to learn how aggressive and competitive they are. You and your coaches also want to observe how they handle failure in games, drills, and offensive situations. Just by watching them play the game, you can easily see how aggressive your players are. After you evaluate those qualities, you and your staff can work to increase or maintain the positive qualities and eliminate the negative ones.

Will one brand of motivation work on all, or does the motivational technique have to be more individually based? I had a tough time when I first got to Esperanza. The school had no tradition and nothing to fall back on as motivational tools—players who had succeeded or teams that had won titles. We had no history of success. At Notre Dame, motivation can take the form of tradition and green jerseys, but few schools have such a history. I inherited some seniors who had bad habits and were resistant to change. I inherited others who were willing to listen and work and saw my arrival as an opportunity for success in their final year. Some of the juniors bought into the program, and, most important, I inherited some sophomores who were fine players, wanted to be a part of the varsity, and were motivated simply by the fact that they had a new coach and a new opportunity. My job was to bring them together. In the process, a number of players fell by the wayside, unwilling to follow the new rules and lacking the discipline and self-motivation critical to a new program.

Motivation Starts With the Individual

In my first year at Esperanza I had one senior tell me that he was going to miss practice to go skiing for the weekend. I reminded him that he had made a commitment to the team and that we were working out on Saturday. "But I go every year," he replied. I said, "You used to go every year." I warned him that he would be dismissed from the team if he missed practice. He went skiing anyway and found his locker cleaned out when he got back. He was done. The next week my pitching coach told me that one of the pitchers didn't want to put in his running anymore and had walked off the field. We cleaned out his locker as well. He, too, was done. The point is that motivation is fine, but it has to start with the individual.

Getting players motivated can involve a variety of methods or one simple approach. The tradition and success of those who came before can be used as a motivator. Talking about or showing the results of a previous success or championship—a ring, trophy, or other award—can be effective. Something as simple as a motivational speech can get a group excited. Some groups are extremely difficult to motivate. These may need extra help in the form of drills or extra work to get them to perform and to show them the importance of their goal. You may want to increase the length or difficulty of their practice to show them the importance of the goal and thus motivate them to be ready.

Being enthusiastic and hands on is a great way to keep your players motivated.

RECOGNIZING AND MOTIVATING DIFFERENT TYPES OF PLAYERS

Every team is made up of diverse personalities. No two people are the same or react the same way to a given stimulant. A coach needs to recognize what he has and how to deal with it. Influencing the self-motivated players is easy, but what about the inconsistent or passive players? Here the experienced coach can rely on the numerous tools that he has used in the past. But the inexperienced coach has to keep trying things until he learns what gets his team going. He gives motivational speeches, relates success stories from throughout history, talks about people who have overcome difficult odds. He shows his players what they can win—pictures of the championship trophy or championship rings. These are just a few ideas that a coach can use to see whether his players respond.

The Competitive Player

Coaches want all their players to be competitive. Baseball is a failure-oriented game that elicits negative emotions and beats down confidence. To learn how his players will hold up, a coach can use competitive games and competitive drills that put pressure on performance and the ability to succeed. These drills and games provide measuring rods for a coach who is attempting to gauge his motivational needs. In this failure-oriented environment, the competitive player always wants another chance to succeed. If a player doesn't have that drive, you need to try to instill it. You can incorporate competitiveness into your practice drills in many ways. One way to do this is to turn batting practice into a competitive game. Divide the players into teams to practice a certain skill so that they are competing against each other. Offer rewards for the team that does best or require extra work for the team that fails. Incorporate a competitive drill (more will be discussed in the practice plan phase of the book) two or three times a week to maintain an edge and foster the influence of the passionate competitive players.

The Passive Player

The opposite of the competitive player is the passive player, but coaches must recognize the difference between a passive player and a quiet player. I've had a number of players who were quiet from a personality standpoint but extremely competitive otherwise. I let them know that in certain game situations they had to be more vocal. The passive player is more of a problem because playing any sport without an aggressive nature is difficult. Here, too, drills can create a sense of aggressiveness. We use a dive drill, which is just what its name implies. The drill forces the player to dive, to lay out, to get dirty. There is no substitute for aggressiveness, and we use videotapes and anecdotes to help the passive player see that. Instilling aggressiveness requires communication, motivation, sensing what a player needs, and providing it.

The Overly Aggressive Player

The flip side of the passive player is the overly aggressive player who always goes full speed in every aspect of the game. We like the aggressive player unless it goes to the extreme, leading to mistakes or an inability to relax, which will restrict the natural flow of talent. The aggressive player needs to be motivated in a way so that he understands the need to play smart and under control. You don't want to restrict his aggressiveness or instincts, but he needs to perform in the context of the team.

This player needs to have a plan. He usually reacts on impulse (reaction without thought). His impulses are out of control. Continue to give this player a plan so that he is under control but maintains his aggressive attitude. For instance, work with an overaggressive hitter to look for a pitch in a specific area. He will hit a pitch only waist high or above. When he sees that pitch, he will be aggressive, but he lays off those low pitches and the pitches in the dirt that he used to chase as a result of his undisciplined impulses.

When Did We Start Doing That?

In 1997 we had a strong team that ended up with a championship. Toward the end of the year we played a highly rated team in a nonleague game crucial to our national ranking. The game opened with our leadoff man hitting the first pitch for a home run. As our player approached second base, he started screaming and yelling as if he were trying to embarrass the other team, rubbing his home run in their face. He continued to yell and scream until he reached the plate. By that time all my players were looking at him as if he were crazy, and I couldn't blame them. We lost that game 2-1, and I will always believe that the opposing pitcher used our player's immature and obnoxious behavior as motivation over the rest of the game, shutting us out after that first pitch because he didn't want to be embarrassed further. I calmly sat my players down after the game and asked them, "When did we start doing things like that? When did we start providing the other team with unnecessary motivation?" I told them that one player had crossed a line and it had affected the entire team and damaged our reputation. That team was self-motivated, but I had to step in. Competitiveness is one thing. Spitting in another team's face is quite another. We couldn't tolerate that behavior.

The Smart Player

This takes us to the next type of player—the smart player. Although this player may not be the most talented on the team, he can excel with his brains and knowledge of the game. Most important, he understands instinctively what the coach is thinking and can stay ahead of game situations. To motivate the smart player, we tend to make him part of our brain trust, let him participate in planning for an opponent, go deeper with our philosophy and reasons for doing things. As a result, the smart player becomes a liaison between the coaches and his teammates, another instrument for helping motivate and communicate.

The smart player does subtle things. Your clever shortstop, for example, may move two steps to his left after seeing a hitter hit two foul balls down the right-field line. The hitter then hits a ball up the middle that the shortstop can get to only because he made the adjustment according to the hitter's foul balls and tendency to swing late.

Then we take some of our smart players on the bench and have them watch the opposing coaches to pick up their signs. We have often picked the pitching coach's signs and were able to call every pitch for the hitter. After the game, we bring this code breaking to the attention of the entire team. We make a big deal of this—as if this player had produced the game-winning hit. We make him proud of his contribution.

We have players who have natural skills and intelligence that classify them as smart players, but many times we teach them to be smart. A shortstop and second baseman who fake turning a double play when the opposing team runs a hit-and-run can turn a fly ball to right field into a double play. We have to teach them how to do this. When they fake the double play, they are trying to get the runner to slide, which can lead to an easy double play.

The Negative Player

By contrast, some players dwell on the negative. These players represent a motivational problem for the coach in a sport made up of negatives. This kind of player beats himself up over failure, finding fault in any situation. He may throw equipment, use foul language, create disruptive behavior, and generate real problems, particularly if he is one of the team's best players. This behavior can't be tolerated, and the coach has to work with the player to make him understand that failure is a part of the game and that he has to accept mistakes and move on—for the benefit of both himself and the team. I once had an exceptionally negative player and told my coaching staff to put him under a microscope. We told him that we would not tolerate his behavior and that we would pull him from games if it continued—or he would simply not play. In time, through communication and motivation, he came to grips with his negativism and became one of our most positive players.

A coach should always remember that the power of the lineup can be his strongest weapon. If a player is good enough to play but his negative personality and performance make him a problem, sit him on the bench. If sitting does not influence or change his behavior, then you do not want him on your team. I have found that sitting the player usually produces a swift change in behavior.

The Selfish Player

In the same mode as the negative player, and even more destructive, is the selfish player. This player has a difficult time buying into the team concept. He has an "all about me" attitude, and strong motivational methods are required to turn him into a team player. Of course, the strongest motivational tool that a coach has is the power of the lineup. The coach needs to make it clear that if his attitude prevails, he will receive no playing time. If his selfishness persists in practice, the player has to go. No matter how good a player is, the team suffers by selfish behavior—on or away from the field.

Another way to put pressure on the selfish player is to make your best players aware of his negative characteristics. Ask them to talk to their teammate when he acts selfishly. Give them suggestions about what to say to him. Feedback from peers can generally change behavior faster than anything.

The Team Player

The last type of player I'll mention is the team player. This is the player you love and appreciate, the one who puts himself last and the team first, a throwback to another era. Just being part of the team is enough for him, and he'll look for ways to help the team whether he's in the lineup or on the bench. Seldom these days is this type of player the star of the team. Our star players tend to be coddled, and their personality seems to lean more toward the selfish type because of this coddling. Much like the smart player, the team player will benefit from your making him feel that he is an important part of the process no matter what his playing level. You want him to keep expressing his team-oriented approach, helping the team stay positive and picking up teammates when they're down, and you hope that his attitude proves contagious. A team player like this is a tremendous asset.

MOTIVATING THE TEAM

Players are not robots. As we have discussed, every team is composed of diverse personalities, of players with different goals. A coach has to come to grips with these personalities and determine the best motivational course with each.

Some players can motivate themselves. These are the players whose eyes are on you and are listening when you talk to the team. They are motivated by what you have to say and by their self-discipline. Other players have their heads down, their thoughts straying. You need to be able to identify those players and then pull them aside, first figuring the best way to motivate them. If your program has a strong tradition of success, you can draw on pride in the program. You might talk about players who have come out of the program and are now playing successfully at the college or pro level. You might also want to discuss players at the college or pro level who have no association with your program but whose stories illustrate drive and dedication.

Again, when I first arrived at Esperanza, we had no tradition of success. I told my first tryout groups that I wanted guys to come out for baseball only if they eventually wanted to play at a higher level, a goal they could strive for—thus improving in the process. Finding a future level—community college, four-year

If the coach is excited, the players will be too.

college, the pros—was a topic that I constantly stressed with my players so that they would have a goal in mind.

Wally Pipp

One motivating story that we share with our players every year involves Wally Pipp, the first baseman for the New York Yankees from 1918 into 1925. Taking advantage of a combination of factors, a rookie named Lou Gehrig replaced Pipp in the lineup one day and went on to play 2,130 consecutive games, making Pipp a footnote in baseball history. We remind our players every year about the Gehrig–Pipp story as an illustration of what can happen if they don't work hard to protect their position, if they aren't willing to play with small aches and pains. We remind them that there's always somebody waiting to take their place.

The great pitcher Warren Spahn, was once asked which hitter he feared the most. He replied, "Anyone with a bat." We use that remark to remind our pitchers that they can't let up against anyone. Motivation comes in many forms. John Scolinos, my coach at Cal Poly Pomona and a legend in Southern California, used to classify players as puppy dogs, hot dogs, and bulldogs. The puppy dogs were afraid of failure. The hot dogs were showy and flashy but not always productive. The bulldogs knew how to handle failure and never let up, battling all the way. Scolinos would tell his players, "You all want to be bulldogs." This is a great motivational analogy to describe a player in practice or a game.

Besides using stories and motivational sayings, you can also simply talk to your players about certain things that are part of your philosophy. The single most important word should be *we*, the least *I*. They should continually hear that. Ask yourself how you want them to act and what you want them to be.

Another way to motivate your players is to reward them for a good performance. We reward our players for three things during games—shutouts, playing an errorless game, and scoring 10 or more runs. For them to receive their reward, however, we must win the game. This approach reinforces the fact that

the team always comes first. Often our rewards include Gatorade or a soft drink, but it doesn't really matter what the reward is. It's simply a little bonus.

This method has proved successful in game situations. I've coached games in which my team is up by many runs and is shutting out the opponent. Despite the fact that we have a healthy lead, my players are going strong. They want the shutout, the reward. When I first started my coaching career, every February a farmer would plow the field next to our school, and the gophers that lived on his property would relocate to our diamond, leaving divots all over. I told my players that every time they eradicated a gopher, they didn't have to run that day. They quickly became adept at gopher removal. As I pointed out, motivation comes in many forms.

Whatever Works

A few years ago I had a player who would wake up at 5:30 every game-day morning so that he could watch the highlight videotape that we had made of our last CIF championship team. This guy finished the season as the top hitter in our area, helping us win another CIF title. He drew motivation from that film, and I'm glad that he did. I had another player who drew inspiration from watching the movie *Field of Dreams* on the night before every game. This guy has now played in the major leagues for three years. Whatever works.

All players, even the best and most self-disciplined, have to be motivated. How to do it, when to do it, and how to choose the right motivation for each player are key decisions for every coach. At times, of course, a coach needs to let his players motivate and discipline themselves. I've had teams capable of pushing themselves through a season, but I don't expect that to be the case every year. Problems, issues, and negative situations are bound to develop, and the man in charge needs to address them by knowing whether a loud voice or a pat on the back is the right motivational tool for the player or players in question.

With some players a quiet minute with the coach and a pat on the back is enough. With others, it's a daily, ongoing process. The ultimate goal is intensity and competitiveness, but not to the extent of losing poise. Players need to be reminded of the next opportunity and not dwell on the negative in a game of failure. Motivation never stops, during practice and on game day, and although raising your voice is unavoidable at times, a coach is heard best when he's calm.

MOTIVATIONAL DRILLS

Motivating your players takes work. Some players are easier than others to motivate, but with work and practice, every player can learn to give it his all every time he steps on the field. We use the following drills to help develop and motivate our players.

Lightning

Purpose. This drill is called Lightning because the offense and defense must go as fast as they can on each play, executing the drills at lightning speed.

Procedure. The hitting group has five or six batters in a group. The drill starts with a hitter and an on-deck hitter. The other four hitters are at first base. A coach throws to the hitter. The hitter gets three pitches and must execute a hit-and-run on each pitch. If the hitter does not swing at a pitch, he is done hitting that round and the next hitter comes up. The runner at first base must steal on the pitch and look back to react to the ball. If the ball is hit in the air, he needs to stop and get back to first base. If it's a base hit, he must go all the way to third base. If he doesn't go to third and stops at second base, he will not hit in the next round. On the next round you put the runner at second base and have him read the ball to advance to third or hold his ground. On a base hit, he must score from second base. In the third round, the runner is at third base and he tags up on fly balls to score. The players are motivated to execute the offensive skills to avoid losing their cuts in batting practice. Players are always motivated when there is a chance that they could lose their swings. The players also stay motivated to run hard on the bases.

Two Pitch

Purpose. We end practice with this drill when we want to motivate our players to compete at full speed.

Procedure. A coach divides his team into two teams. Each player on each team hits every inning. If a team has 10 players, all 10 bat before they go out on the field. The players get a point for every base they reach safely. For example, if a hitter hits a double and reaches second safely, his team gets two points. If the defense makes an error, the defensive team has a point deducted from its total. For example, if a hitter hits a ground ball to the shortstop and he throws the ball away so that the runner is able to take second base, the hitter's team gets two points because the hitter reached second base and the defensive team loses a point because of the error. This drill motivates your offensive players to try to take the extra base. The defense is motivated to play well because they are penalized for making errors. We add a point for the defense if a player makes a great play. Of course, the coaches decide what constitutes a great play. To provide additional motivation, we subtract a point from the offensive team if any player doesn't run hard for 90 feet to first base on an out. The coach can further motivate the players by giving a reward such as soft drinks to the winning team. Alternatively, he can punish the losing team by having them work on the field or do some extra conditioning. This method motivates the teams to compete. In this drill you have each team hit until they've gone through the entire lineup. They then switch to defense. You usually have each team hit two or three times.

Bunt Off

Purpose. This is another drill that will motivate your players and get them competing at full speed.

Procedure. For this drill we set up cones to designate an area where a good bunt will land and an area where a bad bunt will land. For every good bunt, the player receives a point, but only if he sprints to first base. Anyone who doesn't sprint loses a point. In all our drills and competitions, the coaching staff orally reinforces positive performance. We provide the winners with modest rewards and may have the losers perform field work.

Coaches' Keys

1. Communicate your philosophy and motivate your players to follow it. Although you must motivate all players, you should encourage them to motivate themselves and those around them. Remind them that hustle and a positive attitude are the mark of a motivated player and that those characteristics require only desire, not any special skill.

2. Identify the types of players on your team and their various personalities. Among the types are competitive, passive, smart, aggressive, negative, and the team player. Some players can motivate themselves and their teammates; others can destroy the team concept. Motivate your players to improve individual and team performance.

3. Realize, as well, that players have a variety of personalities, so you need to employ a variety of motivational techniques—stories, traditions, sayings, clippings, videos, drills, encouragement, and team and individual meetings. The coach is the prime motivator, and the goal is always *we*, not *I*.

CHAPTER 4

BUILDING A SUCCESSFUL BASEBALL PROGRAM

Constructing a baseball program involves many details—from hiring assistants to fostering school and community support to fund-raising to assisting in the buying of equipment and planning facility improvements. Coaches also need to set rules to sustain continuity and maintain long-term success.

This chapter will walk you through how to put together each of these parts and what your priorities should be. To build your program for the long term, you need to hire good people as assistants, get the school administrators and faculty behind you, and build community support. The chapter will discuss how to choose effective fund-raisers and how to set up rules for your players.

Doing all these things takes time, so you need to be patient and stay the course. You must realize that you will have setbacks as you set up your program and progress through the years. Be patient and keep working at it until you get it right.

IMPLEMENTING A PROGRAM

One of the first things that you should understand as a coach coming into a new program or new school with a new philosophy is that the varsity program is the number one priority. You may have to neglect the junior varsity or freshman programs at times because you must channel your energy toward the varsity program, the most visible level, the level covered in the local sports pages and the level that scouts, recruiters, future players, the community, and the student body will follow over any other. The attention that the varsity level requires often makes planning the overall program difficult because the initial process demands that the best assistants be at the varsity level, meaning that the lower levels may suffer. When I arrived at Esperanza, parents and others complained that our JV team was not successful because the coaching was not up to par with the coaching on the varsity level. I had to explain that our best coaches needed to help get the varsity off the ground and that we'd upgrade the lower levels in future years. Currently, our junior varsity has won nine straight league titles, so you simply set your priorities at the start.

When you come into a program you should give yourself a time frame to work with. How long will it take you to attain the competitive goal? This estimate should be a big part of your plan. I gave myself three years to reach competitive success. Naturally, if you set a time frame for success and don't reach it, you reevaluate and set a new schedule. You must take into consideration the talent that you have and the competition that you will face. You need to be realistic in evaluating those factors when setting your goal.

HIRING ASSISTANTS

As John Scolinos, the great Cal Poly Pomona coach, has often said, "The most important thing you need to do to be a success in anything is to surround yourself with good people." In this case, hiring good assistants is essential, and you should consider a number of traits. Obviously, nothing replaces knowledge of the game gleaned from experience as player or coach. Do your homework. Put the word out. Sometimes all you have to do is ask. A person who you think would not be interested may jump at the opportunity to participate in a building program and working with young athletes. Be flexible. At any level where pay is limited or unavailable, the hiring of a respected assistant may mean that he is available for limited hours. Obviously, practice schedules may be rigid, but you can find ways to work with an assistant's personal schedule and still operate efficient practices. If a high school practice starts at 2:00 and the pitching coach can't arrive until 3:30, run the practice as usual but delay having the pitchers do their bullpen work until 4:00. On game days, of course, the assistants have to be there, and you should make that clear before you hire them.

Sometimes You Can Be Flexible

I had an excellent pitching coach who eventually left the program because the New York Yankees hired him as a scout. The first year that he was coaching for me he had to bring his two-year-old daughter to practice with him because his wife was a teacher and unavailable two days a week. The young girl would patiently sit in a stroller as her dad put our pitchers through practice. The situation was unique, one that I never dreamed I'd confront when I started coaching, but because the coach was an excellent mentor to our pitchers I wanted to be flexible.

Selecting good people as assistant coaches is crucial. Look for people amenable to training and development—people with good character traits who can be taught to coach if those skills aren't at an appropriate level when you hire them, people with positive attitudes who enjoy working with youngsters. Clearly, during the interview process, you need to prepare a set of questions that will provide the information that you want. You might want the potential coach to respond to a hypothetical problem or situation. For instance, you might ask how he would handle a situation in which a player isn't hustling or going through drills at full speed. If you don't have a set of questions ready, you'll be leaving it to chance, operating on whim. Following are some sample questions to consider when interviewing candidates:

- What is your strength as a coach? (Leave this as a general question and let the candidate elaborate.)
- What position do you coach the best?
- What do you emphasize when you coach that position?
- What are your favorite drills?
- How well do you know pitching, hitting, fielding (and so on)?

The answers to these questions will give you an idea of what the potential coach knows. From here you can construct personal questions or hypothetical situations. For instance, you can give the candidate a game situation and ask him what he would do. These questions can supplement the earlier questions and give you more specific information about what the person knows.

A bad hire eventually puts you in the difficult position of firing the assistant or asking for his resignation. Being prepared going in reduces that likelihood.

At Esperanza we want our potential assistants to know that they will be coaching within the parameters of our philosophy, and will not just be yes men. The main way to know whether these interview expectations will be fulfilled is to give the coach the time frame that you expect him to be involved in coaching. Tell him how many days each week you want him at the field. Practice is five or six days a week, a much more demanding schedule than the two days a week that he may have experienced in Little League. See how he responds to considering this commitment. Then tell him that you want him at the field at least a half an hour before practice and one and a half hours before each game. His reaction to making this kind of time commitment will give you some insight about how serious he is about being part of your program. Of course, here you have to use your people instincts, your ability to judge a person's honesty and whether his personality is the right fit for you and the other members of your staff. The new hire will be taking initiative and implementing new ideas. Assistant coaches work best when they have responsibility, an area in which they are in charge. Having a specific, important responsibility gives them the sense that they are helping to build the foundation, that they are part of the whole.

When considering assistants you should also understand that one of the best places to find future coaches can be within your own program. Look for coaching skills and qualities in your players, and don't hesitate to suggest that they might consider a coaching career. Plant the seed based on their personality, and pursue the players whose love for the game is obvious. We've developed many of our coaches this way. In recent years, in fact, every assistant we've had at Esperanza has come out of our program.

Obviously, any new assistant must be aware of the huge commitment. In our system, a potential assistant has to know that we expect him to stay after practices for meetings or field participations. We work out on Saturday, so that's another part of the commitment that can disrupt family life. We also host a national high school tournament during spring break every year, and we expect our assistant coaches to help with it. The point is that you need to make a potential assistant aware of the entire package during the interview process. Doing so later would be unfair to him.

A final consideration in the hiring of an assistant coach is loyalty. If you determine that an assistant has been bad-mouthing you or the program, he has to go. The staff has to be in lock step if it is to avoid sending the wrong message to the players. Loyalty is essential, and good character traits are more important in an assistant than the ability to coach. Again, you can teach a capable, solid person how to coach.

GAINING SUPPORT FOR YOUR PROGRAM

To establish consistency in your program with regard to wins and being competitive year in and year out, you need to gain support from both the school and the community. This section discusses the importance of creating an alliance with your school, including teachers, administrators, and the community that surrounds your school. You want to be able to get the best players out for your sport, and then you need to keep them eligible throughout their four years. In your community you want the Little League and travel ballplayers to dream about going to your school and wearing your uniform. At the college level this feeling in the community would be with the local high schools and junior colleges. You want them to have a goal to stay home and play for their college or junior college with all the local kids.

School Support

Building support among the people who may be affected by your job or who may have a say in your ability to keep the job—superintendent, principal, athletic director, teachers, students—is at least as important as the hiring of assistants. No coach succeeds in a vacuum. Every coach needs the key people on his side, and he gains their support through communicating consistently, establishing the proper priorities and philosophy, and adhering to rules. Developing mutual respect with these key people will help smooth the course when the inevitable problems arise or when the coach needs things for the program.

Make a point to meet your superintendent and invite him to games. Drop a baseball shirt on him. Explain your philosophy. Involve your principal in the program. Let her know that you are aware of her presence at games. In many cases the principal will be fielding any complaints from outside people, including parents, and the more knowledge she has of your program and philosophy, the more likely it is that she will resolve a problem before it becomes a major issue. You want these important people (superintendent and principal at the high school level, president at the college level) to know that you want your players to excel in the classroom as well as on the field. You must have a commitment to education to get the key people in your school behind your program. When your administrators realize that your commitment is genuine, you and your program will gain valuable support.

In my fourth year of teaching and coaching, our principal went to every road game except two. At our end-of-the-year banquet, which he attended, I announced that statistic and thanked him for his support. He was pleased by the recognition and received compliments from many of our parents. Be aware of the principal's power and keep him on your side. He's the most important booster.

After the principal, the athletic director is probably the second most influential person to your job security. He most likely will also be a physical education teacher at your school and will often come to work wearing shorts and some type of athletic shirt. You want the shirt to advertise your program on campus. You want him to write a note to fans in your program, accompanying a note from the principal. You want him to throw out the first pitch at the season opener. Seek his advice with any problems that arise with parents or players. The athletic director is your immediate boss. You want him committed to the program and feeling part of it. He may not be your assistant coach, but he's your right-hand man.

The teachers and counselors are another important group who should feel that your door is open to them at any time. They should understand your philosophy as a coach and be assured of your commitment to academics. At the high school level, of course, nothing should come before the classroom, and you should ask for no exceptions when a player is in academic trouble. Teachers and counselors need to know that you want to be informed of any problems, that you will work with them to resolve the issues, and that you will work with players to prepare an academic schedule that will allow them to move on to college. At the junior high or college level, you want to demand the same commitment to education from your players. The college coach wants all his players to attend class daily. In many cases, at either a large college or a small college, the school has invested scholarship money in a player with the understanding that the scholarship will be withdrawn if the player does not maintain his grades. One of the first indicators that a college student will not pass a course is when he starts missing class. The college coach must have a system of checking on his players and should set up a form of discipline for each unexcused absence from class. The teachers and administrators will appreciate this and will likely be willing to work with the coach to help students who are struggling. This procedure should be standard for every college coach.

As mentioned earlier, coaches don't operate in a vacuum. They need the support of a wide-ranging network, including the student body. A coach should encourage student pep rallies and game attendance. He should meet with the editor of the student newspaper and encourage her to send a reporter to all games. He should ask the band, or a small portion of it, to entertain at games. Baseball will never outdraw football on a high school campus, but the coach who makes himself visible and accessible can stimulate interest and develop more support, which, in turn, will provide his team with a greater home-field advantage.

Coaches should always remember to say thanks, and they should keep in mind that the tentacles of the network don't end where the campus does.

Community Support

The continuity of a successful program depends in large part on community support. Recruiting is now common at the high school level. Student–athletes may not necessarily attend the high school in their district. Parents think nothing of moving to put their sons and daughters in the best athletic program. These trends are an unfortunate aspect of the often misplaced emphasis on athletics and parental concern, but that's the way it is.

Community support can be a tremendous help to the community college or four-year college. The community college needs the local high school players to attend their school. If more than one or several community colleges can recruit at a specific high school, the college must have a good reputation to persuade the local players to go there. At the community college level the ability to recruit talented local players often determines the success of the program. The coach himself is also a factor. He can go out into the community, talk to players, and persuade them to come to his school. Players who like a specific coach often help recruit their friends in the community to boost the talent base. At the four-year college level, community backing and enthusiasm can also be crucial to the recruiting effort. Many colleges offer partial scholarships because they have only 11.7 baseball scholarships a year. Young high school and junior college players who like the school may be willing to take a partial scholarship to attend the local college. A local player may accept books and tuition, a package that is less than a 50 percent scholarship, and this offer can attract excellent high school players who want to attend the local school. By receiving the books and tuition stipend and living at home with their parents, they don't have any major costs. This approach will work only if the good players want to go to the local college, a circumstance that results when the community has a positive attitude toward the program.

The point is that you build a reputation year by year, and you hope that it attracts the interest of neighborhood youngsters from an early age, that they yearn to wear the school's colors as much as they yearn to play for the Yankees. Merely assuming that it's going to happen, however, isn't good enough. You need to promote your program in the community, and you can do that in many ways.

You can hold a Little League Day when you invite local teams to wear their uniforms to a game and be introduced on the field. You can hold a Free Program Day or a Free Hot Dog Day, with players' parents doing the barbecuing. You can have the mayor or a local celebrity throw out the first pitch before a game. And you can integrate the team into the community through drawings, charity events, or other projects.

Every Christmas Eve, for example, we take our varsity players to the Children's Hospital in Orange County (CHOC) to help distribute gifts collected by more than 900 Harley-Davidson riders. If a player can't make it because his family is out of town for the holiday I understand, but we usually have about 95 percent of the team attend in their logo golf shirts to participate in a rewarding experience and promote the program.

We also participate in the Challenger Little League program, helping conduct tryouts and games for physically and mentally disabled boys and girls. Our local Little Leagues also ask our players to help players in their regular programs, instructing and umpiring where needed.

This activity is a great way for our current players to give back to the Little Leagues that many of them came out of, and it's an effective way to promote our program.

The coach and staff should participate as well. We give clinics to Little League coaches and others about how to organize practices and run drills. We often allow travel teams in the area—teams composed of the best young players—to work out on our field or watch our workouts.

Another method that we use to get area youngsters of all ages familiar with our school and hopeful of playing baseball for us at some point in the future is by hosting baseball camps in the summer. We keep them affordable, cheaper than day care for a week, so that we can draw a big group. From our standpoint, the camps serve three purposes. First, they allow the kids and their parents to see the facility. Second, they familiarize the kids and parents with the coaching staff. Third, they allow the kids and parents to become familiar with our knowledge and understanding of the game. We draw hundreds of kids each summer, and the camps have such a reputation that youngsters even come from outside the community. The camps give us an opportunity to see many outstanding players. Who knows where they'll ultimately decide to attend high school?

At the end of each season I ask a number of my graduating seniors whether they would like to work these camps. For a high school kid the chance to work a baseball camp and get paid for it is awesome. The high school kids set up everything for the coaches at each teaching station. They then help the coach at the various stations work with the campers. The parents send their kids because camp is safe, the kids enjoy it, and they learn something. The campers go from station to station, each of which teaches a different skill. The stations consist of hitting, infield play, outfield skills, pitching, base running, and team defense. The kids play games at the end of each day and thoroughly enjoy the camp.

Community support can directly influence your team. The more support you have in the community, the more money you can generate through ticket sales and fund-raising. This money goes to help buy equipment and other necessary items for your baseball program.

FUND-RAISING

Enhancing community support is an ongoing process, and so is the need to improve your program, facility, and equipment. Making these improvements will obviously involve fund-raising, a potentially nasty word but a requirement for building a successful program in the 21st century.

Advertising is an important way to involve the community. Many programs put signs from local businesses on their outfield fence. Community help also comes from the advertising placed in the baseball program books. Many high schools and community colleges do not charge admission to their games. If they do, then their popularity in the community is obviously going to be seen at the gate. The four-year college program that charges admission needs to persuade businesses in the community to buy season tickets that will support their attendance. This kind of community involvement can be a significant asset.

The first question that coaches commonly ask is how to begin to raise funds. First, any fund-

Fund-raising can be extremely helpful in the process of improving your program's facilities, such as new batting cages.

raiser requires an enthusiastic approach by the coach and staff. Without the enthusiastic backing of the coach, creating enthusiasm among the players and community will be difficult. You should start each year by making a wish list of what you want to buy for your program or your facility. From this wish list you will be able to determine how much money you need to raise and what your first purchases will be. Seldom do I raise enough money to buy everything on the list, so I want to be sure to get the items that we need most that year.

First is the basic equipment that programs never seem to have enough of—bats, balls, catching gear, batting helmets. Then there are larger items—scoreboards, pitching machines, lawn mowers, and ancillary salary. Sometimes, you can find help from within. The parent of a player involved with the equipment that you need may be able to supply it free or at reduced cost. We begin every season by asking our players to provide their parents' names and occupations. More than once we've found painters, cement people, landscapers, carpenters, electricians, plumbers, and general handymen within the framework of the team. Often these parents have donated their time or provided it at a discount, or they know a friend of a friend who would be willing to help. All the parents, of course, are likely to be members of your community booster club, another fertile place to satisfy your wish list or at least come up with fund-raising ideas.

When deciding on a fund-raising philosophy, consider two key questions:

1. What kind of fund-raiser would I be comfortable doing?
2. What type of fund-raiser do I think would be a success in my community?

Obviously, if your program has been successful and you have the support of the community, fund-raising of any type is much easier.

In my experience, fund-raising falls into several categories. The first I call "the get something for nothing" fund-raiser in which a successful parent, booster, or perhaps a former player simply donates time, equipment, or money. Maybe calling it getting something for nothing isn't entirely accurate because you always want to acknowledge the generosity with an announcement, a sign at the field, or a note in the program.

The concept of getting something for nothing is an important one. We have one fund-raiser in which each player sends a note to 10 relatives or family friends to let them know that he is on the team and trying to raise money for the program and that any donation would be appreciated. With each letter we enclose a stamped envelope addressed to the school so that the recipient knows that the money is going directly to the program. Before we send the letters out, we first let the parents know we are doing fundraising and ask that they supply the stamped envelopes. We send a note to the parents first. Getting them on board is the most important step because they ultimately provide the names of all other potential donators. The note to them should outline the benefits and specifics of your plan, and also let them know exactly how important their help can be. A sample letter that players can take home to their parents is provided in figure 4.1

Dear parents and players,

We need to raise funds for our baseball team, but don't worry—you won't have to wash cars, sell candy, or go door to door selling wrapping paper or magazines. Last year was the first year for the Family and Friends Fund-Raiser. This fund-raiser alone raised over $13,000. With everyone's help, we can be even more successful this year.

To be successful, we need every player on every level to bring in **10 stamped envelopes** with the names and addresses of friends, neighbors, family members (aunts, uncles, grandparents, either local or out of state), and business associates. Once you have addressed the envelopes, **please turn them in to your head coach by** _____. Donation letters will then be sent to each of these people. (It's nice to add a personal note to go along with the donation letter. Just put it inside the addressed envelope, but do not seal the envelope.) We will then add the donation letter to your personal note. When we receive a donation, a thank-you card and a picture of your son's team will be sent to the friend or family member who made the donation. All money from donations goes directly toward running the program. It is 95% profit for the team.

Thank you.

The Baseball Booster Club

Figure 4.1 A good fund-raising letter should let parents know what you need them to do and how much their help can accomplish.

Among the many other types of fund-raisers are program advertising, outfield fence signage, hit-a-thons, 5K runs, car washes, concession and other sales (such as Christmas trees), raffles, and golf and softball tournaments in which local business people and celebrities participate.

We made a tremendous amount of money one year with a baseball card show in which Hall of Fame hitter Rod Carew came out and signed cards, pictures, and other items. That event was in the early 1990s when baseball cards were in high demand. The card market has slipped some, so it's important to know what will be popular.

We are also fortunate to host the National Classic Tournament, which draws teams from all over the country. The teams are charged a fee, and fans pay an admission fee. We sell T-shirts and other items. The event has been a successful fund-raiser, particularly in those years when we've had a sponsor. Several national and state champions have come out of the tournament, and many future major leaguers have played in it.

At the end of every season you should evaluate your fund-raisers. Were they worth the time, energy, and dollars, or should you go in a new direction next year? Obtain feedback from parents, players, sponsors, and the community. It would be nice if every year you could count on somebody walking through the door and writing a check to cover all the expense that the school budget doesn't, but that's not the reality. Fundraising is the dollars-and-sense reality.

ESTABLISHING TEAM RULES

Over the years I've heard many coaches say that they have only two rules: Be on time and play hard. Maybe that works at higher levels, but at the high school level and below I believe that more is required. Establishing rules and requiring adherence to them make up the backbone of the program. Structure is important. I don't want to leave any doubt about appearance, behavior, or the way we play the game.

Appearance. We start with how we want our players to look. We allow no long hair or beards. We want their hair off the ears and off the collar. Sideburns can go only to the earlobe. Players who fail to pass the hair test after being made aware of the rules are sent home. In an age of liberties, setting an example is important, and although players may not be equal in ability, they can be equal in appearance. Over the years parents have supported us. They are generally happy that we have standards that are sometimes difficult to enforce at home. Our appearance code governs the uniform as well. Players are to dress the same way in practice and games, with no doctoring of the uniform to create embarrassment to the program.

Equipment. Next comes equipment. We accept no excuse for not having glove, hat, and bat at practice and games. Players don't show up at practice without their shoes. They don't mess with another player's equipment, and they certainly don't steal from a teammate. They either respect their teammates' gear and their own, or they are not members of the team.

Alcohol, drugs, and cigarettes. An umbrella of school and campus rules covers alcohol, drugs, and cigarettes. Violations often involve only a two- or three-day suspension from school, but we have separate rules involving drinking and drugs that eliminate a player from the team regardless of what the school does. We are adamant about that.

Academics. As for the classroom, we follow the district policy. Players must maintain a 2.0, or C, grade point average or go on probation for a quarter. If they don't have a 2.0 after the quarter, they are ineligible for athletics.

Profanity. We do not allow profanity, in games or in practice. The staff doesn't use profanity, and players are not allowed to either. Profanity reflects a loss of poise and class. Players should be role models. If a Little Leaguer sees our star player use profanity when he strikes out, what is the Little Leaguer likely to do the next time that he strikes out?

We talk about rules of common sense. We demand, in practice and in games, that when players cross the foul line, they come to play. They hustle, they respect their opponent, and they talk only to their teammates (and in a positive way). Only the catcher talks to the umpire unless a player needs to clarify a rule, the count, or how many outs there are.

Win or lose, on top or bottom, we play with class and react with class. We don't permit any behavior, on the field or off, that embarrasses the program, creates a negative atmosphere, belittles an opponent, or serves to divide the team.

ENFORCING RULES

The last point about rules, and the most important one, is that they serve no purpose if they're not enforced. If there are two standards, or if players see that a violation is not dealt with, the coach can lose control. A rule enforced becomes the law. A rule not enforced leads to the inmates taking over the asylum. When a player violates a rule, we immediately take action. If the violation is something minor such as being late for practice or not being properly dressed (say, in an incomplete practice uniform), we have them clean and vacuum the clubhouse. We don't run our players as punishment. If they come out and don't go hard in the drills, we either make them sit out the drill or send them home. If they don't want to practice, we don't want them out there. If they have problems in the classroom, we monitor it and have them sit out a game if they don't improve. Players who get into trouble at school or are suspended from school are suspended from additional games when they return. Drug and alcohol abuse results in automatic dismissal.

Coaches' Keys

1. Character is as important as coaching skill in evaluating potential assistant coaches. Employ only good people, give them responsibility, and keep them as long as you can.

2. Get the superintendent, principal, athletic director, and teaching staff in your corner and keep them there. They are essential to job security. Communication is vital. They need to understand your philosophy and support it.

3. Strive to enhance support in the community. Make people aware of your facility and team. Conduct camps, clinics, and charity work.

4. Make a wish list of improvements and equipment, establish a fund-raising goal, and be creative and enthusiastic in the type of fund-raisers that you conduct.

5. Create rules that underscore appearance, hustle, and poise in the face of failure. Above all, be consistent in their administration.

Part II

COACHING PLANS

CHAPTER 5 PLANNING FOR THE SEASON

Part II of this book focuses on setting up, organizing, and implementing your practice plans for the off-season. It covers information on conditioning, the weightlifting program, criteria for evaluating talent and making cuts, and evaluating the competition. Part II also emphasizes practice organization, the conditioning program early in the season, and the actual team practice and preparation during the season itself. This chapter then gives you a specific plan for organizing your team's year. It provides an in-depth discussion of choosing a method of conditioning your players, the specific drills and techniques that you should concentrate on, and off-season goals and practices.

GETTING ORGANIZED

The ideal way to plan your season is to sit down with your staff and list what you need to accomplish during the summer, at the start of the school year, in January when you return from winter break, and finally when you start practicing after school in preparation for league games. The goal, of course, is to reach postleague play, and you should have plans and strategies in place for that as well. Often, however, coaches are not able to get together as a staff. If this presents a problem, the head coach must sit down by himself and determine what he wants and needs to do to prepare for the season. Initially, you should compile a list of the things that you want to cover for the year. Beginning with summer ball and into the fall when you return to school, the whole approach should focus on improving your weaknesses and maintaining your strengths. To accomplish this, you need to prioritize your ideas and goals and focus on minimizing your weaknesses so that your team will become more competitive. If you remain weak at certain positions and don't improve, then you have not accomplished what you set out to do. To plan the season and stay organized, you need to make a master plan and then refer to it frequently to ensure that you are staying the course. Your master schedule of drills and your practice plan organization will help you stay on track. This approach will allow the coaching staff to check their progress continually. Figure 5.1 provides an example of a master schedule of drills and fundamentals players will need to succeed.

Something to keep in mind in preparing for the season is dealing with medical forms for your players. Each player should take care of the required physicals. The school provides the paperwork, and completed forms are usually required before the first practice. The school usually monitors this, with the coach's only job being to make sure that the paperwork is on time.

Figure 5.1 Practice Organizer

Practice Organizer

STRETCH AND THROW

IF-Quick hands	IF-Relay throw	C-Pull the bow	P-Dry drills
IF-Four corners	OF-Crow hop	P-Football throw	

INDIVIDUAL FUNDAMENTALS AND GROUP DEFENSE

Outfield	Pitchers	Catchers	First base	Infield
Drop step angles	Covering 1st	Agilities	Rolls	Rolls
Getting behind ball	Picks	Framing	Ground balls	Feeds (5 types)
Over-head catch	Fielding bunts	Fielding bunts	Covering bag	Pivots
Fast-gather-fast	Comebackers	Blocks	Holding runners	Stretch pivots
Round to throwing side	Play at plate	Pop-ups	Toss to pitcher	Short hops
Reverse to throwing side		Pitchouts	Double play	Backhands
Fence drill		Pass balls	Communication	Spin drill
Backup drill		Tags at home	with 2nd	Range drill
Relay drill				Dive drill
				Hit-and-run hold
				Charge and flip
				Pop-ups
				Tag at base
				T-drill
				Leather nuts

TEAM OFFENSE AND DEFENSE

Team defense	Team offense	Team hitting	Conditioning	Offensive execution
Pregame	Hit and run - 1st - 1st and 2nd outs	With runners	Each base instruction	Competition hitting
Picks		5-4-3-2-1	Home/1st/2nd	Pregame hitting
Special picks - Play deep (1st) - No look (2nd) - 3rd to 1st - Windup		Command hitting	Down the line	Clutch hitting
	2nd and 3rd offense	Work ups	Trips	In and out
	3rd gold and red	Count hitting	Catch the rabbit	
	Bunt offense - Squeeze - Push - Drag - Steal - Delay steal		Determination	
Rundowns			Cadillac	
Bunt defense - 1st: 1,2,3 - 2nd: 1,2,3 - Squeeze				
Relays	1st and 3rd - Delay - Go early - Long lead - Safety squeeze			
Double cuts				
Situations				
T-drill				
Machine drill				
No infield drill				
1st and 3rd				

PREPARING IN THE OFF-SEASON

The calendar will dictate your focus. In the summer many players compete on the "school team" coached by the high school coaches. The number of players that you have on this team and the number of games that they play will determine how well you will be able to evaluate and get a feel for the success that your team may have during the regular season. This group should include all the players with the ability to play on varsity, the freshmen who will be sophomores, and even incoming freshmen that have the talent. Get a good look at these players and personalities in the summer. Many teams take their top players and place them in leagues in which they will compete at a higher level in the summer. If you have a returning player or players who were all-league, all-area, or all-state, you may want to put them in a summer league in which they compete against first-year college players, players that have graduated, and other high-level competition. Emphasize to your players that they can't expect to improve unless they play as much as possible against the best competition available. Summer is often the best time to do that. You want to see your players on your "school team," but you also want them to play additional games when possible. Improvement is an important goal for your players in the summer.

Be aware that the player who is not injured but takes the summer off to pursue recreational activities not related to baseball will not progress and improve. In this case look to other players who have made the commitment to getting better by playing more games against tough competition in the summer. When school begins, you are going to change gears and arrange your practice plan to progress slowly and work on the fundamentals that you want all the players in your program to understand and know how to do. You will also focus on your potential weaknesses.

Before school begins you need to allow your players some time off. We like to take the month of August off. We do not schedule any summer league games during this time, and we feel that it's the perfect time for them to rest their arms and take a break from the game.

Players who are competing for an outside team may be in the playoffs at this time. We tell them to take the last two weeks of August off and not to play again until we start school in September.

During the first two weeks in September, we progress slowly, allowing our players, pitchers especially, to rest their arms so that they feel refreshed and ready to go. In the fall, we emphasize the organizational aspect at first. Fall is a time to work on fundamentals. Make sure that all your players—freshmen, junior varsity, and varsity—all know the proper way to execute the drills that your team will use over the course of the year. When coaches rush through the drills and do not emphasize the proper technique, players execute poorly. Take the time to walk your athletes through the various drills. For example, you should walk all your middle infielders through the exact techniques that you want them to use when they turn a double play. You can break down every aspect in a 15- or 20-minute session. These fundamentals can include terminology, cutoffs, relays, positioning, bunt plays, steals, the hit-and-run—all the little things that are important. You can break things up so that you're also giving certain players and areas of concern specialized help. While one of your assistant coaches is working with most of the players on a team-oriented skill, you can work with three or four players on a specific technique such as hitting. During this time of the year you have time to give specific players individualized instruction. Remember, games are won on the practice field. Preparation is the key to victory.

Players Playing Other Sports

Working with multiple-sport athletes can be a challenge. If they play basketball or football, for instance, they will be unable to play in your fall program. Summertime can also be a tug-of-war with these athletes because your games will often conflict with the other sports.

It is tough for today's high school athletes to play three sports such as football, basketball, and baseball. Three-sport athletes are almost nonexistent because of the stress, time commitment, and level of competition. These athletes often end up competing against one-sport athletes for a starting position. This situation can be discouraging, and they often end up quitting one or two sports to focus on the third. As a coach you would like to encourage your players to participate in any sport in which they can be competitive. If you have a tremendous athlete who can play two or three sports, you should want him to experience that as long as he's not sacrificing academics or his health. At the same time, of course, you want to get that player on the field whenever possible to work on his baseball skills.

With the three-sport or two-sport player you're sometimes not going to have him available until his season ends (basketball playoffs, for instance, can keep him away well after the start of baseball practice).

The question is whether the coaches of the other sports will allow him to work on baseball drills while their sport is still in season. At Esperanza we allow the players to do certain things. Pitchers, for example, can throw bullpen sessions and can come out to the field for 15 minutes of throwing if they don't have basketball or soccer practice until later. We feel that this regimen will help them be ready to pitch after basketball or soccer season ends but poses little risk of injury.

We play fall baseball games during football season. Some of the baseball players who are on the football team ask whether they can play in those games, which take place on weeknights or Saturdays. I tell them no because they can be injured by sliding into a base, diving for a ball, or getting hit by a pitch. For the same reason we do not allow them to play in the scout leagues that play on Sundays; we just do not want to jeopardize football by getting them hurt in an off-season baseball game. As soon as football is over, they can come out and start playing right away.

Winter-sport athletes—basketball players, soccer players, and wrestlers—whose season starts in November can play in our fall games before they start their season. If they are pitchers we want them to get a bullpen session in once a week. The coaches of the other sports have been flexible in allowing their players to do bullpen work. These coaches realize that they have less chance of losing the multiple-sport player if they let him engage in limited baseball workouts when it doesn't affect their sport. As a coach, you don't want to put your player in a position where he has to choose a sport. If he makes the wrong choice, you lose him.

You can share multiple-sport athletes, but the amount of time that you share will determine whether they're going to remain multiple-sport athletes. Many players today go to private instruction during the time when they are playing another sport. This is another way to keep them in baseball shape and work on their skills. Realize, however, that no matter how much they have been working on the weekend or with private instructors, they are going to be behind as far as their team-oriented skill and stamina. One hour of private, specialized instruction is not the same as a two-hour team practice.

Evaluating Talent

Evaluating your players' talent is directly related to how you familiarize yourself with both the varsity players and the lower-level athletes. Freshmen and sophomore players whom you were not able to observe as much are now sophomores and juniors. You will now have time to observe them competing with your returning varsity players. The summer program enables you to make a basic evaluation of talent. If you do not run a summer program then, of course, you will not be able to make this initial evaluation. You will have to evaluate these players in the fall when you see all your athletes together at the start of school.

If you have three shortstops—a senior, a junior, and a sophomore—you want to evaluate them to determine which one is best. If the sophomore is quicker and more sure handed, you know that he is the one you need to work with to become your starter. The goal is to win. You don't award a position simply on the basis of seniority.

You should include the following scenario in your evaluation of talent. Incorporate certain drills into your fall practices to allow players to compete for positions. Evaluate each player and determine at what level he will play and whether you plan on his being a starter or a reserve player.

If November and December are bad-weather months and you can't get on the field, you need to do extensive intrasquad work or team work in the months of September and October to make sure that you see these players in game situations, especially if you want to make your cuts before the Christmas break.

Obviously, in evaluating talent, you need to see your players in game situations as often as possible. If your players are in a fall league, you need to attend those games. If you cannot coach your players at this time because of state rules, sit in the stands and evaluate. Write notes about the good and bad things that you see in relation to each person's play. Chart your pitchers, watch your infielders, and diagnose your hitters. Borderline players who you might have to cut could challenge your decision. Record their statistics and document their shortcomings so that you can justify your decisions.

Cutting players, telling them they can't play, is a tough situation for a coach and one of the most difficult aspects of the job. You must handle it in a positive way to avoid conflicts. For instance, you must clarify for the players the evaluation procedure, what will happen to them if they are cut, and whether they can try out again at another time or next year. You must be specific about all these things. The best way to do this for your incoming freshmen and the new players trying out is to have a meeting with them. First, have a meeting at school with the players and have them sign up so that you know each one's name, grade, and position for the tryouts. A week later have a meeting with the parents to explain how you will conduct the tryouts and evaluate the players. Interestingly, parents will in some instances disagree on the position that their son listed as his first choice.

During tryouts, you want to have as many of your assistant coaches on hand as possible to help in the evaluation process. Each coach should have a list of these players, and at the end of each day you should conduct a staff meeting to discuss evaluations. Give each player a letter or number grade on which you all agree. You might assign a number 1 to a player who you believe will be a star, a number 2 to someone who will make the team, and a number 3 to someone likely to be cut. By the end of the week your roster decisions should be clear.

If you have a tryout period that extends over several days, say 10 days, you may want to split those days in half with two cuts. Have 5 tryout days and then cut the players who have no chance. During the second 5-day span, you will have a smaller group of better players, making it easier to determine those who are the best.

The evaluation process is difficult for a coach, and the way it is implemented is important to the player. On the lower levels players must understand that the cut is only for a year and that they can try out again the next year. The coach must be careful to avoid destroying a young player's enthusiasm and spirit. A lot can happen in a year with a young person in terms of growth and change in ability.

We post a list of players who made the team. Those who are cut can meet with any of the coaches to discuss the decision. A young player might find it easier to approach the freshman coach than the head varsity coach. A freshman player might also know one of your coaches from another sport such as freshman football and consequently feel more comfortable talking to him.

In California, where the baseball competition is intense, many of the cut players go out for the golf, volleyball, or track team and do well. A coach can turn a negative process for the cut player into a positive one by suggesting those avenues. All athletes want to play. No one likes to sit. If you can't guarantee playing time to a young athlete—now or in the future—you need to release him and let him do something at which he can be a success. An unhappy, inactive player can become a disciplinary problem during the season.

We interview each varsity player at the end of the fall season, right before winter break. We have three days during which we schedule each potential varsity player for a 10- to 15-minute interview. Each player comes into the coach's office for a meeting with all the varsity coaches. We sit down and tell the player what his strengths are, what his weaknesses are, and where he has to improve. If he didn't make the team, we tell him face to face why he will not be playing with us. We add that he needs a chance to be a success, and it's not going to be in baseball.

We ask some of the marginal players whether they can be satisfied sitting on the bench for a year. Invariably, during these personal interviews in December, most will nod their heads affirmatively and say that being a reserve is not going to be a problem. But come March or April, when you're battling in league and they haven't played for six or eight games in a row, attitudes can change. By clearly putting the issues on the table before the season, you can preempt some of those problems, and you have a basis for reminding the player what he had agreed to in the fall.

As the head coach, it's your program, and you're the final arbiter on decisions and communication. Evaluation is often difficult, and cutting young players is never easy, but there are ways to make it less painful for everyone and possibly turn it into a positive for the player.

Evaluating Competition

Sit down with your assistants, especially if they were with you the year before and saw the teams in your league. Evaluate the competition and determine which teams are going to be at the top of the league standings, which are going to be at the bottom, and where your team fits overall. Decide what your team is going to have to do to be in contention for a playoff berth or league championship.

If you know that players in your league are playing in the off-season or on scout teams, you can watch them, record their tendencies, and make extensive observations. Realize that you will have plenty of time during the season before starting league play to break down the hitters and pitchers you will face. You will get a good look at your opponents then. Scouting your opponents during the off-season is not as useful as scouting your opponent in the preseason. During the preseason you will get a truer look at their strengths and weaknesses.

You should evaluate talent in the off-season in a general sense, not in a specific one. Looking at the players on a certain team might allow you to see them as a potential league champion, so you need to gear up for them as a favorite. Generally speaking, you need to look at how the league stacks up, who you have to be ready for, which team you will open with, and what they like to do offensively. Most of these evaluations are general. You can determine the specific ways in which you will pitch their hitters, the way in which you will position your fielders, and other judgments before the start of league play, not in the fall.

The only uncertainty relates to tournament games because those games are generally set right before the start of the tournament. The rest of the schedule will already be set, so you will know exactly who and where you're playing by the time you end the previous school year in June.

Setting Goals for the Team

We have already discussed individual goals that the player sets for himself or that you establish for him. Such goals include how much weight you want him to lift and how fast you want him to run the 40- or 60-yard dash. You may also include individual goals that relate to baseball. For example, you might want your right fielder to move to center field, or one of your hitters to move from the eighth spot in the lineup to the leadoff spot. You might want a reliever from the year before to become a starter or even the ace of your staff. You can discuss the individual goals that you want each player to strive for during the fall interview or in subsequent meetings and practices. When you tell a player that he has a chance to be a starter, hit in a certain spot in the lineup, or play a certain position, you help to motivate him to work harder in the weight room and on the field during the fall season. Consistently talk to your reserve players to motivate them about working into a starting job and having a successful year.

When you set goals for your team and the season you are not talking about individual goals. As you approach your season, everything becomes about the team. As you start your first nonleague game, let your team know what the goals are. I have found that having three simple goals works well. All are team oriented; none focus on the individual player. If these goals appear too difficult to achieve, adjust them down to a more realistic level. For instance, you may set a goal to have a winning record or to win a series from a team in your league that has equal talent. Give your players a chance with goals that they can achieve.

Our first goal is to make the playoffs. Second, we are going to win the league championship. The third goal is to win the postseason tournament, which will end in a state or section championship. For teams in some states, achieving this goal will mean going undefeated in the postseason. Other states have a double-elimination postseason tournament that allows teams to continue playing with one loss. The key is to attain that third goal.

Beginning with the first nonleague game in February, we consistently preach about the need to improve so that when we start league play we can win enough games to qualify for the playoffs and win the league title as well. This goal should be the motivation, and your team should know what it takes to do it. In California the top three teams from most leagues make the playoffs. If you finish in fourth place you don't qualify. In some states every team goes to the playoffs, more or less playing a new season in a postseason tournament. Make sure that your players know what they have to do to get there.

The players should also know that where they finish in league is going to help them when the teams are seeded for the playoffs. If you are a league champion, you get the best seed from your league, giving you a better chance to attain your third goal of a state or section title. Your team should understand these goals and recognize that all are team oriented.

Of course, teams that get off to a bad start or are struggling might find themselves in a situation where they can't make the playoffs and thus have to adjust their goals. At all times and in all situations, the supplemental goal should be to win one game at a time and to play your best so that you can walk off the field with your head high, win or lose.

Setting Goals for the Coaching Staff

The goals of your coaching staff should mirror the team goals. You want your staff to work toward these goals at practice every day, pumping up the players and getting them excited about routine preparation, about having the chance to improve every day. The staff should be able to handle certain minor problems so that you as a head coach do not have to deal with them, but they should always know where

you're coming from, what the rules are, what the goals are. They are your supporting voices, and you need to remind them each fall what the rules and goals are. As a staff the primary goal is to be able to say at the end of each year that the team improved over the season. You want your staff members, like your players, to be able to hold their heads high.

Setting Schedules

All of your schedules should be finalized before you end the previous school year in June. At Esperanza I'm pretty much allowed to put together the schedule, but all schools are different. At some, the athletic director does it. Scheduling tournaments and nonleague games needs to be done before you break for summer. Your league determines league schedules, and those have already been approved and distributed before the end of the school year. When you start in the fall, all of these scheduling tasks have already been completed.

Reserving Practice Space for the Season

As you progress through the fall one of the problems that may develop is facility availability. Several factors may contribute to the problem. For example, field space itself may be an issue. If the football team has to use part of your diamond for practice, that obviously compromises your practice schedule. All you can do is use the available facilities to your advantage. Some football teams begin practice with a chalk talk, which may allow you an hour or so on the field. If you are not able to use the field, work on strength and conditioning in the weight room. You can't be on the field and in the weight room at the same time.

When a coach plans his practice, he must be prepared for inclement weather. In September most schools will have good weather for practicing. Depending on your location, that circumstance could change dramatically as winter sets in. If you are in a warm-weather state you naturally have an advantage because you are able to continue your practices throughout the fall months.

If inclement weather doesn't permit you to practice on the field, you must be able to secure the multipurpose room or gymnasium, an area where you will have protection from the elements and can continue to work on fundamentals. If no indoor facilities are available in which to practice, then you will need to find a classroom or some room in which you can sit down with the team and discuss a list of things with your players. You want to get something accomplished. You can go over the mental game—discussing with hitters how to work the count and what to look for in different situations, talking to pitchers about pitch selection and game situations, reviewing signs. This is a perfect opportunity to review the fundamentals and reinforce your rules and goals.

Reserving the Weight Room

The fall is also a great time to increase your team strength and speed by working in the weight room. As you set up your weight regimen you must remember to incorporate an evaluation of the players in their lifts. A chart posted in your clubhouse or locker room gives players a visual reference to their improvement and progression. Recording their progress weekly will serve as motivation for them to continue working on their strength. They can also see how they compare to their teammates. Praise those who show dramatic improvement. Weightlifting is an individual activity that players can do on their days off. Encourage them to lift year round. Another important element of a weightlifting program is that pitchers must have a special weight program that works their arms and increases their strength in the front and the back of their shoulders and arms. The objective is to protect the pitching arm by building strength in the proper area. Many of the lifts for pitchers are the same as those for position players, but alternative lifts isolate the pitcher's shoulder, arm, and elbow area, which are most vulnerable to injury. More specific conditioning concerns are covered in chapter 12.

During the off-season you must make use of the weight room when it is available. Check the schedule and know when your team can use it. Look into building your own weight room or converting an empty room or space into a weight room. Sharing the expenses with another sport that will not be using the same time frame for weightlifting is a good option. Another possibility is to check the fitness facilities in your neighborhood. A commercial facility may see a public relations value in allowing a high school team to use its equipment.

Obviously, if none of this works, you can't lift weights in a team atmosphere, which is a significant drawback in an era when all athletes are getting bigger and stronger, and when having a weight program free of steroids and other chemicals is an integral part of high school athletics. Players should lift as a team two times a week during the season to maintain their newly acquired strength. Incorporate a speed and plyometrics program to teach your players the proper way to run and gain quickness.

Most baseball players detest running drills, but you can motivate them by challenging them to improve their times and by letting them know how they compare with their teammates. Place charts for weightlifting and running side by side as a visual incentive for players to monitor their progress.

Most high schools have limited space for weightlifting and other kinds of training, so a cooperative scheduling effort on the part of all coaches is essential. In a competitive business, the stronger and faster athletes will prevail.

DEVELOPING A CONDITIONING PROGRAM

Conditioning for specific positions is difficult, so most programs have a specific program for their pitchers and another for the rest of the team. In their lifts players can be exposed to squats and lunges that will work on their legs and help those who play such positions as catcher, shortstop, or second base. This, like any other part of the game, must be organized and prioritized according to what you want to accomplish. You can do circuit training, which involves going from station to station and lifting for a specific length of time. You can also go to a bulk workout or Olympic lifts using heavier weight. If your athletes are returning from injury, they must go slow and easy with their rehab workouts. Most young players want to get back to their previous workouts right away. Watch them closely, monitor their workouts, and make sure that they take it slow and easy with light weights.

Steroids are not a common problem in high school baseball. I have never even suspected a player of using them. If I did, I would confront the player and want some straight answers. But I don't ignore this issue. I talk to them of the dangers and the fact that the damage steroids do is not worth the gain. Obviously, a player who uses steroids will show dramatic physical change. The coaching staff should also be aware of personality changes. People on steroids can have an extremely aggressive personality. They have trouble controlling their impulses and temper. If you see a striking physical change combined with anger and rage outbursts, steroid use could be the problem.

Another concern is how to structure conditioning during the fall months leading up to the winter break. The key part of conditioning is that the coaching staff needs to determine at what point to start the conditioning program. If conditioning is a priority in the fall, you will need to implement a schedule of running, stretches, and calisthenics that players can do on their own during the two- or three-week winter break. Players who do not condition during this break will lose all the stamina that they have built up during the previous three or four months. To ensure that your athletes continued to condition over the break, the coaching staff should administer a test, a timed one-mile run or other running drill, when they return after vacation.

At Esperanza we really hit the conditioning hard in January when we return from the winter break. We feel that this four- to six-week period before the season starts will give us plenty of time to get our players in shape. We take our players to a steep hill near our school. We time them each time they run up the hill. If they don't make it under the required time, they do extra running. Following the hill run they immediately go on a 20-minute run to ensure that they are getting a strenuous conditioning workout. As a result our players quickly get in shape so that when we begin after-school practices, we can focus on technique and do not have to cut into our practice schedule with conditioning work. When we start practicing after school, we want our nonpitchers to focus their running on the fundamentals and techniques of running the bases. We concentrate on the mechanics of baseball running instead of simply running the players to get them in shape. Figures 5.2 and 5.3 provide examples of effective conditioning

Figure 5.2 A Year-Long Conditioning Program

Month	Emphasis	Description
August	Weightlifting	Start weight program focusing on multiple repetitions (10-15 reps) and 3 or 4 sets of exercises
September, October, and November	Fall practice, weightlifting, plyometric training, and speed work	Practice baseball during school baseball class Weightlifting Monday, Wednesday, Friday Monday: circuit training Wednesday and Friday: heavy lifting Tuesday, Thursday, Friday: plyometrics September: get maximum weight 40 to 60 times
December	Weightlifting, speed workout	Pitchers rest arms Get maximum lifts and record to show progress Record 40 and 60 times to show speed progress Winter break: work out on their own (home training)
January through mid-February	Preseason workout Weightlifting Conditioning workout	Practice during baseball class Monday, Wednesday, Friday: weightlifting (same as fall) Extensive conditioning: 40-yard dash (10), 60-yard dash (10), 20-minute jog or run (no walking)
Mid-February to June	In-season training	Baseball practice Weightlifting 2 days per week Team conditioning with baseball running skills
June, July	Off-season training Summer plan	Individual training for strength building Speed work Aerobic and anaerobic conditioning

programs. Figure 5.2 illustrates a general year-long conditioning regimen. Figure 5.3 illustrates a sample off-season program broken down into daily sessions progressing for the months before after-school practices begin. Once practice starts, conditioning should be incorporated into your practices rather than done separately, with the focus being primarily on developing players' baseball skills. For the weightlifting exercises on Monday and Wednesday provided in the program in figure 5.3, have your players do three to four sets with the first two sets lasting 30 seconds for each player. The third and fourth set can be reduced to 20 seconds. Players should partner up and alternate, having one player spot while the other lifts, then switching places after the designated time. When they both have finished, they should move to the next station in the circuit. The basic lifts should be: bench presses, squats, and regular and reverse curls, with others incorporated into the regimen as appropriate and as time allows. Friday, weightlifting can be one without a circuit. Each group should do three sets with heavier weights before moving to the next exercise. The heavy weight workout should be done at least one day a week. On the days calling for plyometric drills, include a few from the following: butt kickers, leg lunges, carioca, backward running, jumps, high knees, and striders.

If you are running extensively in the fall you must provide your players with a program for maintaining their conditioning over the winter break. No matter what you do in the fall, however, you must have an extensive running program starting in January so that your athletes are in shape by the time after-school practices begin. This kind of program lets you focus on baseball running fundamentals as well as a number of offensive things that you will need to do on the bases once the season starts. By getting your players in shape before the season, your players will be able to get through your practices

Figure 5.3 A Week-Long Off-Season Conditioning Program

September to December

Monday, Wednesday, Friday
- Workout weightlifting (include plyometric drills in weightlifting)

Tuesday, Thursday
- Extension plyometric drills
- (5-10) 40-yard sprints
- (5-10) 60-yard sprints

January to February

Monday, Wednesday, Friday
- Weight lifting and plyometrics
- Long distance running

Tuesday, Thursday
- Extension plyometric drills
- (10) 40-yard sprints
- (10) 60-yard sprints
- (10) 100-yard sprints
- 20 minute run at jog pace

(Work up to these numbers.)

easier and with the proper tempo. Keep in mind that the one-hour preseason athletic period will increase to practices of two and a half to three hours. When players are in shape they have less problems handling the long workouts. They practice with more zip and energy.

Coaches' Keys

1. For planning purposes, you need to divide the year into seasons—summer, fall, and spring. You then outline a conditioning and practice program for each and set the goals for each season.

2. Reserve field and conditioning space early and be willing to share players with other sports. Encourage multi-sport players to find time each week to work on their baseball skills.

3. Evaluate your talent and try to conduct your tryouts before the winter break so that you will be ready to go in the spring.

4. Meet with your players personally to tell them where they stand and what your expectations are for the season—as individuals and for the team.

5. Scout opposing players in the off-season but recognize that you can do more definitive scouting in the preseason.

6. The ultimate team goal is to win a state or sectional title, but the goal for coaches and players is always to perform to the best of their ability.

CHAPTER 6 ORGANIZING PRACTICE

This chapter emphasizes practice organization. It incorporates practice progression, consistency, and the occasional need for a special practice to prepare for an opponent's specific strengths or weaknesses. It will also touch again on conditioning.

The chapter starts with how to organize a practice and why it is important to take the time to organize each practice, and this chapter talks about what to emphasize when you sit down and brainstorm with your staff, according to what skills you should cover. The proper method to progress as you move through the season is also covered. A complete and well-rounded practice uses various approaches to conditioning players.

First, I believe that every day at practice should have a theme. One day it could be defense; on the next, offense. A general principle early in the season is to take the field assuming that your players know nothing. Start with this premise and build on it, emphasizing fundamentals even with returning varsity players.

Another key starting point is attitude. Players should be willing to practice at game-speed tempo. We instruct our players to go full speed in all drills, emphasizing that anyone can perform at half speed. We tell them that practices should mirror the tempo at which we'll expect them to perform in games.

A plan is imperative and should be carried with you throughout the practice. Time is limited. You shouldn't be guessing. Some things are automatic, no matter what the level of talent and results to that point. For example, your infielders need to get ground balls every day or nearly every day to reinforce their defensive skills. Your pitchers need to throw their bullpens on a regular basis scheduled around your game dates. Batting practice will occupy a certain amount of every practice as well.

In and around those baseball basics, the practice and game performances of your team will dictate the things that you need to work on and emphasize. Your plan should all be there on your clipboard each day, as basic as the belief that every day you and your assistants take the field prepared to coach and teach. If that seems automatic, well, I've seen too many coaches merely grab a chair and a bottle of water, and spend their entire time sitting near the batting cage chatting with people who have dropped by practice. Too many times, coaches neglect their responsibility to coach and teach, to set a tone, to provide an example of hard work. A coach should be out there to coach, not socialize.

Even with experienced players, the coach should take the time to demonstrate how to perform skills properly. You never know what previous coaches have left out.

PRACTICE ORGANIZATION

The first thing to do when organizing a practice plan is to meet with your coaches to brainstorm, discuss what you want to accomplish, and decide how you want your players to look or dress at practice. Again, communication is essential. A coach should let his players know everything for which they will be held accountable. If you want your players dressed in a special or specific way for practice, let them know. If you don't care, tell them that also. I personally like to have my players come out in uniform appearance.

Uniforms

A player's appearance at practice may seem trivial, but pride in appearance is important and you need to control it. The first decision related to their dress, of course, is what apparel you want them to wear. Do you want your team in shorts or baseball pants? If you have a Little League team, the younger guys will often show up in jeans. You'll need to tell them to get some baseball pants if that's what you want them to wear—and if the league allows it. If you're going to have them sliding on the bases at practice, tell them not to wear shorts. Otherwise, mom is going to send them to practice any way she wants.

The same uniformity should hold for high school and college players. Sometimes all the players at a high school practice are dressed differently. They are wearing different shirts, some of which have no affiliation with the school, or they may be wearing different colored pants or shorts. I believe that your program's practice organization should start with a uniform dress code. Wearing shorts on certain practice days is fine, but the shorts should be uniform and include the school logo. In our fall program, for example, our players wear our baseball shorts with an Esperanza shirt. If we are going to play an intrasquad game, they have to wear baseball pants. When the season starts in February, we practice in pants every day. On a special day with a shorter practice or lighter workout, we might permit shorts. Those are our first decisions in organizing practice. I personally feel that the uniform dress is where discipline starts. Players take pride in what they wear and they need to be organized, especially if they are wearing a different shirt on certain days. Our players, during the regular season, wear gray baseball pants. On Monday, Wednesday, and Friday at practice they wear our cardinal colored practice shirt, and on Tuesday, Thursday, and Saturday, they wear their gray practice shirt. This may seem like an inconvenience, but the kids seldom violate this dress policy. They take pride in their practice uniform. Another positive is that requiring them to wear a uniform helps them be organized. As a result of having to be prepared for each practice, they are better organized with their uniform and equipment on game day.

Setting a Periodized Schedule

The next step is obvious. You need to list the items that you want to cover at practice for the day, week, month, and season. Your assistant coaches should be involved in that process. The list, of course, can change over time as certain needs and situations develop, but basically you should never take the practice field without the time being structured and a plan in place for the team generally and each position specifically. Figure 6.1 provides an example of

Figure 6.1 A sample practice plan

Daily Practice Plan

2:00-2:10 Stretch and run
2:10-2:15 Throw

Date: January 29, 2005
Opponent: Santa Marguerita

Time	Pitchers	Catchers	Infield	Outfield
2:30	Infield or outfield	Roll	Rolls	Fundamentals
2:45	Infield or outfield	Catch or fungo	Ground balls	Ground balls
3:00	All players	Defense vs. T		Hit off T

3:00-3:15

Team defense:

Situations (Alternate 3 groups)

2 on 1 defense hitting

Offensive execution:

Work on "slash" with runners at 1st and 2nd

Round 1	Hit-and-run—drag—squeeze	Announcements
Round 2	7 cuts—slash	Go over signs
Round 3	3-2-2	
Round 4	Base hits	

HITTING GROUPS				FINAL NOTES
Group number and location				
Hitter	Dickerson	Larson		
On deck	Aguilar	Hines		
2nd on deck	Bono	Tilly		
Runner at 3rd	O'Hail	Daly		
Runner at 2nd	Hunter	Montgomery		
Bagman	Muhlsteff	Slater		
Runner at 1st	Burns	Youngdale		

Competition: 2nd pitch   Late hitters:

Conditioning:

Tag at 3rd

Determination"

how to structure a practice. The actual drills a coach decides to run on any given day will depend on what skills he recognizes his team needs to work on.

Neither the head coach nor his assistants should be without a copy of the plan when they go on the field. Posting a copy on the bulletin board each day isn't a bad idea. Seeing the plan helps the players be prepared and seems to build their respect for the coach's organization.

Don't Be Afraid to Change

In 1986 I hired an assistant coach, Doug Domene, who had been a head coach at a small Christian school for three years. Doug recommended some subtle changes in our practice approach, but we mostly stayed with the previous plan. We won the CIF Championship in California that year and were voted the nation's number one high school team by *USA Today*. The following year we lost eight starters, and Doug surprised me by saying that we needed to make major changes in a practice format that had produced a national title.

Sticking with what we had been doing would have been easy, of course, but Doug saw the need to fix certain things, and we went to work, basically revamping our whole practice plan, from playing catch at the beginning of practice through conditioning at the end, all with a specific structure and purpose.

Despite the loss of the eight starters we returned to the CIF title game that year and came within a run of repeating as number one in the nation. We made it to the CIF title game again in 1988.

I attribute a lot of that and our ensuing success to the organizational structure that Doug brought to our practices and our willingness to adapt, to recognize that practice structure and approach often relate to the needs of a particular talent level. We are always trying to improve our practice plans because that's where success starts.

Progression and Consistency

The goals of progression and consistency start with a plan as well. When teaching progression, you as a coach want to have goals that you stick with as you organize your practices. The primary goal, of course, is to build toward a finished product. In that process, we'll talk about starting with fundamentals and then moving through more complex drills until your team achieves game execution.

Start your progression with a simple teaching system. Begin by introducing your skills or drills to show how to do them properly. Next, reinforce them through repetition until doing them correctly becomes habit. Last, review what you've done. Keep coming back to the skill or drill so that your players do not forget it. This is an important philosophy in our practice progression and consistency: introduction, reinforcement, review.

At Esperanza we spend a lot of time structuring our practices so that they progress consistently and logically. We begin our practices with stretching, standing legs, sitting legs, arms, and light running. Our stretching has no tempo. We have two players in front and the rest of the team in lines. We stretch legs and arms. During this time, we want them to be thinking and talking baseball. Although this may seem

Working closely with your players will not only help them develop the skills they will need to succeed, but will also help them feel like they are part of a team.

unimportant, we want our players to focus on baseball as soon as they take the field. No one talking about girlfriends or anything except baseball. After stretching, the players take a loosening-up run. One of our coaches is out in front, acting as a pitcher. The team works on getting quick takeoffs as if they are stealing a base. Following this, our players are ready to get their arms loose by playing catch. We consistently have the same players play catch together—middle infielders together, corner infielders together, and so on with outfielders, catchers, and pitchers.

If I were coaching a team below high school level, I would watch my team play catch on the first day and then pair the players based on talent level, with the best together and so on down the line. When you have a player with a strong arm playing catch with a player whose catching skills are poor, the chance for injury is greater. Pair players at the Little League level on ability, not position.

At Esperanza we try to structure our throwing. We start by putting players on their knees and taking 10 throws that way. All players do this except catchers, who are in their game crouch for the 10 throws. Next, from a standing position, we put a player on the foul line, and after each throw his partner backs up a step so that they are lengthening the distance and strengthening their arms. We want our players to throw from a distance every day to increase accuracy and arm strength. We then shorten it up again and continue throwing until their arms are loose. We then implement some type of throwing drill—Four Corners, Quick Hands, or any of several drills that we have on our fundamental list. Kids play catch from the time that they begin to walk, but it is never too late to learn new techniques and never too late to improve.

As the rest of our team plays catch, we use this time every day to have a coach work with the catchers on their fundamentals—blocking, framing, and so on. Catchers are often the least coached players, so you need to set aside time daily to work with them.

After our team has stretched and played catch, we progress to our fundamental period. Players at each position work on fundamentals specific to their position. Some drills are done daily; others are done once or twice a week. This

progression is covered in chapters 7 through 12. You can refer to those chapters to see each drill or fundamental. During the fundamental period our pitchers are working on flat or dry drills. They are on flat ground in the outfield working on their form and technique, working out of both a windup and a stretch. We describe these drills in depth when we talk about pitching in chapter 12.

Following our fundamental time we progress to our group skills. Our players work in small groups. We can have our shortstop and second baseman working together while our third basemen are throwing to our first baseman, or we can have our pitchers working with our infielders on fielding bunts and grounders back to the mound. We can also have our catchers working with our corner infielders, the first and the third basemen, on pickoffs, while our pitchers, second basemen, and shortstops are working on pickoffs to second base. We can do a number of things with our group skills. In another effective drill, our lower-level players hit grounders off the tee while our infielders and pitchers play defense.

The outfielders at this time are working on their ground balls, fly balls, and backup drills in smaller groups. Remember to group outfielders together and infielders together during these small-group drills. This period gives our pitchers who at times play other positions a chance to work with their colleagues at those positions.

The next progression takes us from small-group skills to team skills. We practice our cutoffs and relays as a team and practice team situations off live pitching or against the pitching machine or tee. At Esperanza, when we finish this first part of the practice, having focused primarily on defense, we meet behind second base on the outfield grass for a 10-minute break. During this break, which we call announcements, I talk to my players about various topics that I want them to understand. This talk can include techniques, signs, or perhaps something that happened in a recent game. I may talk about something we're going to work on next. For example, I might tell my players that after announcements we're going to work on our first-and-third offense. I explain what I want them to concentrate on so that they know where the focus should be.

After we finish our work on team skills and announcements, we move on to batting practice. We hit as a team. We like to divide our team into three groups. One group is hitting live on the field, another is hitting in the batting cages, and the third group is playing defense and fielding each batted ball live. The batting cage hitters rotate to live hitting on the field and then on to defense. The defensive players move to the batting cage. This is our daily batting practice, although we mix up the type of batting practice and how we hit.

After batting practice we are either finished with our baseball skills or ready to involve the team in a competition drill. We divide the players into teams and watch how they compete against each other in various drills and games. We will discuss these hitting and competitive drills in greater detail in the hitting section.

The final thing we do is conditioning work or running. Sometimes we break off and have our pitchers go with the pitching coach to run separately for extra conditioning. For the position players, conditioning is always related to the game. It may involve stealing a base, learning how to get jumps on the pitcher, or base-running techniques, including going from first to third and second to home. There is no reason that conditioning can't be tied to learning how to run the bases and play the game better offensively. Our conditioning may also be tied to a reminder of how to sprint on and off the field. We do not have our team run to the foul pole a certain number of times because that activity doesn't enhance baseball skills. All our running relates to technique and hustle.

SPECIAL PRACTICES

We use special practices for two reasons. The first type of special practice prepares us to counter an opponent's strength or exploit an opponent's weakness. In the second type of special practice we deviate from the routine or usual practice to send the team a specific message, either a positive one or a negative one.

We have this second type of special practice after games in which we have performed poorly or embarrassed ourselves. During these prac-

tices the coaching staff makes the point that we will not tolerate the negative or embarrassing behavior. We reinforce this concept with extra running, extra work, or some other tedious activity that clearly illustrates to the team that their behavior must change.

A special practice may take the opposite approach by enhancing a positive atmosphere. This type of practice can be short and quick or have some type of reward after the practice. We might treat the team to a soda or sport drink to let them know that they did a great job. For a bigger accomplishment, such as winning the league, we might shorten our practice during the next week and maybe even have a barbeque or bring in pizzas to let the players enjoy their achievement.

These special practices do not happen every week. I don't like to prepare for an opponent with special practices. The philosophy I like to take in our team approach is to focus on our own execution, not our opponent. If we do see a glaring weakness in an opponent, we will point it out so that we are prepared to take advantage of it, but if we're doing our job on a daily basis, working on fundamentals and preparing for any situation, we shouldn't need a special practice based on an opponent's strengths or weaknesses.

At the same time, we may on occasion want to charge up our players with a special practice. One year we had our next game scheduled against an outstanding team that was winning our league. We needed a special practice to give us confidence against them. I told our players that I thought we could steal home against those guys and that we were going to have a special practice to work on doing that. We made a big deal about stealing home, and our players really got into it, creating an energized practice. We came out to play the game with electric enthusiasm. We did a tremendous job that day and won the game. We didn't steal home, and I knew that we probably wouldn't even try, but we gained the confidence and enthusiasm that gave us an emotional shot in the arm. This approach does not always work, but at times it can provide a much needed boost.

Your special practices can be designed to prepare specifically for your opponent or to reward or punish your team. At Esperanza we limit our special practices because we feel that we should be able to handle anything that our opponent does based on our preparation.

CONDITIONING IN PRACTICE

The last section of this chapter involves conditioning. By the time we start our first practices in February in preparation for the season, our players are already in shape because of what we did in the fall. Two months before we start our season we take our players to a street near campus that has a steep incline. We have our players jog over to this street and run up it in a certain time, according to my stopwatch. I time their first trip up the hill and then make them run that time each trip or they run an extra one. We start the first day by running the hill 3 times. At the end we are able to run it 10 times under the designated time. Following this run, we have the players run for 20 minutes around the school. This session is great at getting them ready for the season. It has nothing to do with baseball running skills, but it builds their stamina and gets them into running shape. Then when the season begins, we just need to maintain this level. Keeping this in mind, we design all our conditioning to incorporate learning and refining our baseball running skills and techniques. We work on how to turn first base on a double and the angle that the batter takes out of the batter's box. We go over the steps that players take when stealing a base, how to open the hips and cross over with the left foot. We practice it repeatedly so that it becomes second nature and our players can do it automatically.

Many coaches, especially at the Little League level, take it for granted that their players know how to run the bases. Many of these players have never been taught the proper technique. Review all your base-running skills. Teach your players how to tag up on a fly ball using their own eyes and how to get a jump after the catch. Show them how to line up on the base and push off to get a great jump when they tag up. A Little League coach may not want his players to tag up and use their own eyes to react. The coach may want to tell his players when to tag and when to leave. That's fine, but make sure that you practice it. Don't just talk to your players about tagging up and expect them to get it.

We spend a lot of time with our players to make sure that they understand where to go and how to help the base runner. We have a batter at home, a runner at second base, and an on-deck hitter. The batter at home swings the bat and runs out a double, the runner at second runs home, and the on-deck hitter picks up the bat and tells the runner from second base to stand up or slide. This is a running drill, but it also shows the on-deck hitter where he needs to be in that situation and how to signal the runner to stand up or slide.

Sometimes we divide our players into three groups to condition them. We have a group at first base working with a coach on stealing second base, a group at second base working on stealing third base, and a group at third base working on stealing home or on our squeeze bunt. We then rotate so that each group has a chance in each situation. We don't emphasize the conditioning aspect of any drill because that takes care of itself.

In our baseball program our varsity team works out six days a week during our season. We play two games a week, and Saturday is a practice day. On Saturdays, we do not condition. We have a light workout. We usually hit, some players get ground balls, or we might have our pitchers throw live to our hitters. This extra day of working out is beneficial, but we do not need to stress conditioning as part of it, although our pitchers do go on a long Saturday run to keep their legs strong. Otherwise, our position players over the years have seemed to respond well to this light format, and our Saturday workouts have been some of our best.

Coaches' Keys

1. Practice organization begins with a brainstorming session by the coaching staff. Your practice plan needs to cover all the skills and situations that will prepare your team to play. Having a checklist will ensure that you know what to emphasize daily, weekly, monthly, and for the season.

2. Implement a system of progression and use it consistently throughout your practices. This progression should include stretching and throwing, individual time, small-group work, team defense, team offense, hitting, and conditioning tied to technique.

3. Special practices can prepare you to capitalize on an opponent's weaknesses or offset an opponent's strengths. You can also use a special positive or negative practice to reinforce or discourage a particular behavior. To maintain their distinctive quality, employ special practices infrequently.

4. Condition your players and get them in shape before the season. When the season begins make sure that your players stay in shape by training them in baseball running techniques and skills.

Part III

COACHING OFFENSE

CHAPTER 7 TEACHING HITTING SKILLS

Hitting a baseball may the most difficult skill to learn and master in sport. Before he begins tutoring, a coach must get this point across to a young player. Teaching the skills that are necessary to becoming a good hitter is much easier when the player understands just how difficult hitting is. That way he is less apt to become frustrated with failure. Even a .300 hitter fails 7 out of 10 times, and even when a hitter makes solid contact the odds are that he will make an out. Once a hitter understands the negatives involved with hitting, he has taken the first step toward becoming a successful hitter.

In teaching the basics of hitting, the coach should stress how important it is that the hitter have a plan when he steps into the batter's box. With a plan in place, the hitter can adjust as he gets into the ball-and-strike count. Besides considering the effect that the count has on adjustments and approach, the hitter has to adjust to the pitcher and the type of pitches that he is throwing. Know when the count is in your favor and when you have an advantage. Also be aware of when you need to "battle" at the plate, because the advantage is with the pitcher. Table 7.1 illustrates how the count affects the batter's chances of getting on base.

After a coach gets these concepts across, he is ready to lay out the skills involved with hitting.

Table 7.1 Hitting With the Count

Count	BA	AB	Rank
0-0	0.337	698-2073	5
1-0	0.380	520-1368	1
2-0	0.328	162-494	6
3-1	0.353	171-484	3
2-1	0.367	299-814	2
1-1	0.341	397-1163	4
3-2	0.234	269-1148	8
0-1	0.327	357-1092	7
2-2	0.186	336-1810	9
0-2	0.134	127-946	11
1-2	0.171	321-1879	10

The statistics on over 15,000 ABs were used to create this chart.

THE ABSOLUTES OF HITTING

Hitting can be a personal thing, or it can be a general skill. The techniques are endless—from the stance through the swing to the follow-through, or finish. In working with a hitter, a coach needs to know that. The other important thing that a coach needs to know is that a hitter must execute certain absolutes to be successful. This section will explain good hitting techniques.

Stance

Among the hitting absolutes, the first is balance in the stance, the position of the feet. The feet can take three different basic positions.

• The first is the closed stance, in which the front foot is closer to home plate than the back foot (see figure 7.1a). This stance helps keep the front shoulder closed and with any luck prevents it from flying open, an action that leaves the hitter vulnerable to breaking balls and pitches away.

• The second stance has the hitter's feet even, with neither one forward or back from the other (see figure 7.1b). In this stance the hitter is basically balanced.

• In the third stance, the open stance, the front foot is open or farther from home plate than the back foot (see figure 7.1c). A hitter may use this stance for several reasons. Some hitters believe that they can see the pitcher better. Other hitters think that the open stance keeps them from getting jammed with the inside pitch, and some hitters use it to dive into the pitch and hit the ball away. Still other hitters do it as a loading device. In other words, as the pitch is delivered, they take a stride with the front foot toward the plate, putting the feet on a more parallel plane.

In all three stances the hitter wants his feet to be just wider than shoulder-width so that his stride is not too long. The closer his feet are together in his stance, the longer his stride is apt to be. A long stride will make it easier for the pitcher to get the hitter off balance. With this in mind, the hitter wants his feet to form a wide base and take a stride from one to six inches, but no longer than six inches.

The hitter should bend some at his knees and waist. A coach should check to see that the hitter has his knees over his feet and his shoulders over his knees. The hitter's weight should be on the balls of his feet. This positioning will make his toes point inside and his heels point out. An important part of hitting is keeping the eyes level and the head not tilted so that the back eye, the right eye for a right-handed hitter

Figure 7.1 (a) Closed stance position, (b) even stance position, and (c) open stance position.

and the left eye for a left-handed hitter, can see the pitcher. A hitter often doesn't realize that his head is tilted in his stance in a way that he cannot see the pitcher with his back eye. A great deal of hitting is based on keeping the head and eyes level.

Rhythm and Timing

The next technique of hitting involves rhythm and timing. All good hitters have a rhythm that involves synchronizing the trigger movement of taking the hands back as the pitch is delivered and striding with a closed front foot. The hitter takes his hands back to generate rhythm and increase power. The hitter starts movement with his hands and front foot when the pitcher breaks his hands to take the ball out of his glove. As the pitcher gets to his release point, ready to let go of the ball, the hitter's front foot should be down and his hands back, ready to come forward and hit (see figure 7.2). The pitcher, of course, tries to disrupt this rhythm and timing by delivering pitches with a variety of speeds and movements to get the hitter off balance. To stay on balance, the hitter

needs to keep his weight and hands back when he strides. A coach can help a hitter keep his weight back by instructing him to stride softly with no weight on his front foot.

The Swing

The next technique in hitting is the swing itself and the path that the bat takes in the swing. When the hitter starts his swing he should have the barrel of the bat above his hands and his hands above his elbows. The hitter should try to swing down on the ball, and when he gets the bat on the plane of the ball, he keeps the bat on that plane and hits through the ball. In bringing his hands into the hitting zone, the hitter should be turning his back hip an instant before he starts his hands forward. Keep in mind that every swing has the goal of getting the fat part of the bat on the ball with hands in a position that has the inside hand wrist down and the outside hand wrist up (see figure 7.3). When the hitter throws his hands inside the ball as he swings, he has a better chance of getting the fat part of the bat on the ball. These are all components of a good swing.

Figure 7.2 When the pitcher breaks his hands, the hitter's front foot should be down and his hands back.

Figure 7.3 At contact, the inside hand wrist should be down and the outside hand wrist up.

Many instructors say that the important point to emphasize is "path to ball," putting the hands and barrel into a position to hit, which allows even an off-balance hitter to have a swing left. Many of these coaches say that hitters don't swing the bat at this point as much as bring it into a position out in front of the chest with their hands and their pivot. The barrel hasn't started to move to the ball yet. The hands go first, the barrel second. Hitters who start the barrel first will likely be long and slow with their swing and probably under the ball.

Point of Contact

The next technique in the hitting progression relates to the contact point where the bat meets the ball. In basic instruction, a coach wants to instruct his hitters that home plate is divided into three parts—inside, middle, and outside. The location of the pitch in these three areas dictates the point of contact. When the hitter makes contact, he wants to hit the ball on the fat part of the bat with the wrist facing up on his top hand and his bottom hand on the bat flat with the palm facing down. The hitter wants to get the barrel of the bat into each zone—inside, middle, and outside—and wants to make contact on this fat part with his elbows slightly bent to allow him to extend his arms after the initial contact (see figure 7.4). Although achieving it is difficult, we want extension to the inside of the ball on contact. As the hitter makes contact in this perfect rendition, his back knee and belly button will point to the direction of the hit. So if the ball is pitched to the inside of the plate, a right-handed hitter will swing and get the bat out in front so that he can hit the ball on the barrel of the bat. He will drive his back knee to the ball and his hips will turn so that his belly button is facing left field when he finishes.

If he is hitting a ball thrown down the middle of the plate, everything is the same as it is with the inside pitch except that his bat will face toward center field, as will his right knee and belly button. When a right-handed hitter hits a pitch on the outside of the plate, he will have the barrel of the bat and his hands pointing to right field. As he makes contact, his right knee and belly button will be facing right field. When

Figure 7.4 Having the elbows slightly bent will allow the hitter to extend his arms after the initial contact.

a hitter makes contact with his hands in the proper form and hits the ball on the barrel of the bat, he will be in a power position, driving his back leg to the ball.

Follow-Through

The final technique of hitting a baseball involves what is known as the follow-through. This stage, the finishing point of the swing, occurs after contact is made. In the follow-through, the hitter's wrists turn with the swing but they do not roll. The hitter wants his wrists to remain flat without rolling for as long as he can. His weight should not be on his front foot but against it, so that his weight stays back and balanced. The batter finishes his swing with his head down so he is able to see the ball hit the bat (see figure 7.5).

An important aspect of the follow-through is that the wrists turn but do not roll. For a right-handed hitter, the right wrist does a left turn, but the knuckles on the right hand do not roll to the top. The left hand turns under, and the knuckles face the ground. The coach

Figure 7.5 The batter should always keep his head down.

should emphasize that no swing is complete without this turn.

All these technical components of the perfect swing are important, but a hitter can't go to the plate thinking of each one, worried about, for example, where his knuckles are. All the actions of the body must be addressed in workouts and batting practice, and a coach should avoid loading up a young hitter's mind with so many technicalities that he freezes at the plate. A hitter has to be relaxed and comfortable at the plate. Not every swing will be the perfect swing, not every hitter is going to look the same at the plate, and many players have delivered hits with one-handed, off-balance swings. Providing a young hitter with the rudiments is important, but the coach should allow him to find his own comfort zone. Figure 7.6 provides the most important aspects of the swing.

Figure 7.6 Mechanics of the Swing—Hitting Fundamentals

Loading Phase

Many young batters swing the bat after the ball is past them, and many times this happens because they don't get into the load position in time. Load position refers to the position that the body and bat need to be in just before the swing. The loading phase refers to striding and the positioning of the bat. This phase is important because, if done properly, it can help the hitter make solid contact with the baseball on a more consistent basis.

The Load

- This is the part of the swing that prepares the body or coils the body to swing the bat.
- Set the hands in place by moving them back slightly toward the right ear (right-handed hitter) or left ear (left-handed hitter). (Do this when the pitcher takes the ball out of his glove during the windup.)
- The player also sets or "loads" his weight on the back foot. (Weight distribution is about 70% on the back foot and 30% on the front.)
- Side view of a player in the load position should form a vertical line from the back ankle to knee to hip to shoulder.

The Stride

- From the load a player should stride. There are three components to the stride (three Ss):
  1. Short. Short is literally a short step.
  2. Soft. Soft is as if testing the water in the pool.
  3. Straight. Straight toward the pitcher, not open or closed.
- During the stride, it's very important for the player's head to remain still.

(continued)

(continued)

Fire and Follow-Through
Fire and follow-through refers to the process of hitting the ball and following through with the swing.

Turning the Hips
If lower-body strength and bat speed are to be maximized, it is essential that the hips be turned during the swing.

- To turn the hips during the swing, the hitter should pivot on the ball of the back foot.
- Back foot turns at the same time as the hands start toward the ball. Back foot rotates into a heel over toe.
- Front leg straightens at the knee joint. It's called hitting against a stiff front leg.

Getting the Barrel to the Ball

- Hand path is to take the knob of the bat to the ball. That will keep the front arm bent.
- Straightening the front arm will create a "barring out" and not allow the hitter to stay "inside the ball."
- To ensure that the player stays "inside the ball," the hands must pass through the contact point before the bat head. If the bat head arrives first, the player has "cast the bat" around or "outside the ball."

Getting to the Power Position

- The batter should swing the barrel of the bat *down* and directly at the ball and should try to hit the ball with the sweet spot on the bat. The sweet spot is generally the area between 2 and 6 inches from the top end of the bat.
- The batter's arms should be slightly extended right before contact is made with the baseball. *Extension of the arms happens after contact!*
- The bat should be on the same plane as the baseball when contact is made.

Keeping the Eyes on the Ball

- Hitters should keep the eyes on the baseball until contact is made.
- The hitter's head should not follow the body when it turns.

Following Through

- After contact is made with the ball, the barrel of the bat should maintain a smooth, slightly upward path, which ends with the hands rolling over, up, and toward the front "ear."
- The handle of the bat should stop around the left shoulder for a right-handed batter and around the right shoulder for a left-handed batter.
- The barrel of the bat should wrap around the upper back.
- The hitter's chin should be over the shoulder area at the completion of the swing.

Reading Pitches

Besides proper swing mechanics and timing, the ability to read, or pick up, the pitch is crucial to allowing the hitter to stay balanced and have the best chance to hit the ball. Reading pitches starts with picking up the ball at the pitcher's release point. If the hitter picks up the ball right out of the pitcher's hand, he will have more time to read the pitch.

The rotation of the ball is different on a fastball than on a curve. The curveball rotation is in a tumbling form. A hitter can see the seams rotating down with the break of the ball. The fastball rotation is tighter and does not have downward rotation. The hitter needs to identify these rotations right away and then react to them.

The third pitch, the change-up, can be hard to pick up because a good change-up will have the same rotation as a fastball but will be 10 to 20 miles per hour slower.

A fourth pitch commonly thrown is the slider. This pitch is hard to pick up because it is thrown so hard. A slider is usually about 5 miles per hour slower than the fastball. The slider has a side rotation, but it is thrown hard with a sharp, late break that offers little time for the hitter to react.

After your hitters understand what the pitch rotation looks like, they must work on picking it up at the release point.

Reading the Pitch

Purpose. This drill gives hitters practice reading pitches.

Procedure. Put your hitters in the bullpen when your pitchers are throwing live to a catcher. The hitter will not know what the pitcher is throwing. The hitter must call the pitch as soon as he can pick it up. If a pitcher throws a curve, the hitter loudly calls, "Curve" as soon as he recognizes the pitch. This drill forces the hitter to identify each pitch quickly. They can take this drill into the game and be more efficient at identifying pitches. The hitter must first understand what each pitch looks like and then be able to identify it quickly. This drill will work to develop these skills. Next, have your team scrimmage live where your pitchers are mixing up their pitches. The hitters must identify the pitch and hit it if it's a strike, just as they would in a game.

COMMON FAULTS AND CORRECTIONS

Knowing the basic techniques of hitting a baseball is not the only thing that young hitters must know. When hitters are struggling, the coach must identify the problem and have a solution.

The most common problem for a young hitter, maybe any hitter, is swinging and missing. A swinging strike usually occurs when the hitter takes his eye off the ball or tries to pull the ball, which in turn pulls his head off the ball. Another factor could be that the hitter is swinging under the ball or simply not getting his bat into the zone in time, which may be the result of a loop or uppercut in his swing.

Estimates are that 80 percent of all swings and misses result from swinging under the ball. To alleviate this problem, the hitter needs to change the angle of his swing to hit down on the ball. Doing this will allow him to eliminate an uppercut or loop in the swing. Another remedy would be to keep his weight back, wait longer on the pitch, and try to hit the inside of the ball, which will help keep his head on the ball and prevent him from pulling off.

Hitting High on the Ball From a Tee

Purpose. Drills to help the hitter achieve that downward hitting action start with the batting tee.

Procedure. Put the ball on the tee with the seams up high on the baseball. The hitter must hit the seam. To do this, he must swing with the proper downward angle to hit the top part of the ball.

Hitting High on the Ball With Soft Toss

Purpose. This drill forces the hitter to focus on a specific aspect—the top of the baseball instead of a general part.

Procedure. Soft toss and tell the hitter to hit the top part of the ball. By focusing on the top part of the ball in this drill, the hitter will develop a habit that will carry over into the game. At batting practice and during a game, you want your hitter to be able to hit that specific top part of the ball with a downward swing, keeping his hands inside.

Another factor in swinging and missing and another common problem is swinging at bad pitches. This problem may result from a number of causes, but it starts with not knowing and recognizing the strike zone, and not recognizing what type of pitch the pitcher has delivered.

A hitter who swings at bad pitches may also be pressing, trying so hard to break a slump or get a hit that he swings at almost anything, especially high pitches out of his zone that he simply can't handle. A coach can tell a hitter to relax, wait on the ball, and stay off high pitches, but following that advice is easier to think about than do.

Any drills to work on overcoming this poor habit involve discipline, seeing all types of pitches, both strikes and balls, and making the judgment about which ones to swing at after recognizing what pitch is being thrown. A great aid here is a pitching machine called the Home Plate Machine. This device can be programmed to throw various pitches—fastball, change-up, curve, and slider. The coach working the machine can also change the location so that some are strikes and some are balls. Drilling with this machine is a tremendous help in working on recognizing various pitches and judging whether they are strikes or balls.

A frustrating fault for a coach to observe is the hitter who continually takes good pitches for called strikes, watching good pitches go by without swinging. The hitter may be afraid of the ball and not even wanting to be at the plate, unsure of his strike zone, or guessing and obviously guessing wrong. A way to solve this, or attempt to solve it, is to encourage the hitter to be aggressive in the strike zone. Encourage him to go to the plate and jump on the first pitch in the strike zone. The hitter must want to hit, and ultimately success breeds success.

Another common problem that a coach is likely to encounter is the hitter who consistently pops the ball in the air, most often caused by swinging under the ball and dropping the barrel of the bat in the swing. To help solve this problem, the hitter needs to keep both his front shoulder and his front hip closed. When the hitter opens his front hip early, he immediately tends to drop the barrel of the bat. The premature opening of the front shoulder can cause the hitter to drop the barrel and swing under the ball. To fix this problem, start by getting the hitter to keep his front shoulder and hip closed at the start of his swing. Another way to fix this is to have the hitter work on hitting down on the ball, striving to hit the top half of the baseball. By focusing on the top of the baseball and trying to hit that specific part, the hitter may start to avoid hitting the pop-up, although even the best hitters will hit pop-ups and weak ground balls, which is another common problem.

The drills for this flaw are the same as those used for the hitter with the uppercut swing. Use the tee, soft toss, and batting practice with the emphasis on hitting the top of the baseball, which will create a downward swing.

Also, during batting practice, you can have a round of hitting called No Pop-Up, No Pull. Here, the hitter gets to continue to hit as long as he hits a ground ball up the middle and doesn't pull the ball to his power side. By executing this drill, the hitter must get on top of the ball to hit a ground ball and keep from opening up his front hip, which creates a loop in his swing. If he doesn't execute the ground ball and doesn't keep his hip and hands in, his turn in the cage ends.

For the hitter who makes consistent contact but consistently hits weak ground balls, a couple factors could be in play. First, the hitter's stride may be too big, meaning that he gets out on his front foot ahead of his body, stripping his power. Another common cause of the weak grounder is that the hitter's trigger may be too big, producing a long swing that circles or goes around the ball, prompting his top hand to roll over, again stripping power. A hitter should work in practice on hitting with no stride, hopeful that doing so will translate in a game to a short stride with the hands and weight back, and wrists and palms flat.

Wide Stance, Short Stride

Purpose. To help hitters who are hitting weak ground balls.

Procedure. Spread the hitter's feet, widen his stance, and have him work off the tee to get accustomed to using a short or no-stride stance. From there, the coach should soft toss to the hitter from the side, watching his stride to ensure that it is short with no weight on the front foot. The coach can even fake the soft toss and hold on to the ball to check the stride and balance and make sure that the hitter stays balanced and doesn't get out on his front foot.

One-Hand Swing

Purpose. Another drill to correct weak ground balls is to have the hitter swing with only one hand to work on keeping the wrist from rolling over.

Procedure. Soft toss to the hitter, who swings one-handed, first with the top hand and then with the bottom hand. Here, if the hitter rolls over the wrist, it really shows. Make the hitter stay flat in the power position with his hands. That will help him get the feel of how the hands should be when he makes contact with the ball.

Whenever possible, a coach should try to get time to work with his players one on one. The sheet on problems and remedies tells a coach what is wrong with the player and how to fix it, but keep in mind the saying "easier said than done." In other words, you can't assume a problem is fixed unless you work with the hitter yourself to help fix it. A coach can tell any player what is wrong with his stance, swing, or approach, but to fix it, the coach must provide him with the necessary drills. One-on-one work can accomplish this. Even just 10 or 15 minutes of drilling during, before, or after practice can be a great help in getting the hitter on track. The head coach should try to rotate during the course of a week so that he is able to work with each player at some time. As I mentioned earlier, include in your schedule a list of players who will come early or stay after practice to do this individualized work. One-on-one work is a necessary and important part of improving your hitters. Figure 7.7 provides a simple reference for common hitting problems and remedies.

Figure 7.7   The Hitting Formula: Solving Your Own Problems

Symptoms	Causes	Remedies
Swinging and missing	Taking eyes off the ball, overswinging, trying to pull, uppercut, swinging under ball.	Learn to wait, hit inside out, swing down on the ball.
Being jammed	Overstriding, pulling out, letting ball get on you, striding at too sharp an angle to the plate, standing too close to the plate, trying to lift.	Keep weight back, drive from back side, be ready, stride into the pitcher, position after stride should provide plate coverage, be quick with hands.
Weak on breaking ball	Trying to pull, circling the ball, not waiting, overstriding.	Use opposite hitting, learn to wait, look for breaking ball on occasion, hit inside and out.
Weak on change speed	Not waiting, trying to pull, overstriding, not seeing the ball.	Learn to wait, learn to hit the ball the other way.
Swinging at bad pitches	No plan in mind, not waiting, too tense.	*Wait, wait, wait,* consciously relax, stay off the high pitch.
Popping up	Late on ball, pulling out, trying to lift, swinging under the ball.	Keep front shoulder and hip closed to start swing, hit slightly down on ball.
Weak grounders	Overstriding, circling the ball, not waiting.	*Wait, wait, wait,* keep hands inside flight of ball, hit through the ball.
Taking good pitches	Not swinging on each pitch, guessing.	Always swinging, have a plan in mind, visualize your strike zone.

HITTING DRILLS

Many hitting drills are available. The key is to identify a specific problem and prescribe the right drill. A coach also needs drills to help his hitters execute skills that they will need in the game. The first three drills are drills used to correct common hitting problems. The next three drills address common hitting skills needed in game situations.

One-Knee, One-Hand

Purpose. The purpose of this drill is to put the hitter in a position where he can focus only on his hands getting into and through the hitting zone with flat wrists

Procedure. In this drill, the hitter should have his front leg extended out and his bottom hand on the bat handle. A coach on one knee should soft toss the ball to the hitter, who should try to keep his hand inside the ball with a short swing, with his wrist flat and palm down (see figure 7.8). If the hitter's swing is too long or he rolls his wrist, the coach should spot the problem easily.. By having the hitter on one knee, he does not employ the hips or stride and he can focus entirely on using the proper technique with his hands. A good drill to help keep

Figure 7.8 Watch to make sure the batter's wrist is flat and his palm is down.

the wrists flat and build strength in the wrists and forearms is to have the hitter, on one knee and using only one hand, swing with a shorter, smaller bat than he normally uses. After 10 swings with the bottom hand, the hitter should do 10 with the top hand.

Front Inside Soft-Toss

Purpose. Another soft-toss drill to encourage a fast bat, this drill trains the hitter to increase his hand quickness by shortening his swing. At the same time, this drill will make him use the proper technique of having flat wrists in his swing.

Procedure. With the hitter standing, both hands on the bat, the coach feeds pitches from behind a screen, trying to keep the ball on the inside half of the plate. This pitch placement forces the hitter to be quick with his hands as he attempts to hit the inside half of the ball. If the hitter drags the barrel of the bat with slow hands, the pitch will jam him. The hitter needs to work not only on having quick hands to hit the inside pitch but also on getting the bat in a power position with flat wrists so that he can hit the ball on the fat part of the bat. The feeder in this drill makes sure that the hitter does not roll his wrists or jam himself with a long swing. A good coaching point for this drill is to hold the ball on every fourth or fifth pitch. By doing this, the coach can observe whether the hitter is on balance and not stepping away or opening up his stride too soon. The swing should be short and powerful to the ball with good technique to achieve good contact on the fat part of the bat.

Stride and Freeze Tee

Purpose. One of my favorite drills addresses the hitter who gets out on his front foot and has trouble keeping his weight back. He is unable to load his hands in a trigger by taking the bat back. Hitters who do not take their hands back before hitting get on the front foot and thus generate no power.

Procedure. In this tee drill, the coach or feeder sets up the tee so that the hitter can hit the ball straight up the middle. The ball is not on the tee. The hitter takes his stride, releases his hands back, and freezes. The coach checks the hitter's balance and form to see that he has his hands and weight back. When the coach sees that the hitter is balanced with the proper form, he puts the ball on the tee and the hitter hits the ball from that position. The coach then checks the hitter's follow-through to make sure that he is on balance. After the hitter swings 10 or 15 times in that sequence, the coach can put the ball on the tee and have the hitter take his swing from the beginning. This drill progresses from a stop position that allows the coach to correct the hitter's flaws with his hands and balance to an overall view of the swing that allows the coach to ensure that form and approach are close to perfect.

Slider Soft-Toss

Purpose. This drill is designed to show the hitter the movement of the slider, how to track the pitch, and the proper way to hit the pitch to the opposite field—right field for a right-handed hitter and left field for a left-handed hitter.

Procedure. To start the drill, the coach sits on a chair or stool with a screen in front of him. He is right in front of the hitter with the screen as protection. For a right-handed hitter (opposite for a left-handed hitter) he throws the ball underhanded across the hitter to the outside part of the plate. The hitter tracks the movement across his body and hits the ball where it is pitched. The right-handed hitter will drive the ball to the opposite field. If you are working on a right-hander's slider you do the same drill with a left-handed hitter and the ball coming in to him. You can also work it away from the left-handed hitter and into the right-handed hitter, which is the break of a left-handed pitcher's slider. This simple drill helps a hitter work on a pitch that can be extremely frustrating. The hitter can track the ball, and the coach can see whether he is executing properly to drive the baseball the other way.

Fastball, Change-Up

Purpose. This drill trains the hitter to hit the fastball to the opposite field and stay back to hit the off-speed pitch. The hitter uses the same technique for a change-up, curve, or any other off-speed pitch.

Procedure. The coach or pitcher in this drill is behind an L screen throwing to the hitter from a chair, sitting down or standing up. The hitter in this drill wants to hit the fastball to the opposite field and stay back for the change-up. You want your hitters to use this approach at the plate when they face a pitcher who can throw both pitches for strikes. The coach or pitcher randomly throws fastballs and change-ups so that the hitter does not know what to expect. The coach or pitcher does not need to know how to throw curveballs. All he does is change the speed so that the hitter must stay back to hit the off-speed pitch.

Fastball, Curveball Soft Toss

Purpose. This simple drill is executed using soft toss to simulate the fastball and curveball.

Procedure. Positioned behind a screen, the coach underhands the ball on a fast line for a fastball or on a big slow loop for a curveball. The hitter in this drill must react quickly to the fastball, which is thrown to him with velocity. When the coach lobs up the ball on a big arc it has the downward movement of a slow curveball. The hitter has to wait to hit the ball on the downward path, just as he does on the curveball.

SITUATION-SPECIFIC DRILLS

The easiest way to drill for specific situations is to set them up during hitting practice. For example, put a runner at each base. In the first situation, have the runner at first break to second on a hit-and-run, requiring the batter to work on hitting the pitch to the opposite field. Then inform the batter that a runner is at second and with no outs, requiring the batter to hit a ground ball up the middle or behind the runner so that he can advance to third. Then, with the hitter aware that a runner is at third with one out, he must try to score him by driving a deep fly ball. Thus, the hitter has worked on a variety of executions in that one practice at-bat. All the base runners move up when the next hitter comes to bat. The runner at third base becomes the on-deck hitter, the runner at first goes to second, the runner at second moves to third, and the hitter becomes the runner at first. A coach can give points for execution, punishing those who fail and rewarding those who succeed.

BUNTING TECHNIQUE

Bunting may be a lost art, but anyone can learn the skill and technique needed to bunt, and a team that can execute the bunt puts tremendous pressure on the defense. By perfecting your players' bunting technique, you can effectively use the bunting game in your offense. Certain situations call for certain types of bunts, and each requires a different technique.

Sacrifice Bunt

The term *sacrifice* means that the hitter is going to sacrifice his at-bat to move the runner to the next base. To execute a successful sacrifice, the hitter must first move up closer to the pitcher in the batter's box, giving himself more fair territory in which to get the bunt down. The hitter should also crowd home plate, making it easier to bunt the outside pitch because it is already easy to bunt the inside pitch.

The hitter should turn to face the pitcher either when the pitcher comes set in his stretch or when the pitcher breaks his hands from the set position. The coach decides when he wants his hitters to turn and face the pitcher. The hitter turns to face the pitcher with the front foot open from the back foot. His hands hold the bat with the bottom hand on the knob or slightly above, cocked firmly. His top hand will be just below where the label would be, and his top hand should grip the bat with his thumb up and the bat between his index finger and thumb. A coach can tell his players to act as if they are

hitchhiking with their top hand and put the bat between the thumb and index finger. The bat should be out in front of the body slightly tilted so that the ball will go down on contact (see figure 7.9). The hitter should have his bat at the angle that will aim the ball in the direction he wants. His angle for a bunt to third will be with the barrel toward the shortstop. The hitter should just catch the ball with his top hand to get the ball bunted to third base. To bunt to first, the barrel of the bat will be facing the second baseman so that the bunted ball will travel down the first-base line. If a runner is on first base, the hitter would want to bunt the ball to first base because the first baseman, holding the runner close to the base, cannot break early to field the bunt and the third baseman can. If a runner is on second, the hitter usually wants to bunt down the third-base line, forcing the third baseman to charge and field it, leaving third base unprotected. In the initial situation, with a runner on first, the hitter uses a bat angle that will prompt the ball to roll toward first. The hitter wants to get on top of the pitch so that he doesn't pop it up, and he wants to pretend that he's actually catching the pitch softly with his bat, taking it back slightly before contact so

Figure 7.9 When bunting, the bat should be out front and slightly tilted.

that he deadens the ball, getting a short roll on the field that will be tougher to field cleanly and will ensure that the runner advances.

Squeeze Bunt

The squeeze bunt is used to score a runner from third base and should be executed as a surprise. The stance and technique are the same as those used with the sacrifice bunt. The major difference is that the hitter will not turn and face the pitcher until the pitcher has the ball at the top of his motion, ready to release it. This late turn by the hitter keeps the pitcher from throwing a pitch out of the strike zone to foil the bunt attempt, and it delays an early charge by the first and third basemen. The hitter just needs to turn and bunt the ball down to the pitcher's glove side on the infield grass. The runner will be coming full speed, so the only way that the pitcher can throw him out is to barehand the ball and flip it to the catcher, and he can't do that if the bunt is on the glove side. So the bunt directed to the pitcher's glove side should score the runner every time. But the runner must be sure not to break too early. If he gives the play away, the pitcher can step off the mound and trap him in a rundown, or he can throw a pitchout so the hitter will not be able to bunt the pitch.

Bunting for a Hit

Whether it is called a drag bunt or simply bunting for a hit, the batter can try to catch the defense on their heels by bunting when they don't expect it. Unlike the sacrifice and squeeze bunt, the drag bunt requires a different technique for right- and left-handed batters.

The right-handed hitter moves up in the batter's box first, as if executing a sacrifice bunt. He steps back with his right foot. He uses the same grip on the bat that he uses with a sacrifice bunt. The batter then puts the bat out in front of his body with the bat angled so that when the ball hits it, the ball will roll toward third base (see figure 7.10). As the hitter makes contact he pushes off his back foot and runs to first base. As with any bunt, the hitter should bunt a strike that is up in the strike zone, from the thigh to just above the waist. The hitter is

Figure 7.10 At contact, the bunting hitter pushes off his back foot to get moving to first base as quickly as possible.

trying to bunt the ball near the baseline on the grass. If he makes a mistake, he wants it to be a foul ball. He executes the entire movement in a continuous motion rather than in a slow series of movements. The batter is in motion, heading to first base as he puts the bunt down.

A coach can teach his left-handed hitters two techniques to drag a bunt to third base. The first technique gives the hitter a better chance to get the ball down with good direction. Again, in this technique, the first move is up in the batter's box. The hitter turns and faces third base with his shoulders. As the pitch comes he jab steps with his back foot toward third base. This movement will give him the perfect angle to bunt. He then bunts the ball and runs to first base.

The other technique, which is more difficult but allows a faster start out of the batter's box, is for the hitter, after moving up in the batter's box, to step toward the pitcher's mound with his back foot as the pitcher lets go of the baseball. The hitter must angle the bat to bunt the ball at the third-base line. This technique is difficult because his back foot is stepping toward the pitcher's mound. If his bat is facing the pitcher at the time of contact, the bunt will go right back to the pitcher for an easy out. So, in using this technique the hitter must get the bat angle to face third base. He is then ready to step with his right foot toward first base. As I said before, this technique gets the hitter to first base quicker but requires precise execution to get good direction on the bunt.

BUNTING DRILLS

These various bunt techniques can be executed by anyone if they work at it and use proper form. Players who practice these bunting drills can dramatically improve their ability.

Chorus Line Bunting

Purpose. A coach can use this drill to show a large group of players the proper technique for the various bunts. The drill progresses slowly, making it easy to correct faults.

Procedure. We use this as the first bunting drill every year. We line up the players side by side in a chorus line and walk through the technique. The coach demonstrates the form and walks them through each step. The coach then acts as the pitcher and, without a baseball, feints a delivery to determine whether the players know when to turn in preparation to bunt. This drill is useful in the early season because it can be used indoors.

One-Hand Bunting

Purpose. This drill helps a hitter get the proper angle with his bat and keep the barrel up so that he does not pop the ball in the air.

Procedure. You can use hard balls for this drill, but for youngsters who are just learning the best method is to use softer balls tossed underhand. The hitter holds the bat at the proper angle with only the top hand, label height, thumb up. Have each player bunt 5 to 10 balls to first base and then 5 to 10 more to third base.

Bunting Versus Chalked Area

Purpose. This drill determines how precise players can be in putting down bunts, and helps develop precision. A coach can employ live pitching or a pitching machine.

Procedure. The first thing to do is chalk or paint an area close to the baseline and home plate with the number 3. This will be the highest number and the best place to bunt. Mark a second area, close to the baseline but farther out, with a 2. Then mark a third area even farther out with a 1. The goal is to deaden a bunt in the area marked with a 3. A bunt in area 2 is above average if it is close to the 3 and average if it is close to the 1. A bunt to area 1 is average to below average. The areas close to the mound are not marked; a bunt to those areas does not score any points. A coach may want to keep score to identify which players are most successful at bunting to the proper area. He can include rewards or punishment for the best or worst scores, making it a productive and competitive exercise for the players.

Machine Bunting

Purpose. This drill uses the pitching machine, usually in the batting cages. By doing this drill daily, a coach can make sure that his players get constant work on their bunting skills.

Procedure. In the cage the hitter works on his sacrifice, drag, or squeeze bunt technique, essentially doing three drills in one.

Players Throw to Each Other

Purpose. This drill gives players more work on the skill and technique of bunting.

Procedure. This drill can be done at any level in an open area. Players throw to each other while the rest of the team is taking batting practice. Four to six players find an open area, perhaps down the right-field line. One player is the bunter, another is the pitcher, one simulates the first baseman, and one is the third baseman. The players bunt to third and first three to five times each and then rotate to the next position until everyone gets his bunt work.

Pressure Bunting Versus Live Defense

Purpose. This drill puts bunters into a live situation.

Procedure. Use defensive players at all positions except the outfield. A pitcher throws his full range of pitches. Use base runners to create different scenarios for the bunter, who takes signals from a third-base coach. This drill provides insight into how each player will respond to a bunt situation in a game while giving extra work to backup pitchers.

The preceding are just a few of the drills that will improve bunting technique and a team's overall bunting game. Many other drills have been developed, and an imaginative coach can create his own.

Coaches' Keys

1. Hitting a baseball may be the most difficult skill in sport to learn and master.
2. Teaching hitting skills involves a number of absolutes—balance, rhythm, swing path, contact point, and follow-through.
3. Handle hitting problems by identifying the problem, its cause, and the proper remedy.
4. The coach should use the drill that focuses most closely on the hitter's specific problem.
5. With practice and hard work, anyone can execute the skills and technique used in bunting. Used consistently, bunting drills can improve individual ability and a team's ability to put pressure on the defense.

TEACHING BASE-RUNNING SKILLS

One of the first things that a coach needs to understand is that base running and the teaching of it are neglected parts of the game. From Little League through high school and into college, coaches assume that everyone knows how to run the bases. Consequently, they do not focus on teaching the proper technique, knowledge of the rules, and other points that enable teams to gain an added offensive edge.

THE ART OF BASE RUNNING

Good base running starts with correct form and technique. Pay close attention to your players' form. Do they run with their arms moving straight ahead, or are they pumping their arms across their bodies, hindering speed? Quickness and speed are generated by getting away from the plate and getting the arms moving toward first base with the same form that a track athlete would use. If a player is not pumping his arms in the direction that he is going, he cannot run at maximum speed.

The drills that we provide in this chapter will show you how to work with your players to improve their running form and running skills. Another thing that you want to do is teach your players the rules that pertain to running the bases. Do they know the proper way to tag up and advance to the next base? You must explain every situation involving a fly ball from the viewpoint of the offensive player who is tagging up. This gets back to the coaching philosophy of expecting your players to know nothing. When you yell, "Tag," you want your player to go directly back to the base and either find the ball and advance on his own or listen to the base coach say, "Go" and then advance.

Do your players understand the infield fly rule? If they don't know the rule, they can run into an out on a dropped pop fly with runners at first and second or the bases loaded. They must know that they don't need to advance. So your base-running rules can involve taking extra bases, but they can also involve not advancing when there is no need to advance. For players to understand these distinctions, you need to explain the appropriate rules.

When you're teaching base running, you start by working from home plate. You start with running technique from home to first, then from first to second, from second to third, and finally from third to home plate.

Players can increase their speed by learning how to run the bases. The key to running the bases is to understand that you run the bases making left turns and that to get to the next base most quickly you must take the proper angle when making those turns. The better your technique, the faster you run the bases. Teach players how to take the right angle and how to hit the inside corner of the base when running to the next base.

Base running starts at home plate with swinging the bat and getting out of the box. Teach your players the attitude of being aggressive, taking the extra base, going full speed. Too many players watch today's professionals go half speed, jog, trot 90 feet to first base. Some imitate this lazy, nonaggressive form of base running. You want them to be aggressive all the time.

BASE-RUNNING FUNDAMENTALS

To be good base runners, players must master the techniques involved. They must know how to tag up properly, turn the bases, lead off, and slide. You can teach all these techniques, which are covered in the following sections.

Tagging Up

The proper technique to tag up on a fly ball and advance after the catch is for the runner to be stationed on the base in a track sprinter's stance with his foot ready to push off at the moment of the catch (see figure 8.1).

The technique that can differ when tagging does not involve the runner's footwork, but how he decides when to leave the base. For older players, those in high school, college, and at the professional level, most coaches let their players use their own eyes and take off on their own after the catch. But with younger players at Little League age, the coach may want to have them tag up and leave the base when the coach says, "Go." This method keeps the players from making a mistake on their timing. The runner at third base with the coach next to him can use the coach's command to avoid leaving early.

Turning the Bases

The proper technique for running the bases involves making left turns and hitting the inside corner of each base while advancing around the bases. When leaving home plate the runner starts out of the batter's box straight toward first base. When he sees that he will round first base or run to second, he runs at a wider angle that will take him toward the first-base coaching box. When he gets approximately to the box, he dips his left shoulder slightly and hits the inside corner of first base with either foot (see figure 8.2). This approach to the base allows the base runner to have a direct line to second.

Figure 8.1 Proper technique for tagging up on a fly ball.

Figure 8.2 If the runner is going to round a base, he should hit the inside corner so he will have a direct line to the next base.

If he is going to round second base or run to third, he takes a route out toward right-center field, staying on the infield dirt, of course, and hits the inside corner of second base as he did first base.

If the runner continues to third, he again angles wider than that base, hits the inside corner, and is in position to move directly up the baseline toward home. Figure 8.3 illustrates the proper running paths for rounding the bases.

Leading Off

The base runner use the two types of leads, the primary and secondary leads, at every base.

At first base and second base the technique is similar, if not the same, on the primary and secondary leads. At third base the technique is different because we do not want the pitcher or catcher to pick off our runner. The pickoff is a big concern at third base. We'll start the discussion with primary and secondary leads at first and second base.

Primary Leads

The primary lead is the lead that the runner takes when he steps off the base. Before he does this, the runner looks at the coach who is giving the signs and responds by showing with his fingers how many outs there are. Next he steps off the base and slide steps to his lead

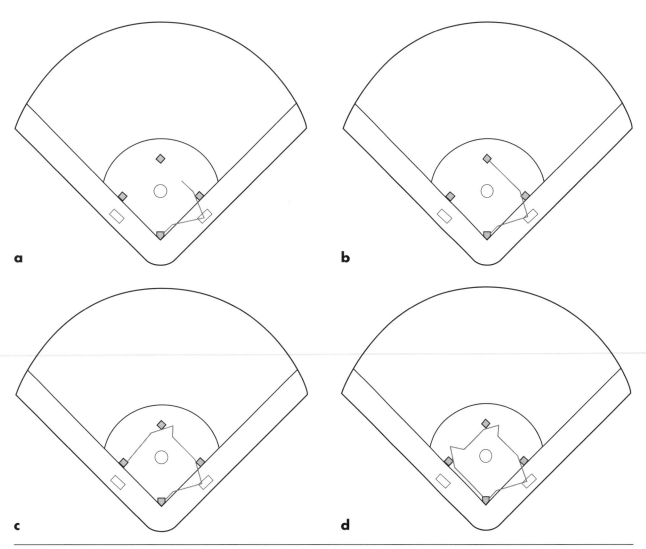

Figure 8.3   The proper running paths for *(a)* a single, *(b)* a double, *(c)* a triple, and *(d)* and an inside-the-park home run.

(see figure 8.4). He does not cross over his feet but instead slides his feet two or three times to extend his lead. This slide movement involves a right, left, right, left action that inches his lead longer and longer, enhancing his ability to steal the next base. From the moment he steps off the base, his eyes must never come off the pitcher. If he takes his eyes off the pitcher just as the pitcher tries a pickoff to the base, he can easily be put out in an embarrassing way. With this understanding, we tell our players to take the sign from the coach and tell us how many outs there are while standing on the base. The runner must never look at the coach when he is off the base. When your runner steps off the base you want his eyes glued on the pitcher. He should step off the base with a shuffling type of footwork, never allowing his feet to cross over. A pickoff move by the pitcher can be successful if the runner is crossing over with his feet.

We teach our player to slide step to the length of the primary lead, which should be a dive length away, or a step and a dive length away if we feel that the pitcher cannot pick off the runner. The size of the lead depends on the effectiveness of the pitcher's pickoff move and the game situation as far as the score and the number of outs. If we are down by a lot of runs late in the game, we shorten the lead and reduce risks.

When the runner establishes the distance of his lead, he is then in his primary lead. A key point here is that the runner should be balanced with his hands between the waist and the numbers (see figure 8.5). The runner should not have his hands hanging low or his hips low. He should be in a linebacker or basketball guard's stance. If his hands are below his waist or hanging down, he needs more time to get them into runner's position and form. You want the runner to be able to get into sprinter's form as quickly as possible.

Remember as well that the length of the primary lead depends on whether the runner has the steal sign. If the runner has a bunt sign in a situation where the sacrifice is obvious, he must be aware that the pitcher is likely to try a pickoff. The length of the primary lead also depends on whether the pitcher is right-handed or left-handed. Most runners are more cautious against a left-handed pitcher and will shorten their primary lead.

The primary lead at second base is going to be a step or two longer than it is at first because the runner has no one holding him on the base. The one thing that the runner must be aware

Figure 8.4 The runner should slide step to the lead, not cross over.

Figure 8.5 The proper leadoff stance.

of with the primary lead at second base is that he wants to be able to get back to the base on reading the pitcher's pickoff move to second. The base runner will get help from the third-base coach, who will be telling him where the infielders are. If the pitcher makes a pickoff to second, the base runner must be able to see it coming and get back to the base, but at second he will always have a longer primary lead than he does at first because neither the shortstop nor the second baseman is standing on the base holding him on.

The primary lead at third base will be similar in length to the lead at first base. A right-handed pitcher will make the runner at third base feel as the runner at first base does against a left-hander. The runner on third should take a lead that will allow him to get back to the base safely.

With a left-handed pitcher on the mound, a runner at third will have an advantage because he can read the pitcher's move early. Most, if not all, teams from high school baseball on up do not hold the runner on at third base. In Little League, at both first base and third, teams hold the runner on, so the runner may want to shorten his lead at third base.

So, the base runner establishes his primary lead when he comes off the base. When the pitcher releases the ball, he goes into his secondary lead.

Secondary Leads

The base runner moves into a second type of lead, called the secondary lead, as the pitcher releases the ball. To do this, the runner uses a shuffling technique to stretch his lead to a point where he feels comfortable in his ability to get back to the base on a snap throw by the catcher. He shuffles to a position that will give him a good jump to the next base on a batted ball while not being so far off that the catcher can pick him off. If the ball is hit in the air or on the ground, the runner is then in position to advance or go halfway to the next base. The secondary lead gets the runner to a position where he can react. The runner gets to the secondary position and then reads the ball.

The problem that runners may have with the secondary lead is that they end their shuffling movement facing the next base as the ball is getting to home plate. In this case, the runner is in a position where the catcher can pick him off. Make sure that when the runner reaches his secondary position, he is facing home plate with his weight on the balls of his feet and waiting for the ball to get into the hitting zone. He can then react quickly to the batted ball or a catcher's pickoff attempt.

A key benefit of the secondary lead is that it puts a runner in position to advance on a pitch in the dirt. When your runner sees the ball bounce or go in the dirt, he takes off knowing that even if the catcher blocks the ball, he will be on his knees, making a throw difficult. If the runner reacts right away from his secondary lead, he can advance easily. Pointing out the possibility of advancing on a ball in the dirt is an excellent way to make your players more aggressive with their secondary leads at first and second base.

A runner at third base in his secondary lead will take his jab step back and then take two or three steps toward home plate, putting his weight on his front foot and leaning toward home. Here, with the secondary lead, the runner is in position to steal a run if the ball gets away from the catcher. At the same time he can get back to the base if the catcher attempts a pickoff.

If the pitcher goes from a windup rather than a stretch at all three bases, the runner should walk into his secondary lead. This technique is easy to teach because once the pitcher is into his windup, there is no chance of a pickoff. The walking lead is the most effective way to get a secondary lead against a pitcher in his windup. Make sure that your runner does not run off the base or walk so far or fast that he runs the risk of getting picked off by the catcher.

Second and Third Base Leads

Leads off second and third base involve concerns that differ slightly from leads off first base. The following sections discuss considerations and proper techniques.

Leading Off Second

The leadoff from second base is totally different from the leadoff at third. I say this because at third base the runner is 90 feet from scoring a run, whereas at second base he is one hit from scoring a run, provided that he can go two bases on that hit.

The lead that the runner at second base takes depends on the game situation—how many outs are there, and what the score is. With one out he wants to try to make it to third, but with two outs, getting to third may not be worth the risk. The presence of other runners is also a factor. Is a runner on third or first? If runners are on first and second, the runner at second is the lead runner and will play the game as if he is the only runner. If a runner is at third base, the runner at second base can take a slightly larger lead but he must always be aware of pickoffs.

If the batter is trying to sacrifice bunt, the runner at second must be able to read the bunt and get a good jump to advance to third base. He must first see that the ball is bunted on the ground rather than popped up or missed entirely, which might leave him vulnerable to being picked off second if he has gone too far. Only when he sees the bunt down successfully should he get a good jump toward third base. If the runner is going to steal the base on the pitch, he wants to get a moving lead so that he can get a jump on the pitch.

For the runner to understand how to get and secure his lead at second base, he must watch the pitcher at all times, not the second baseman or shortstop who might be trying to sneak in behind him. The pitcher will dictate when the pickoff will come by turning and pivoting to second base. The runner must get back to second base when he sees that. The base coach must keep the runner aware of the actions of the shortstop and second baseman so that the runner can lean back to second if either fielder is harassing him or inch farther off the base if neither is paying attention to him. The base coach talks to the runner with the following calls. If the defense is not trying to pick him off, the coach can call, "You're OK," or to be more specific, "You're OK, nobody near you." If the shortstop or second baseman comes near second for an attempted pickoff, the coach just tells the runner who is there. For instance, he says, "Heads up shortstop" to tell the runner that the shortstop is near the base. "Heads up second base" means that the second baseman is near the base.

In a bunting situation, you want the runner at second to have a good lead, but not an over-extended one. You do not want him to lead off so far that he can be picked off. Your runner must be under control because a bunting situation provides the middle infielders with their best chance to put on a pickoff. Because the shortstop usually has the responsibility to cover second in a bunting situation, he is already moving to the base when the batter shows the bunt. If the runner is careless or overaggressive with his lead, the catcher can easily pick him off on a missed bunt. Many teams put on their best pickoff plays in a bunting situation. The catcher may also be looking to pick off the runner in this situation.

If the coach gives a steal sign, he wants his runner to inch off the base as far as he can and keep his feet moving. The runner must be aware that a good pitcher stops movement either by stepping off the rubber or trying to pick off the runner, but when stealing third the runner should continue to move his feet. The best chance to steal third arises when you get the pitcher or middle infielders into a game situation where they basically ignore the runner. The runner doesn't really do anything to get the defense to ignore him, but he and the third-base coach recognize that the middle infielders are forgetting about the runner and aren't showing any movement for a pickoff. Many times they're simply too focused on the hitter or the pitches and simply forget about the runner. An alert coach and runner can take advantage of that inattention. Stealing third can be easier than stealing second because the runner can get a bigger lead. The third-base coach can help here by constantly talking to the runner, making him aware of where the shortstop and second baseman are. The coach is saying, "You're OK, you're OK," and the runner is inching off toward third base or moving his feet in place. If the shortstop comes toward second base, the coach says, "Heads up shortstop," and in response the runner takes a jab step back and leans back toward second base. While the third-base coach is talking, the runner is watching the pitcher to make sure that the pitcher does not pivot to pick him off. When a middle infielder breaks to second base to attempt a pickoff, the third-base coach yells, "Back," but the runner should already be diving or moving back to second because he was watching the pitcher and leaning back as the coach talked. His lead at second base is dictated by his eyes and aided by his leans, which are helped by the voice of the third-base coach.

Leading Off Third

When you focus on the runner at third, start with the basics. Tell the runner at third that he needs to take his lead and subsequently run in foul ground, returning to the base if necessary in fair ground to prevent a throw from the catcher. Taking a lead at third varies depending on whether the pitcher is using a windup or stretch and whether he is right-handed or left-handed. With a left-handed pitcher, the runner at third reads the pitcher as a runner at first would against a right-handed pitcher. The runner usually has little concern because the third baseman does not hold the runner on and the left-handed pitcher usually doesn't try to pick off the runner. But a right-handed pitcher in his stretch can attempt a pickoff at any time. You must make your players aware of this.

At Esperanza we had a situation years ago that showed how important it is for the runner to be aware of this pickoff. The play that occurred made us change our secondary lead technique. We had a runner at third base with two outs, trailing by one run in the last inning. The right-handed pitcher was in his stretch and, as he lifted his front leg, our base runner at third took two steps toward home plate and looked at the catcher. The pitcher stepped toward third base and threw to the third baseman. My base runner was staring at the catcher, wondering what happened to the ball and became an easy out. Game over. I decided immediately that we were going to change our technique at third base. Now, any time we face a right-handed pitcher in his stretch, we have our runner at third base take a jab step back to third when the pitcher lifts his foot. The runner leans back to third base, reading the foot of the pitcher. If the pitcher moves his foot toward home plate, the runner shifts his weight toward home plate and takes two or three steps in that direction. If the pitcher steps toward third base to pick off the runner, the runner already has jab stepped to

third and is leaning on his left foot so that he can easily get back to the base.

The other key here is that when the runner reads that the pitcher's front foot is going home, signaling that he is delivering the ball to the plate, the runner takes two or three steps toward home and faces the catcher with his letters facing home plate. He is leaning on his front foot. The runner does not jump around or run toward home plate, which would get him too far off the base and give the catcher an opportunity to pick him off. With this technique, if the ball gets away from the catcher, the runner is ready to advance.

The technique at third base is different when the pitcher is working out of a windup. Once the pitcher starts his windup, the runner walks toward home so that he can beat the pitcher to the plate on a passed ball or wild pitch. When stealing home, the runner will sprint toward home as the pitcher starts his windup. The key is for the runner to get off the base as far as he can before the pitcher starts his windup and to face home plate so that he is ready to sprint.

To do this, you want to look for a pitcher who is going to ignore the base runner. In that situation the runner can take a big primary lead before the pitcher starts his windup.

Sliding

Another skill related to base running is sliding. A player who can execute various slides to take advantage of an off-target throw has an edge. Even on a good throw, the base runner may be able to surprise the fielder handling the throw by taking a different angle to the base. Adroit sliding can be an extra weapon for your offense. For instance, a runner sliding into home who sees the catcher blocking the plate might be able to slide to the outside of the plate and reach back to touch it as he goes by, slipping his hand under or between the catcher's legs.

Similarly, a runner stealing a base can slide to the outside of the base so that the fielder will have to reach farther to make the tag, giving the runner more time to be safe.

Runners should learn to execute another type of slide, the pop-up slide, when they see that they will be safe at the base that they are approaching. In this slide the runner tucks his leg under and uses it to pop up when his front leg hits the base. He is then in position to advance and run to the next base if a bad throw occurs.

Pop-Up Slide

Have your player practice the pop-up slide on the outfield grass so that they slide more readily and are less likely to be injured. The best time to practice is after a rain when the grass is wet. Put a base on the outfield grass and have the players slide into it. To start, line up all the players in a straight line and have them tuck one leg under the other, which is straight, so that the two legs make the figure 4. From this position they will hit the base with the straight leg and pop up by pushing up on the bent leg. Then have your players slide one by one into the base, popping up when they hit it. Figure 8.6 illustrates the proper pop-up slide technique.

Figure 8.6 The pop-up slide.

Hook Slide

The hook slide is executed with the left foot bent to hook the base on the outside. To start, line up your players and have them put their legs in the hook slide position with the right leg straight and the left leg bent. Then have them practice sliding to the base, hooking the outfield side of the base with the bent left foot. As the players practice they should concentrate on sliding away from the base with the body, hooking it with the left foot so that the fielder has only that small part of the runner's toe to tag. Figure 8.7 demonstrates the hook slide.

Figure 8.7 The hook slide.

Rainy Day Sliding

Purpose. This drill allows demonstration and practice of the pop-up and hook slides.

Procedure. One of the best times to practice sliding is when rain has fallen on your field. On rainy days, or following a rain, we like to work on our sliding technique. Because players do not slide on the dirt, sliding is not painful and the risk of injury is small. Most coaches and teams never work on sliding. With the grass still wet, take your team out to the outfield grass and put down bases. Then have your players slide into the bases, executing the various types of slides that we've discussed. Work on hook slides and pop-up slides. Your players will enjoy this drill and get much needed practice at a little used skill.

SMART BASE RUNNING

Doing things intelligently on the base paths can help you score runs and prevent running into stupid outs. You must teach your players to execute smart baseball on the bases.

The 45-Foot Rule

The first point—and I can't stress this enough—is talk to your players about the rules at length so that they understand them. Doing this will give them the knowledge of how to be smart on the bases. If you are starting at home plate and working your way around the bases, one of the first rules that you want to coach is the 45-foot rule. Any ball hit in front of home plate requires the offensive player to run the last 45 feet to first base in the chalked box on the foul side of the base line. If the runner is inside the line, he is automatically out, whether the first baseman catches the throw or not. Your players must work on getting to the outside at the 45-foot point. This skill is easy to practice, and you don't need to do it often or with different methods for your players to get it.

45-Foot Rule

Purpose. Use this drill when you want to practice the 45-foot rule.

Procedure. Put everyone at home plate. One by one have them take a swing and sprint to first base. When they get to the 45-foot mark, they run outside the line. To make sure that they do this, draw a line in the dirt to show them where the 45-foot mark is so that they know to get outside. You can also chalk the line as they do for a game. Another method that works well is to have a coach stand at the 45-foot mark on the inside. The players get to the outside or they risk running into him, an occurrence that really gets the point across.

Running on an Overthrow at First

The next base-running skill is reacting to an overthrow at first base. On an overthrow you will often see a base runner automatically turn toward second base. He then looks back and realizes too late that the catcher is backing up or the ball has bounced right back to the first baseman. He is in no-man's-land where he can't get back to first base and he can't get to second safely. A simple toss from the first baseman or catcher to one of the fielders results in an easy out.

We use a technique that helps minimize this predicament. Our base runners turn on the overthrow toward the foul side of first base. We have them pivot to the right shoulder and find the ball. If the catcher has the ball backing up or the ball bounces back to the first baseman, the runner has not turned to second base, so he walks back to first base. If an overthrow occurs that our runner can advance on, he turns to his right, finds the ball, and quickly accelerates to second base. On most overthrows at first base, the decision whether to go to second base or stay at first is easy. Few bang-bang plays occur at second. Knowing this, we want our players to get a good look before making that decision. With this technique, your players will not run into an easy out. Turning toward the foul side of first base is the smart base-running technique on an overthrow.

Avoiding No-Man's-Land

Purpose. We use this drill to emphasize how to decide quickly whether to move to second base. In this drill, the runners use the proper technique and read the ball when they make that turn to find the ball.

Procedure. Start all the players at home plate. They take an imaginary swing and sprint through first base. After they hit the base, they chop their steps and turn inside with the proper technique to find the baseball. A coach stands by the fence where the overthrow would land if it got by the first baseman. The coach is holding a baseball. The players make that inside turn and find the coach. If the coach steps toward them holding the baseball, the runners walk back to first as if the catcher had backed up the play. If the coach drops the ball out of his hand to the ground, the runners read that as a ball on which they can turn and run to second base. Used once or twice a week at the end of practice, this drill can ensure correct execution of the technique.

Runner at First

Now we work on the basics of having a runner at first base. The runner at first must look at the coach, who is flashing the offensive signs. The runner holds up his fingers to show how many outs there are. This rule applies to our runners at every base.

A coach will often tell a base runner that he has one out and receive in return an affirmative nod of the head, only to have the batter hit a fly ball and see the runner sprint past the next base, soon to be doubled up. Later, the head coach will ask the runner whether he knew how many outs there were, and the runner will always answer that he didn't know. If your base runner is holding up his fingers to show one or two outs or a fist for no outs, he has to think about how many outs there are. This little mental device may sound simple or trivial, but using it helps your players avoid making running mistakes because they don't know how many outs there are. With this technique, the player is less likely just to nod his head and tune out the coach.

Runner at Second

Another part of smart base running is advancing a runner from second to third on a ground ball to third base. When a player hits a ground ball to third base with a runner at second, we are going to take third base. We do this by having our runner at second shuffle off the base when a ground ball is hit to the third baseman. When the third baseman looks at the runner to check him, the runner leans back to second base but still has a large lead. The key is for the runner to execute this lean when he is exactly on a line

between the third baseman and second base. By leaning in this location between the fielder and the base, the base runner creates an optical illusion that makes him appear closer to second base than he actually is (see figure 8.8). On the release of the ball by the third baseman to first, the runner breaks to third base. He has a good lead, gets a great jump, and makes it safely to third every time.

Figure 8.8 The optical illusion the base runner creates by leaning on the line between second and third can let him take a bigger lead.

The essential elements for this play are for the base runner to get a big secondary lead from second base and place himself directly between the base and the third baseman when he leans toward second. He does not take steps back to second; he just leans that way and then breaks to third when the third baseman turns to throw to first. The lean creates an optical illusion that keeps the third baseman from accurately judging how far off the base the runner is. This play gives your offense an advantage because now the runner stays at second only on a ground ball hit to the pitcher or shortstop. Any ground ball hit to first base, second base, or third base will get the runner over to third.

Second Base Lead and Lean

Purpose. This drill is used to practice the lean between second and third in the leadoff to create the optical illusion discussed earlier.

Procedure. First, have all your runners go to second base. Have a coach or someone else at third base. A coach rolls a ground ball to third, and the person there fields it. When he catches the ball, have your runners get off the base in line with the third baseman and lean toward second base. At this point you can even take your team, all the other runners, to the third-base coaching box so that they can see the illusion that the runner appears to be closer to second base than he actually is. To finish the drill, the third baseman, after looking the runner back, makes an imaginary throw to first, at which point the runner breaks to third. Running this drill only once or twice a week will keep your players sharp.

Runner at Third

The next base that we cover is third base. Explain how you run when at third and why. You need to instruct your runners to take their lead at third and stay in foul territory if they're running. They do this, of course, so that any batted ball that hits them is a foul ball. A runner hit with a batted ball in fair territory is out. So have your runners at third start in foul territory but return to the base, if necessary, in fair territory. This positioning will make it more difficult for the catcher to make a good throw on a pickoff to third.

When your base runner gets to third, the last thing you want is for him to get picked off by the pitcher. To protect against this, we have our runners take a jab step (a short, quick step that pushes off on the ball of the foot) back to third when a right-handed pitcher lifts his front foot. We have our runners hold that jab step to read the pitcher's move. If the pitcher steps to third to pick off the runner, the runner dives or otherwise gets back to third base. The runner has already taken the jab step, so he should be able to avoid being picked off.

If the pitcher steps toward home plate with his lead leg, the runner takes his three steps toward home and reads the pitch. If it bounces or gets past the catcher, he can then attempt to score. This technique will help your players avoid being picked off third base by right-handed pitchers.

Third-Base Tag-Up

Purpose. This drill works on tagging up at third.

Procedure. Position a coach in left field and throw him fly balls with safety balls. Players tag up, use their own eyes, and sprint home when they see the outfielder make the catch. We use soft safety baseballs so that the players will not be hurt if they get hit by the throw.

BASE-RUNNING DRILLS

If you want to take advantage of base-running opportunities and avoid giving up outs on the bases, you must be able to coach technique and form.

Three-Group Base-Running

Purpose. To work on base-running skills at each base. In this drill you divide your players into three groups so that your coaches can work with smaller groups, making explanation easier and allowing every player on your team to be working on something.

Procedure. We often start our practice, after we stretch, with base running in three or four groups. We usually work with the players in three groups—one at third base, one at second base, and one at first base. If you have 18 players on the team, you put 6 at each base. If you have 18 players and 3 of them are pitchers who don't run the bases, at each base you can put 5 players and a pitcher for your runners to work against. At first base we work on a variety of things—the proper angle when turning the base and going to second, finding the ball on an overthrow before turning into fair territory, picking up signs from the coach and responding by showing with the fingers how many outs there are, taking primary and secondary leads, and various steal techniques such as the straight steal and the delayed steal. Naturally, we don't do all of this on one day. Each time we run this drill, we have the players work on one of these techniques, a different one or two each time.

The coach at second base, meanwhile, also talks about how to take primary and secondary leads, how to pick up the coach at third on a base hit to the outfield, how to react to bunt situations and ground balls to the left side of the infield, and how to steal third by reading the pitcher.

Our runners at third base work on the jab step back to third with a right-handed pitcher on the mound. We tell our pitcher either to pick to third base or to deliver the pitch home. Runners must read this and react from the jab step. We will also have our players work on tagging up on fly balls to the outfield, returning to the base, using their eyes to judge when to leave the base, and using the technique of pushing off to get maximum speed.

We have the players spend five minutes at each station. This drill gets our players a tremendous amount of base-running work in only 15 minutes. We also do a lot of work starting at the plate. Players practice dropping a bunt and getting quickly into good running form, or doing the same after taking a full swing. They stay in the outside chalk lines over the last 45 feet to first base and run hard through the base, being aware of a possible overthrow. We work hard on the running angles that players should use when they hit a potential extra-base hit and must run to second base. We put a coach right near the first-base coaching box. After swinging the bat, the runner must come out of the batter's box and go hard at this coach to get the proper angle. When he gets to the coach he turns, dips his shoulder, and hits the inside corner of first base on his way to second. With this technique, the player is on a straight line to second base after he hits first base.

Right-Field Line Stealing

Purpose. Another drill that we commonly run works on stealing second base and reading the pitcher.

Procedure. We have our players go down the right-field line. One of our coaches is the pitcher, and we run our steals—the straight steal and the delayed steal. We work on the technique of leaving first early on a first-and-third double-steal situation. We have the players practice taking off on the steal and getting into running form, facing the next base as soon as possible by stepping across the body with the left leg as the first step in the steal process.

Determination Drill

Purpose. We end our practice at least once a week, usually the day before a game, with a drill that we call Determination. The drill works on both technique and conditioning.

Procedure. The runners all start at home plate and run half speed to first and second base. In running the bases they must hit each base with the proper angles and perfect technique. Coming around second they run three-quarter speed to third base, again hitting the base with the proper angle on the inside corner. When they hit third, they sprint full speed up the line to home plate. They must hit home plate with the ball of the foot squarely in the middle of the plate, not on the black part of the plate. If even one player misses the middle of home plate, the coach or coaches who are judging the foot placement wait until all players finish and then have them start all over. Everyone on the team must hit home directly in the middle. This drill reinforces technique and form and builds morale because the players cheer for each other so that they do not have to run the drill several times.

The drills that we have presented all work to improve your players' technique on the bases. You can use some every day and others once or twice a week.

Coaches' Keys

1. Teaching base-running skills involves instructing your players in both base-running technique and the rules that pertain to running the bases. Work with your players on running form, properly running the bases, and sliding at each base.

2. Smart base running refers to doing things intelligently on the base paths. Talk to your players about relevant rules such as the infield fly rule, the 45-foot rule, and turning to avoid being put out on an overthrow at first base.

3. A primary lead is the lead that a runner establishes when he steps off the base. A secondary lead is the extended lead that he takes after the pitcher releases the pitch.

4. Runners use different leads at second and third base. At second base the player must read the pitcher while listening to his coach tell him where the middle infielders are. At third base he should jab step back if the pitcher works from a stretch position. If the pitcher is working from a windup, the player should walk facing home plate.

5. Base-running drills should teach both technique and skill. Start your players at home plate and work your way around the bases. Mix up the drills and the frequency with which you use them.

6. The goal is to get your players to run the bases smartly and aggressively.

CHAPTER 9 TEACHING OFFENSIVE STRATEGIES

To teach offensive strategies, a coach must first teach his players offensive skills. One of the first skills that the players should be able to execute is the bunting game, starting with the sacrifice bunt, then the drag and push bunts, and finally the squeeze bunt. If your players can execute all these skills, you can work your strategy according to the game situation.

The next part to look at, work on, and incorporate is the running game. You want your team to be able to steal bases and take advantage of opportunities when the opponent makes a mistake. If the opportunity is there, your players should take the extra base. They should be able to steal second base, third base, and home when the defense allows it. You need to instruct your players on reading the pitcher and using the proper technique to run the bases. A good running game can turn a walk into a double, a double into a run. A good running game puts constant pressure on the opposition and complements a team-oriented offense that emphasizes hitting behind the runners and executing the hit-and-run.

Your players should understand all the parts of the game that can affect your team's offensive strategy. Obviously, they need to know the number of outs, and we talked earlier about how they show the coach that they are aware of that. The score is also important, of course. In a tight game, the players need to know that you may use any part of your offense—steal, bunt, hit-and-run. If your team is behind by five or more runs late in the game (after the fifth inning in a seven-inning game, from the seventh inning on in a nine-inning game), you want your runners to play it safe to save your outs. To reduce the risk of being thrown out, your runners would move up one base on each hit.

The defensive skills of the opposing team can also influence your offensive strategy. Drag bunts for hits can be executed on slow third basemen or pitchers. Runners can go two bases on base hits to outfielders who don't throw well.

FORMULATING AN OFFENSE

A coach can only do so much. His team's talent level is the basic barometer, telling him what his players need to work on and what strategy fits their ability.

If you have players who can run and make contact, you can implement a number of the offensive strategies that we have already talked about, which include the steal, hit-and-run, and the bunting game. If you have a group more apt to hit for power, then you will more often play for the big inning.

Throughout our tenure at Esperanza, I have always stressed an offense that puts pressure on the defense. I want my players to be on the attack rather than wait for the one big hit. With each inning and each base runner, I want them thinking in an aggressive fashion.

To get a runner on base, we will look to drag bunt or push bunt if the defense gives us this opening by playing their third baseman or first baseman back. The adage that you can't steal first base is true, but your bunt offense, your little ball offense, can put your opponent on their heels. A key point to note here is that you can have the greatest offensive strategy and ideas, but if you don't get runners on base you can never use them. The key is using the right offense for the right players. You must know the offensive strengths of each of your players. You can teach just about anyone to bunt, but some players will have better ability to drag bunt and push bunt. You need to know which players can execute those skills. No aspect of coaching is more important than putting players in position to succeed.

Most coaches at the high school level do not like to give up outs to advance a runner. In constructing your offense, however, keep in mind that if you score a run an inning in a high school game, you will end up scoring seven runs, which should be plenty. If you score a run every time you give up an out, you may score even more.

As you evaluate your talent and the individual skills of your players, you must also think in terms of your bench. These reserve players can give your offense a significant boost at an important time. The coach who is able to substitute with a player who can produce a key hit through his contact ability or execute a crucial bunt puts his team in better position for success.

When formulating an offense, coaches should always keep in mind that title and playoff games often come down to that key bunt or stolen base that produces a one-run victory. Playing for a big inning is fine if you have the talent to do it, but remember the baseball adage that speed never goes into a slump. Fundamentals and execution are paramount for teams at every level, especially in the abbreviated seven innings of a high school game. Every out and every base runner are pivotal. If the big hit fails, you have to be able to play little ball. We've had a lot of success at

Esperanza playing to our motto "Get them on and get them home."

THE HIT-AND-RUN

A team capable of executing the hit-and-run can increase its offensive playbook. Successful hit-and-runs result not so much from great speed but from bat control and contact hitting. Coaches should always be aware and take advantage of situations that play into their strength, but they should never ask a player to do something that he's not capable of doing. With a count of three balls and one strike or three balls and two strikes, the hit-and-run can be a low-risk strategy if you're confident that the hitter has the discipline to read the pitch and make contact. Your hitter can take a ball for a base on balls or hit a strike to put the ball in play with the runner moving. By knowing your players' capabilities, you can use the hit-and-run to generate offense without relying on pure speed.

Hit-and-Run

Purpose. Use this drill to practice the hit-and-run during batting practice.

Procedure. End each round of line hitting with a runner on first base or runners on first and second base. Have the runners stealing, obliging the hitter to try to hit the ball on the ground. You don't want a big-hop ground ball but a sharp ground ball that is difficult for the infielders, moving to cover their bases as the runners steal, to react to. You can adjust this drill to make the imaginary count three and one or three and two so that the hitter works on taking ball four, ensuring the advance of the runners. I also like to tell my hitters on a normal hit-and-run to swing at any pitch. My thinking is that even if they don't make contact, their swing will distract the catcher enough to allow the runner to get an extra step or two and steal the base. I tell my hitters that the one pitch they do not swing at on a hit-and-run call is the pitch in the dirt. The runner or runners should be able to steal the base on any pitch in the dirt, so the batter doesn't have to sacrifice a strike.

PLAYING FOR THE BIG INNING

There are definite advantages and disadvantages to playing for the big inning. Coaches use this strategy when their players don't have the speed to steal bases and cannot execute the hit-and-run or bunt. They resort to playing for that big inning, waiting for the home run or extra-base hit, rather than giving up outs trying unsuccessfully to execute a more aggressive game.

The disadvantage of this big-inning philosophy is that the team may never get the home run or extra-base hit, or the series of hits, needed to produce a big inning. In addition, because of the lack of speed and the inability to steal bases, the team is more vulnerable to the double play.

All this puts an emphasis on fundamentals and execution. Some coaches simply prefer to play for the big inning. The only strategy involved is simply taking pitches to put pressure on the opposing pitcher to throw strikes, with the goal being to put as many runners on base as possible and look for the big hit. I like to think that there is a strategy that combines both approaches and is based on recognizing the strengths and weaknesses of the opponent and having players who have learned how to execute the fundamentals—the various bunts, the hit-and-run, hitting behind a runner at second base, and producing a scoring fly ball with a runner at third. We want our players to be thoroughly prepared so that they can think along with us and aren't surprised by any strategy we employ.

SET OFFENSIVE PLAYS

Coaches can have their teams execute several different offensive plays to put pressure on the opposition. We've already talked about the standard bunt and hit-and-run offense that everyone knows and uses, but let's talk about some other plays that can give your team an advantage.

Advancing Runners

When a coach wants to advance the runner at first base to get him into scoring position, he can use a number of methods—the sacrifice bunt,

drag or push bunt, hit-and-run, straight steal, or slash (fake bunt and hit). The consequences of these will affect the decision-making process of what the coach will do.

The sacrifice bunt gives up an out to advance the runner. If a team is trailing by more than two runs in the last two innings, this is not a smart strategy. Coaches want to save their outs, not give them up. So instead of using the sacrifice bunt when trailing by more than two runs, the coach may have his hitter bunt for a hit. This attempt may be unsuccessful, of course, giving up an out, but the runner has still advanced into scoring position.

The hit-and-run is another way to advance a runner. If the batter makes contact he has a chance to get on base and advance the runner two bases. The runner at first stealing on the pitch will probably be able to go to third base on a hit to the outfield. The hitter wants to hit a hard ground ball or a line drive. The infielders are moving when they see the runner trying to steal, so if the hitter makes contact the fielders on the move will have trouble fielding the ball. A key coaching point is that the hitter needs to swing at any pitch not in the dirt. On a ball in the dirt the hitter has virtually no chance to make contact and the runner should be able to steal the base on his own. A coach who wants to use the hit-and-run should also see that the pitcher is around the plate with his pitches so that the hitter will get a good pitch to hit.

Of course, a coach can always use the straight steal, but to be successful this strategy requires having a runner with speed or the ability to get a good jump. The situation changes if the batter has a three-ball count. The runner at first will get help if the subsequent pitch is a ball because the hitter will have walked.

Another method, probably the least used, is the fake bunt slash. Here the hitter sets up as if he is going to bunt, but just as the pitcher gets ready to release the ball, the hitter pulls the bat back and swings. This technique is effective if the defense is moving to cover the bunt. The hitter can then put the ball in play against infielders who are out of position. The key here is not to hit the ball in the air to the outfield. The outfielders are not moving so they will not be out of position.

Coaches can use several strategies to advance a runner into scoring position. A coach must know his players, size up his opponent and what they are trying to do defensively, and then decide how to attack their weaknesses.

Using the Delayed Steal

Even if your team does not run well, you can put your players in motion. The delayed steal, in which the runner at first shuffles into his secondary lead after the pitcher releases the ball and then shuffles twice more before taking off to steal second base, is a powerful weapon when you see the defense slip into any of the following:

- A catcher who frames the pitch too long, looks at the umpire after close pitches, or goes to his knee after each pitch.

- Middle infielders who turn their backs and face the outfield after a pitch. The second baseman should be walking into the base path, and the shortstop should be moving toward second after the pitch. If they are late or lax, the delayed steal is there for the taking.

Bunting With a Runner on Second

Another offensive play that can be successful is the bunt with a runner at second base and no one out. In this situation the normal sacrifice is a bunt to the third-base line. The first thing to do is note where the first baseman is playing. If the first baseman is playing behind first base, the hitter squares late and bunts the ball to first base. The first baseman will break late to the ball, and if the batter gets the ball down anywhere near the line, the runner at second will advance easily with the possibility that the bunter will also be safe without a play.

In relation to that situation, with a runner on second base or with runners at first and second and no one out, a good play to run instead of your sacrifice bunt is to have your hitter drag bunt. When you drag bunt, you open up a number of advantages. First, depending on the bunter's technique, the defense has less reaction time than it does with a sacrifice bunt when the hitter squares away early. When you have a hitter squaring late to drag bunt, the defense must react quickly and is more apt to make a mistake. The

second advantage is that you are not automatically giving up an out to advance the runner. The batter is bunting for a hit when the defense is not expecting a bunt, possibly even after he has taken a full swing to get the defense thinking that he will not be bunting. Even if he fails to reach base, as long as he gets the ball down he will move the runner or runners over. The third advantage is that by drag bunting, the defense almost always has to hurry a throw, possibly creating an overthrow that will allow a runner to score. Figures 9.1 and 9.2 illustrate where to bunt the ball for right- and left-handed batters and the common infielder movements.

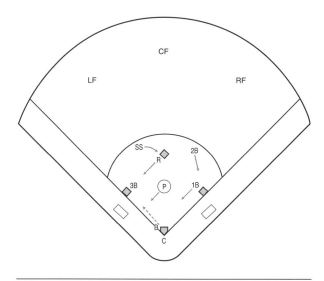

Figure 9.1 Right-handed drag bunt to third base with runner on second.

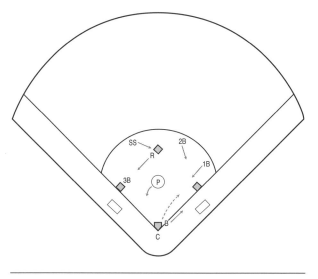

Figure 9.2 Left-handed drag bunt to first base with runner on second.

A Drag Bunt Wins the Game

I recall a 1987 game in which we were trailing 3-1 in the bottom of the seventh. The opposing pitcher had been dominating. We were down to our last three outs, and things looked bleak. But we got a leadoff walk, and the next hitter was hit by a pitch. We had runners at first and second with no outs and our number nine hitter coming up. We called for a drag bunt, and he got it down. The third baseman charged the ball and threw on the run. The ball went all the way down the right-field line. Both runners scored, and the hitter ended up at third base. We had tied the game without hitting a ball out of the infield, and we went on to win, with the big play being that drag bunt.

Squeeze Plays

With a runner at third base, several run-producing plays can be effective. First, of course, is the squeeze play, a bunt that will score a runner from third base. The suicide squeeze calls for the batter to bunt any pitch no matter where it is because the runner is coming full speed on the pitcher's release of the ball. In the safety squeeze the batter bunts only at a strike and the runner waits to see whether the bunt is down before he breaks to home. In this situation, if the batter gets the bunt down where he should (see figure 9.3), the run scores and there is a strong possibility that the batter will reach base, maybe even without a play. Naturally, the score of the game dictates whether a squeeze is appropriate. I generally favor the idea of giving up an out for a run, although not when we trail by several runs in the late innings.

The squeeze does not have to be restricted to a situation in which you have only a runner at third base. Executed properly with runners at second and third or with the bases loaded, the squeeze can and should produce two runs. In this situation, your runner at third waits and does not break until the pitcher's front foot hits the ground. Meanwhile, your runner at second leaves when the pitcher starts his windup or as he starts his delivery to the plate from his stretch. When the ball is bunted, the runner from third should score easily and the runner from second base rounds third and

Figure 9.3 Proper safety squeeze bunt placement and technique with a right-handed pitcher.

keeps coming to the plate. The defense seldom thinks about the trail runner and almost always throws to first, allowing the second runner to score without a play.

Another play is the bases-loaded squeeze with three balls on the hitter. In this situation you want your runner at third to leave when the pitcher starts his windup. If the pitcher works from the stretch, the runner at third leaves as soon as the pitcher delivers to the plate, as if the runner were stealing home (see figure 9.4). The hitter squares and shows bunt right away as the pitcher begins his windup or when he is set in his stretch position. Showing the squeeze early, with the bases loaded, puts tremendous pressure on the pitcher. Keep in mind that the pitcher has a three-ball count on the hitter with less than two outs. Most pitchers are taught to throw a pitchout when they see squeeze. If he does that with a three-ball count, it's ball four and the run scores automatically. If the pitcher is rattled and throws a wild pitch, two runs could score, depending on how the ball bounces. If the pitcher throws a strike with all the runners going and the batter bunts the ball properly, it's one run and possibly two. Again, you must know your players and know that the batter is capable of getting a bunt down, but the bases-loaded squeeze with a three-ball count is an exciting and often smart play.

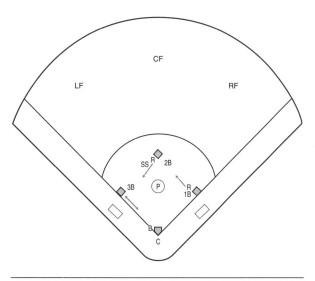

Figure 9.4 In a bases-loaded squeeze play situation with a 3-1 or 3-2 count, all runners leave right away and the batter squares early. The batter only bunts if a strike is thrown.

Grounder With No Outs or One Out and a Runner on Third

Another play with a runner at third is designed to send the runner home on a ground out with no outs or one out. This play can be run in two ways. The first way is to have the runner break on any slow roller hit to the first baseman, shortstop, or second baseman. The runner has to read it and take off full speed to home. Usually the throw will go to first, and you will have cashed in a run for an out. Most teams do not work on throwing out runners at the plate. In this situation, your runner stays at third on anything hit hard at an infielder but tries to score on the slow roller to first, second, or short. The second way is to tell your runner at third to go on any ground out. He doesn't have to read hard or soft, but there is a risk. He is likely to be thrown out on any hard-hit grounder to the pitcher or a corner infielder. The advantage is the runner gets a great jump and can really put pressure on the infielders.

Sacrifice Fly

The team that consistently produces a run-scoring sacrifice fly with a runner at third is likely to be successful. Teams at all levels of baseball waste these opportunities. With a sacrifice fly, a ball hit deep to the outfield that is caught or shallow to an outfielder with a weak arm, the runner tags or touches third base and leaves after the outfielder makes the catch, arriving at home plate before the throw gets there. When a runner is at third with one or no outs, the hitter is trying to hit the ball in the air (preferably deep) to get the run home. The runner needs to be reminded to tag up at third base on any line drive because his natural reaction on a line drive is to take a step or two toward home plate. These misdirected steps may delay him enough that he cannot tag up and have a chance to beat the throw. Third-base coaches should consistently remind runners at third base to tag up on a line drive or fly ball.

SIGNS AND SIGNALS

Baseball used to be the only sport in which signs were given. Now, coaches and players in virtually all sports flash signs and signals in some form. Baseball teams still run their entire offense with signs, and signs are the system of communication between pitchers and catchers. At the major league level, the manager in the dugout flashes signs to the third-base coach, who in turn flashes signs to the hitter and base runner or runners. Everyone in the stadium may be watching the coach as the offensive players look to see what play might be put on, so the signs must be complicated enough that the opposition can't steal them but simple enough that the offensive players won't miss them.

At the high school level and college level, the third-base coach or the head coach in the dugout gives the offensive signs. If the third-base coach is the head coach, he flashes whatever signs he wants. If the third-base coach is an assistant coach, he may have the liberty to flash his own signs or he may relay the signs from the head coach in the dugout.

We instruct our base runners to be standing on the base when they look for a sign so that they can give full attention to the coach without worrying about being picked off. The coach relaying the signs can have a variety to choose from, to make it more difficult for the opposition to steal them. We remind our players that they should look for a sign before and after every pitch. If the only time we flash a sign is when a play is definitely on, we make it easier for the opposition to steal the sign.

We use various types of signs. One is the indicator. The coach has an indicator that he touches—perhaps his cap or cheek or uniform letters—in the process of flashing an assortment of signs. The next touch after the indicator is the sign. So if the indicator is his cap, the coach can flash an assortment of signs that mean nothing until he touches his cap. Once he touches his cap, he may touch his leg for a steal or his belt for a bunt. He may also erase the sign by wiping his hand across his letters. In other words, if he has gone to his cap and leg, meaning that a steal is on, he may then erase it just to confuse the opposition.

Another system uses pump signs. A pump is any tug or touch at the coach's uniform or body. So as the coach hits his arm, tugs his ear, brushes his leg, he is performing pumps. The pumps are counted after the indicator is touched. So if the indicator to set off the pumps is the cap, the players count pumps after the coach touches his cap. The cap, which is the indicator, is zero. One pump is one word—*squeeze*. Two pumps means two words, *hit-and-run*; three pumps stands for the three-letter word *run* (steal); four pumps means the four-letter word *bunt*; and five pumps is the five-letter word *slash*. If the coach ends on his indicator, it's back to zero, which means that nothing is on. If your players know what each sign stands for, as they should, all they have to do is count after the coach goes

to the indicator. These signs can be extremely difficult to steal.

In addition, we use what we call automatics. These signs are relayed by a coach's movement. As an example, every time the coach gives his base runner a fist, that signal is a green light to steal a base. The coach may tug his belt, and that is the automatic for drag bunt. The automatics do not need any other sign or movement to implement the play. A coach can also use automatics that work only when he calls the player's number.

You need to pick a style that you feel comfortable with and that your players will understand. You can also use a combination, but remember that if you make them so difficult that your players don't understand them or miss them, you might as well not have any signs.

Coaches' Keys

1. In formulating an offense and teaching strategy, it all comes down to the talent level of your team. You have to put players in a position to succeed, and you can't ask them to do something they are not capable of doing. Successful teams are those schooled in fundamentals and execution. Most often, successful teams incorporate both a power game and a little ball approach that employs various bunts and uses an aggressive style on the bases.

2. Your players should know how to think along with you, but you are in charge and can employ various signs and signals to implement plays. The key is to make them simple enough for the players to understand and subtle enough that the opposition can't steal them.

Part IV

COACHING DEFENSE

TEACHING DEFENSIVE SKILLS

Defense is the key to success in any sport. Hold your opponent scoreless and you win. As a coach, putting your best defensive players on the field is a must. Your team must be prepared to defend in any situation, which means that you must practice and prepare consistently. This chapter covers all the components of putting together a good defensive team. We start with the basic fielding skills and the important parts of how to teach those skills. We then progress to infield skills, stance, and positioning. We provide drills to improve your infielders' catching, throwing, and fielding execution.

From there, the chapter moves on to discuss the catcher, using the same format to cover all the components and drills necessary to make your catchers better. The last group covered will be the outfielders. Here the footwork, skills, and drills for playing the outfield will be expanded on so that you can improve your outfield defense. We also show you how to move a player from the infield to the outfield so that he can compete and excel at this change of position.

All this will show you how to improve the defensive ability of your position players, which translates into good team defense.

TEACHING FIELDING SKILLS

When you start teaching fielding skills as a coach, you are looking for players to demonstrate specific skills to show that they can play the various positions effectively. At the college level, coaches usually make few changes in position outside of moving a shortstop to second base or switching an outfielder from one field to another. When a high school coach puts his team together, he often makes a number of defensive changes. These can be as drastic as putting a center fielder at shortstop or having his best pitcher catch when he is not pitching. The Little League coach may face a more difficult task. He probably has players who have never played the position that he wants them to play or, even more daunting, he may have first-year players who have never played the game at all.

Fielding skills start with the simple game of playing catch. Make your players understand from the start that more throwing errors occur during the season than errors of any other kind. A good rule for organizing players during warm-ups is to pair them on the basis of differing priorities.

At the younger levels you want to put players together according to their skill level to avoid injuries. Older players can be paired according to positions—the shortstop with the second baseman; the third baseman with the first baseman; and the catchers, outfielders, and pitchers with their own. This grouping will allow them to learn from each other.

Teaching fielding skills involves improving technique and building confidence. This task requires constant supervision and repeated work on fundamentals.

In playing catch, there's more to it than the simple act of making a throw and making a catch. Players should focus on making accurate throws, keeping the arm up so that the ball doesn't sail or sink on a sidearm throw, and catching the ball with the glove in the right position. By concentrating on what they're doing, their throwing and catching become more automatic. You need to monitor this part of the warm-up process and provide drills that improve arm accuracy and glove dexterity. The goal is to deliver chest-high throws and perform two-handed catches with the palm up on a ball below the waist and the palm down on a ball above the waist.

After turning the routine of playing catch into more of an art form, the next important step, of course, is teaching your players to field ground balls. All defensive players must be able to handle the routine ground ball reliably. Again, technique and footwork require practice, with ground balls as well as with pop flies and fly balls. In all instances, proper positioning is the key to making the fielding of a ground ball or fly ball easier. If you're dealing with younger players who may be timid about fielding the ball or if you're concerned about the potential for injury, use a tennis ball in practice to help develop technique and confidence.

The bottom line is that good defensive skills result from the often-taken-for-granted routine of playing catch. Do it right and the rest of it comes easier.

DEVELOPING INFIELD SKILLS

This section will focus on the specific skills and drills that your infielders will need. The most important skill is the ability to catch a ground ball. Everything else builds from that basic skill. If you are a Little League coach and no one appears able to catch a ground ball consistently, you can only do the best you can, looking for the players with the best hands or those unafraid of the ball.

At higher levels, high school and up, you go back to the player who can best catch a ground ball. If two or more players have equal ability, you put the one with the best or quickest feet at shortstop, the best arm at third, and the weakest arm at second. Your best fielder should be at shortstop because it is the most challenging defensive position, requiring a player who can cover a lot of ground, make difficult off-balance throws, and, in most cases, be the infield captain. Third base requires a better throwing arm than second base because of the distance involved. Obviously, your first baseman must be able to catch throws from the infielders, whether high, low, or in between.

That is a general view of what skills the various infield positions require from a player. After your players have a set position, you can begin working to improve their skills through the drills in this section.

Stance

When working on infield skills you should focus on certain absolutes on which to drill your players. First, put them in a good stance. You want infielders to have their feet approximately shoulder-width apart, with their toes pointing straight ahead. A right-handed infielder should have his right foot slightly behind his left, with his right big toe opposite the instep of his left foot. The left-handed infielder should be just the opposite. An infielder should hold his hands just below his waist, similar to the stance that a linebacker in football or a guard in basketball would use. Don't allow him to hunch too low, which would inhibit his ability to move quickly in either direction.

After infielders become comfortable with the form of the proper stance, they should know when and how to take it. Some infielders become so focused on the stance itself that they become rigid in it, almost afraid to relax and come out of it, and they forfeit their quickness in the process. You want your infielders to back off and then take three or four steps to get into their stance, ready to field the ball. They should take their stance when their pitcher's arm is at the top of his delivery, just before he releases the ball. They should be thinking, "Hit it to me," and they should be aware of the situation (how many outs and how many base runners) if the ball comes to them. Little League coaches may want to have their players say aloud, "Hit it to me."

Positioning

The next step in developing infield skills is positioning. An infielder wants to catch a ground ball with his feet in the same comparative position as he took in his stance. His feet should be shoulder-width apart, and his foot on his glove-hand side should be slightly in front of his other foot. His glove should be out in front of his body with his glove on the ground. A line connecting the two feet to the glove should form a triangle. If the glove is not in front in this triangle, the infielder will not be able to follow the ball into his glove with his eyes. A coach should be able to see the button on the top of the infielder's cap when the player has this triangle and is looking the ball into his glove. If the infielder's glove is back between his feet in a straight line, he cannot look the ball into his glove and is more apt to field it on a bad bounce, allowing the ball to play him.

The triangle technique (see figure 10.1) provides the infielder with better vision, permitting him to look for the good bounce. Most ground balls take three bounces, or hops. We call these the big hop, the short hop, and the middle, or in-between, hop. All ground balls are different, and predicting a bad bounce is impossible, but if an infielder knows these hops and can recognize them, he will often react to field the ball on the best one. The big hop, of course, is generally the best because it's the easiest. When an infielder catches a ground ball on the big hop, he is usually upright in his stance, can glove the ball easily, and is in good position to make a throw.

The big hop, of course, progresses to a short hop through a progression of bounces and is still comparatively easy to field. The in-between hop, neither big nor short, is much more difficult. Usually, the fielder has to play the in-between hop because he has let the ball

Figure 10.1 Triangle technique.

play him by remaining back on his heels rather than being aggressive.

Most coaches believe that they are improving technique simply by hitting their infielders ground ball after ground ball. This routine doesn't work if the fielder is using improper technique and the coach isn't stopping to correct it. A coach should always be reinforcing proper stance, glove position, aggressiveness in reading the hop, soft hands in fielding the ball, and looking the ball into the glove.

The player reads the hop when the ball is hit. After taking his ready steps, he is prepared to charge the ball to get the good hop. But if the ball is a line drive that is going to bounce in front of him, he may need to back up to get the big hop. Players can practice this in the drill called 18 or 21 that appears later in the chapter.

After they get the right hop, players must look the ball all the way into the glove, executing this action with what is known as soft hands. The term *soft hands* refers to the give action that an infielder uses with his glove so that he does not knock the ball out. He catches the ball and squeezes it easily with his glove—thus the term *soft hands*. These techniques will also be explained with the Secure the Catch drill later in the chapter.

Forehand and Backhand Catches

The forehand catch is the most frequently used catch when fielding a ground ball. The infielder has his glove down with the palm of his glove facing skyward when he catches a ground ball. His throwing hand is set above the glove, ready to meet the glove and ball after the ball hits the glove. The throwing hand secures the catch. The fielder can also make the play on a ground ball without securing the catch with the throwing hand by just squeezing the glove on impact from the ball. Again, the player should use the soft hands technique to execute this squeezing action. Figure 10.2 illustrates the proper forehand catch technique.

Figure 10.2 The forehand catch.

The backhand is a technique for catching a throw or ground ball when the fielder will catch the ball with his glove in a position with his palm facing home plate. The player should use the backhand on any ball that he fields outside his body on his throwing side. If a ball is hit to his throwing-arm side and the player cannot get in front it, he backhands it by reaching across his body to secure the catch (see figure 10.3*a*) and then uses the right, left throwing technique described later in the throwing techniques section (see figure 10.3*b*).

Diving Catches

Players can make outstanding plays by diving for a ball to make the catch. On a ground ball the fielder must scramble to his feet and release the throw quickly. The first part of the dive is to extend the glove as far as possible to catch the

Figure 10.3 *(a)* The backhand catch and *(b)* the right-left throwing technique.

ball (see figure 10.4a). After the fielder makes the catch, he can scramble to his feet to make the throw or throw from his knees for a quicker release (see figure 10.4b). The throw from the knees will not be as strong as the throw from the feet, but it will be quicker. The fielder must decide which technique to use.

Figure 10.4 When diving for a catch, first the player extends his glove as far as he can *(a)*, then makes the throw from his knees *(b)* for the quickest release.

Catch and Tag at a Base

To catch the ball and tag a runner sliding or running into a base, the fielder must first get his feet into position to make the catch. Making the catch so that the ball doesn't fly into the outfield and allow the runner to advance a base is the most important part of the catch and tag. The fielder wants to get to the base with his feet on each side of it so that he can be ready to tag as the runner approaches the base. If the runner comes in standing up, the fielder simply steps toward the runner and tags him in front of the base with two hands holding the ball (see figure 10.5). If the runner slides into the base, the fielder catches the ball and makes a one-handed tag with his glove and the ball inside it. The tag action is down and then up right away with the glove so that the runner can't kick the ball out of the glove (see figure 10.6).

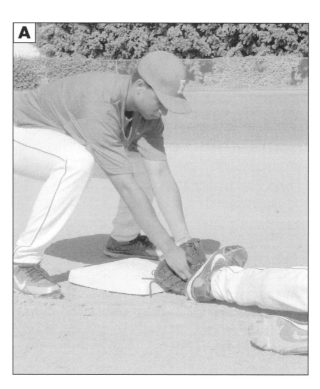

Figure 10.5 If the runner is standing, the fielder steps forward and tags him in front of the base.

Figure 10.6 The proper tag action for a sliding runner will prevent the runner from kicking the ball out of the fielder's glove.

Throwing Technique

After catching the ball out in front of the tri-angle that I described earlier, the player needs to use the proper throwing technique. He takes his glove to his throwing side and removes the ball as quickly as he can. He then gets his arm into throwing position by separating his throw-ing hand from the glove as he takes the ball to ear level to prepare to throw it. His footwork is to step with his right foot (or left) toward the base (see figure 10.7). Practice may not always make perfect, but in time practice will allow the fielder to turn all these individual steps into habit. He will be doing what comes naturally rather than worrying about whether his feet or hands are in the right positions. Sidearm throws are not a good technique and can hurt the arm. Most players don't throw sidearm unless they are executing a charge and flip play. Snap throws are the same as regular throws, but with quicker arm action and footwork.

Figure 10.7 Proper throwing technique.

Double Plays

The double play is the most decisive defen-sive play in baseball (of course, triple plays are the ultimate defensive play, but they are extremely rare). With a double play, the defense gets two outs for one hit ball. The double play can be a tremendous rally killer against your opponent.

The primary and most common double plays are made by the shortstop or third baseman to the second baseman for the force play, with the second baseman relaying the ball to the first baseman for the second out. The second baseman turns the double play using a tech-nique known as the pivot. He must catch the ball facing the third baseman or shortstop and then pivot or turn on his right foot to throw to first, often pushing off the bag while avoiding the sliding runner.

The first thing that a shortstop and second baseman do when a runner is at first (or first and second, or bases loaded) is to reposition themselves four steps closer to home plate and three steps closer to second base (see figure 10.8). This positioning gives the middle infielders more time to get into position to turn the double play. Some people note that they are giving up a lot of ground and opening holes for the batter by this position move. True

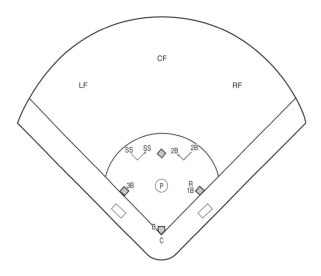

Figure 10.8 Standard double-play positioning.

enough, but they have to give up something if they want to get to the base in time to turn the double play.

After your middle infielders have moved into double-play depth, they are ready to turn a double play on any ground ball. If the ball is hit to the third baseman or shortstop, the second baseman takes the throw and relays it to the first baseman. He does this by coming to the left-field corner of the base with both hands up as a target. Doing this is important because the eyes of the third baseman or shortstop will go right to the second baseman's hands. If he doesn't have his hands up, the third baseman or shortstop will not focus on his hands but will look at his whole body, a larger target, and thus tend to throw less accurately.

The second baseman commonly uses one of two kinds of footwork. The first is to catch the ball, step on the side of the base facing first base, and throw to first. This technique is quick and simple. The problem with it is that the runner is sliding into the first-base side of the base and can easily cause a bad throw to break up the double play.

With the other technique the second baseman comes across the base with his left foot on the third-base side of the base (see figure 10.9a). He steps to catch the ball with his right foot off the base and then steps with his left foot to finish the throw to first base (see figure 10.9b). This is the ideal way to turn the double play from the high school level on down because if the runner slides into the second baseman when he has cleared the base, the result is an automatic double play. The runner cannot make contact with the fielder out of the direct line to second base.

In other situations, depending on who fields the ground ball, the shortstop may take the throw from the pitcher, first baseman, or second baseman. When any of them feeds or throws to the shortstop, he tries to catch the ball on the outside of the base. He then kicks the base with his right foot and finishes with the throw to first. The only time that this may change is when the first baseman fields a ground ball. If the first baseman fields the ball playing deep or behind the baseline between first and second, the shortstop will stay with

Figure 10.9 (a) The second baseman comes across the base with his left foot on the third-base side of the base, catches the ball with his right foot off the base, and (b, c) throws with his left foot.

the outside move on the double play (see figure 10.10*a*). But if the first baseman fields the ball on the inside of first base, the shortstop will come to the inside of second base to take the throw from the first baseman (see figure 10.10*b*). The shortstop and first baseman should practice this because the first baseman must instinctively know where the shortstop will be. The first baseman often has a difficult throw to make to second because the runner who is going to second is directly in his throwing path.

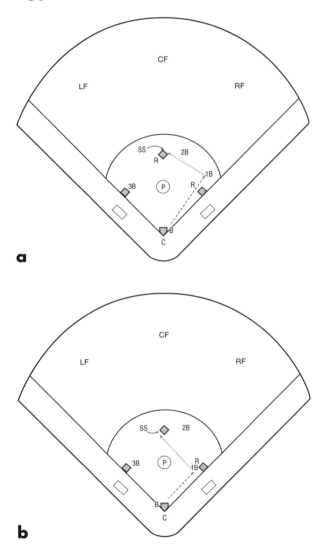

Figure 10.10 (*a*) Outside and (*b*) inside shortstop movement on a double play.

Infield Drills

Here are a few drills that you can do every day or a couple times a week. These drills will demonstrate the skills necessary to play all the defensive positions. Coaches should be able to recognize which players excel at which skills and then put them into or change them to the proper positions.

Secure the Catch

Purpose. This drill teaches your infielders how to use both hands or only the glove hand to secure the ball in the glove with the proper technique.

Procedure. Have infielders roll balls to each other, catching it with the glove and feet in the triangle position, keeping the head down, and using soft hands. They do not throw. This drill simply reinforces fielding technique.

Range or Dive

Purpose. This drill will increase your fielders' range and encourage them to be aggressive, diving for ground balls when necessary.

Procedure. Perform this drill on grass to diminish the risk of injury. For this drill the players line up in a straight line behind one another. They are about 10 yards from the coach. After each player, one by one, takes his ready steps, the coach rolls the ball hard to either the right or the left. The player must react quickly, moving his feet and diving when necessary. If he fails to field the ball, he must scramble to his feet and find it. Again, players do not throw.

Short-Hop

Purpose. This drill enhances the first baseman's ability to dig out short-hop throws, but you can use it with all infielders.

Procedure. For this drill, spread your infielders out approximately 30 feet apart. Pair them up and have them throw short hops to each other. Have one player throw 5 or 10 throws while the other player catches the short hops with soft hands, moving toward the short hop. Then switch assignments. Have your first basemen do this drill the same way while keeping a foot on the base so that they can work on their footwork as well as their short-hop technique.

18 or 21

Purpose. This drill teaches your infielders how to play the ground ball to get the big hop or short hop. We talked about reading the hop and aggressively going after the big hop or short hop to avoid being caught in between. Players can practice this with a simple drill in which you put each infielder at his position with a bucket or small crate next to him.

Procedure. As the fielder catches each grounder, trying to get the big hop, he calls out the number of hops on which he caught it, calling no number if he dropped it or didn't get to it. When the player catches the ball, he lines up to throw to first base but instead of throwing it drops it in the bucket or crate. The focus is strictly on the hop, and the drill is called 18 or 21 because that is the number of balls that we usually hit to each infielder.

Roll Double Plays

Purpose. This drill is aimed at working with second basemen to improve their double-play pivot.

Procedure. The second baseman should come across the base with his hands up so that the infielder throwing to him gets a clear view of his glove. The second baseman should have his left foot on the base and be stepping toward the throw with his right. He then brings his left foot off the base to evade the runner and position himself for the throw to first. In this drill the second baseman should take throws from both the shortstop and the

third baseman on balls rolled to them, to get adjusted to the pivot. Similar roll drills can be used to enhance the technique of corner infielders as they field bunts and to improve the shortstop's technique coming across the bag as the middle man on double-play grounders hit to the pitcher or right side of the infield.

Leather Nuts

Purpose. Your players will love this drill, which will improve their quickness and ability to catch a ground ball.

Procedure. Use softer balls or safety balls for this drill. Have the infielders line up one behind another approximately 10 to 20 yards from a coach, who hits hard grounders in a rapid fashion to the player at the front of the line. If the player fields the ball cleanly, he goes to the end of the line. If the player drops the ball, he is eliminated. Ultimately, a champion emerges. The safety balls help keep players from getting hurt, and they love the competition.

Multiple Fungo

Purpose. This drill permits you to get a lot of work done in a short time and gives players a lot of practice catching ground balls.

Procedure. Using fungo bats, one coach hits grounders to the third baseman, and another hits grounders to the shortstop and second baseman. For the first part of the drill (figure 10.11a), the third baseman works on coming across the bag and throwing to the first baseman, who is protected by a screen. For groundballs to the shortstop and second baseman, the shortstop throws to the second baseman at second and the second baseman throws to the shortstop. After a while, the third baseman has a turn to work on his throws to second base, and the shortstop and second baseman throw to first (figure 10.11b). Many teams use this setup while they take batting practice. Others do it separately.

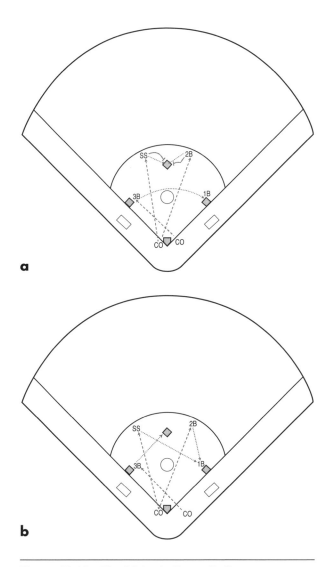

Figure 10.11 The Multiple Fungo Drill.

DEVELOPING CATCHERS' SKILLS

Catching may be the most important defensive position, but it may also be the least coached. Like a middle infielder, the catcher needs to be quick with soft hands and short arm action on throws. The first skill that a coach needs to look for in a catcher is obvious—the ability to catch the ball. At the Little League level, you want to find someone who is not afraid of the ball and is excited about putting on the catching equipment. A good arm for throwing out runners is a big help, but many catchers have been effective with an average arm, compensating with quick feet, a quick release, and good athletic ability.

Stance

When the catcher gets in his stance, he wants to have a wide base. His feet should be wider than shoulder-width so that movement to the outside and inside corners to set up a target is subtle and not obvious to the batter. If his base is wide enough, the catcher does not need to move his entire body to one side of home plate or the other to set up a target. He subtly shifts his glove and does it late so that location cannot be relayed to the hitter. A wide base also allows the catcher to spring toward pitches to his left or right. With no runners on base, the catcher can drop one knee and catch or receive the ball in a stance with one knee on the ground (see figure 10.12*a*). When runners are on base, he can make a minor adjustment from that basic stance by getting his butt up a little so that he is able to come out throwing quicker (see figure 10.12*b*).

Catching Technique

Catchers should receive the ball in a relaxed position and try to catch each pitch between the thumb and index finger. A good catcher allows the ball to come to him, following it from the release point and working each pitch to the middle of his chest if possible (see figure 10.13).

Blocking

This same thinking applies when a catcher must block a ball in the dirt. The difference is that the catcher will "catch" the ball with his chest protector rather than the glove, which he uses to plug the hole between his legs. The catcher will improve his ability to block pitches in the dirt only through continual practice. The object in blocking the baseball is to get the chest as close to the ball as possible (figure 10.14). Catchers do this on balls in the dirt whether they are right, left, or directly in front of them. When the ball hits the chest protector or glove, the catchers wants it to deaden and drop so that he can pounce on it immediately. Quick feet are essential behind the plate. Catchers who can block the ball can keep bad pitches from being wild pitches.

Figure 10.12 *(a)* Catcher's positioning with no runners on base and *(b)* his positioning with runners on.

Figure 10.13 The catcher should work the pitch to the middle of his chest.

Figure 10.14 Proper blocking technique involves getting the chest as close to the ball as possible.

Framing

Catchers must work at the art of framing, the process of keeping the glove steady and giving the umpire a good look at the pitch, perhaps subtly moving a pitch on the corner into the strike zone in the hope of getting a strike call (see figure 10.15). To do this, the catcher must follow the ball from the pitcher's hand and catch it with his thumb pointed toward the pitcher. The only exception is on a low pitch, where the catcher must maneuver his glove to make the catch and then bring it up into the strike zone.

Catchers should frame only strikes or pitches that could be called strikes. Balls that are way out of the strike zone should just be caught and thrown back to the pitcher. Nevertheless, a catcher adept at framing and reading how an umpire is calling a game can often steal strikes as it goes along, making a key difference. For the catcher, however, there is still more at which he must be adept.

Figure 10.15 Framing the pitch.

Throwing Out Runners

Two time factors are involved in thwarting base stealers. First, the pitcher must do a focused job of holding runners on base and then be quick to the plate in his delivery. The catcher needs to remind his pitcher of those responsibilities. The second factor involves the time needed for the catcher to get the ball out of his glove and into the glove of the infielder. The faster all this transpires, the better the chance of throwing out the runner.

Quick feet are critical. The catcher has to move his feet quickly after he catches the ball and as he prepares to throw. He should step with his right foot to where his left foot was, gaining ground in the process (figure 10.16a). He should take the ball out of his glove much as an infielder does when he throws. He separates his hands in front of his body, aims his shoulder at the target while keeping his shoulders closed until he releases the ball (figure 10.16b), and aims for the middle of the infielder's body from his waist to his knees. Most throwing errors by a catcher result from hurrying and a breakdown in mechanics, so practice and drills are essential.

Signs

One of the major responsibilities of the catcher is to flash signs to the pitcher. In the process, the catcher must make sure of a couple things. His knees must be pointing at the shoulders of the pitcher. If his knees are too wide, the opponent's first- or third-base coach will be able to look in and see the sign. In addition, the catcher should flash the signs with his fingers buried in his groin area and hidden between his legs. If he drops his fingers lower, the opponents can see them under his legs, and if they are too far out front, opponents can spot them as well. With his fingers buried while giving the signs, the catcher should also put his glove on the outside of his left knee to shield the third-base coach from getting a look. The pitching coach or the head coach flashes the signs to the catcher for whatever pitch he wants to call. The coach usually taps some part of his face or hat to call the pitch. There are many styles or types of signals for calling pitches.

Figure 10.16 Quick movement is necessary for the catcher to throw the runner out. *(a)* He should step with his right foot, gaining ground, and *(b)* aim his shoulder at the target while keeping his shoulders closed until releasing the ball.

Catcher Drills

The following drills are designed to develop catcher-specific skills.

Crouching

Purpose. A catcher needs to have his legs in shape so that he can maintain a crouch for nine or more innings, move quickly in both directions, and come out of the crouch to make a quick throw.

Procedure. To start, have your catchers play catch in the crouch position. Have them walk a distance in the crouch position. Have them work on strength, quickness, and spring by jumping over the plate from one batter's box to the other.

Framing and Glove Work

Purpose. As discussed previously, framing is an essential element in a catcher's performance. This drill works on helping the catcher learn to effectively frame a variety of pitches.

Procedure. Have your catchers start working behind the plate without a glove while you throw tennis balls or soft safety balls. The catcher works on catching the ball with a bent elbow, holding it in front of his body so that the umpire gets a good look at location. In time, the catcher can work on the same drill and technique with his glove on. The coach can throw balls high and low, in and out, with the catcher in his crouch, framing the ball as he catches it.

Blocking

Purpose. This drill is aimed at improving a catcher's ability to block pitches with his chest protector.

Procedure. Initially, instruct the catcher to keep his hands at his side or behind his back as balls are bounced toward him or off him. Then, with his glove on, he can work on dropping his glove between his legs in the proper form to block pitches in the dirt. After each block, he should get to his feet, find the ball, and scoop it up.

Throwing

Purpose. The most important throw the catcher makes is to second base. We talked about the technique earlier—proper footwork, quick release, shoulder alignment. This drill reinforces those fundamentals by simulating game conditions with a batter in the box.

Procedure. The coach should use a stopwatch to time how quickly the catcher releases his throws after catching the ball. A good time for a high school catcher is 2.0 to 2.2 seconds. Any thing quicker at that level is outstanding. The batter can swing over pitches to make throwing more difficult for the catcher.

Pop-Ups

Purpose. Pop-ups can be difficult for even the most experienced catcher in full gear, and that's how a catcher should practice as his coach hits pop-ups with a fungo bat.

Procedure. The steps for the catcher are these: Find the ball in the air, throw the mask away, and make the catch while moving toward the ball. Almost all pop-ups fouled behind the catcher will drift back toward the playing field, an important consideration.

Blocking the Plate

Purpose. This drill ensures that your catcher knows how to block home plate when the runner is coming home on a tag play.

Procedure. The first thing to do is show the catcher the proper positioning of his feet so that he is facing third base out in front of home plate. The catcher should use the fact that he is wearing protective equipment. This gives him a tremendous advantage because with the equipment on he can stand in front of home plate with limited fear of being hurt as he blocks the sliding runner from getting to the base. If he catches the ball early he wants to step toward the runner so that the runner cannot slide around him. To run this drill, have your catcher in the proper position and throw him the ball. He catches it, takes a step toward third, and then makes the imaginary tag.

Fielding Bunts

Purpose. A catcher needs to be able to field bunts out in front of home plate. This drill has the catcher field the bunt with the proper technique and use the correct footwork to make a throw to the proper base.

Procedure. Your catchers should have all their catching gear on for this drill. Stand behind the catcher where the umpire stands during a game and from there roll balls out in front of home plate. The catcher runs to the ball and scoops it with his glove and bare hand together. If the ball is bunted (if you roll it) toward the third-base line, the catcher uses the same technique with his hands and glove but he has his back to third base as he turns and steps with his left foot to first in a good throwing technique. With this drill, you can have the catcher field the ball and throw to any base, not limiting his technique work to first base.

Bullpens

Purpose. I believe that any time a catcher warms up a pitcher in the bullpen, he should simulate game conditions by doing it in full gear and framing or blocking every pitch to gain experience. Bullpen work provides an excellent opportunity for the pitcher and catcher to develop game tempo.

Procedure. The last part of each bullpen session should be to have the pitcher throw a pitchout, which is designed to make it easier for the catcher to throw out a potential base stealer in a possible running situation. The catcher and pitcher need to practice working together on throwing and catching the pitchout. The catcher must wait until the pitcher releases the ball to move wide of the plate. He then catches the ball and uses his footwork for throwing to second or third base.

DEVELOPING OUTFIELD SKILLS

Outfielders employ different techniques than infielders do, although there are some similarities. As the pitcher goes through his windup, outfielders take three or four ready steps just as infielders do, but they stand a little taller so that they can turn quicker to go after balls over their head or in the gaps. An outfielder should possess at least average speed. The faster the outfielder, the better the chance that he can run down balls hit right, left, or over his head. Outfielders must be able to catch and judge fly balls. The outfielders with the best arms are generally put in right field or center field so that they can prevent a runner at first from advancing two bases on a base hit. The outfielder with the weakest arm usually plays in left field. The center fielder should be the fastest and best defensive fielder because he has the most ground to cover.

Drop Step

One of the key skills that outfielders should be taught initially is the drop step (figure 10.17). The outfielder uses the drop step when going after a ball hit over his head or a ball that he has to go back on to either side. The outfielder must immediately step back to the side on which the ball is hit. This first step, known as the drop step, is the key to quickness and the ability to run down deep drives or balls in the gap.

Ground Balls

An outfielder, like an infielder, must be adept at fielding ground balls and recognizing hops. On a clean hit in front of him, he should charge the ball under control to get either the big hop or the short hop, staying away from that in-between hop that could skip past him. The difference, of course, is that an outfielder has much more time to read the hop than an infielder does. The outfielder should use a technique that I call fast, slow, fast. He takes off quickly when the ball is hit, slows to read the hop, and then accelerates when he sees that he is going to get the good hop. He uses

Figure 10.17 The drop step.

this technique when he charges any ground ball or ball that drops cleanly in front of him. Outfielders should never use one hand to pick up or catch the ball unless the ball has stopped moving. In that situation he can reach down with his hand and grab the baseball.

On a ball hit to his right or left, the outfielder needs to use the crossover step footwork (figure 10.18). He uses the crossover step and then takes the proper angle to field the ball, trying to get the good hop so that he can get his glove down easily and prevent the ball from getting past him. The crossover technique is good for getting to the ball hit in front of the outfielder but at an angle to his right or left. On balls hit in the gap, the outfielder must take his drop step and then judge how hard the ball is hit and how fast it is traveling. On a hard-hit ball, the outfielder must take an extreme angle with his drop step so that he can cut off the ball before it gets by him.

An outfielder should not drop to a knee to catch a ground ball unless he feels that he will

Figure 10.18 The outfielder's crossover step footwork.

Figure 10.19 The crow hop or kick step.

otherwise misplay it. Dropping to a knee slows him down and may allow runners to take the extra base. But on a hard-hit or difficult ground ball, the outfielder may need to drop to one knee to block it. In any case, an outfielder never wants the ball to get by him.

Fly Balls

When an outfielder moves into position to catch a fly ball, he should catch it on his throwing side moving forward, giving himself the best chance to release it quickly if the situation calls for a throw. In this situation he should take a crow hop, or kick step (see figure 10.19), into the catch, to put momentum and strength behind the throw. The crow hop, or kick step, is the large running step that an outfielder takes with the right foot and then the left (for a right-hander) to get more strength on his throws

At times, on a do-or-die play, an outfielder must slide into a sinking line drive as if he is slid-

ing into a base or lay out totally, fully extended. Outfielders can't afford to go to sleep. They have to be aware of situations in the same way that infielders are. They have to do their best to keep balls in front of them, cut off balls in the gap, and remember to back up bases in case of an errant throw by an infielder. Outfielders are the last line of defense, and a coach on the bench should be in constant communication with them regarding positioning and changing situations, either orally or with hand signals.

Priority for Outfielders

When pursuing a batted ball, two outfielders will often get to it at the same time. Here they must communicate with one another to avoid collision. The best way to avoid collision is to set up a form of communication with all your players. The player who wants to make the catch should call, "I got it," and the other player or players should answer, "Take it, take it." By answering, the other players let the outfielder who has called for the ball know that they will not run into him. That way, the outfielder who called for the ball can be more aggressive going after it because he knows that the other fielders are not going to impede him.

When outfielders go after a fly ball and two of them call the ball at the same instant, the center fielder always has priority over the other outfielders. All outfielders charging on a shallow fly ball have priority over any backpedaling infielder.

Backing Up Outfielders

When two outfielders get to a ball at the same time, the one who calls for the ball should pursue it aggressively. The other outfielder will back him up in case the ball gets by. On a ground ball, the backup fielder wants to get approximately 10 yards behind the fielder who is making the play. From that location he has plenty of time to react to the ball that gets by his teammate. On a fly ball, the backup outfielder wants to get as close as he can to the fielder who is making the catch. If the fielder bobbles or drops the ball, the backup outfielder may be able to reach in and catch it before it hits the ground.

Outfield Drills

As with infielders, many drills can be used to improve outfield skills.

Drop Step

Purpose. This outfield drill works on the outfielders' footwork to get to balls hit to their right or left. Balls hit in the gap area between the outfielders require them first to take the proper step to get a good jump on the ball, then to use the proper technique to get to the ball quickly, and finally to take the correct angle to cut off the ball or make the catch.

Procedure. In this drill the coach has his outfielders in a straight line, one behind another. They take turns doing the drill. After the outfielder takes his three ready steps, the coach points to the right or left. The outfielder steps back at a 45-degree angle and runs in that direc-

tion, pumping his arms before reaching up to make an imaginary catch. The coach has the player work to both sides to learn the proper footwork, technique, and angle when cutting off or pursuing balls hit in the gap. With the same drill, the coach can throw fly balls to the outfielder or hit balls with a fungo bat. Here he watches the outfielder run to the ball, checking to make sure that he does not run with his glove out but instead chases it with proper running form, reaching out only at the last second to make the catch. Besides having his outfielders go left and right, the coach can work on deep drives directly over their heads. We do this drill every day.

Line Drive

Purpose. At Esperanza we also call this the Make a Great Catch drill. This drill helps outfielders with the low line drive and forces them to work on putting their gloves in basket form.

Procedure. Again, we have the outfielders take turns. This time, the outfielder takes his ready step and runs directly at the coach, who directs something of a line drive throw at his knees. As the outfielder moves to catch the ball, he has his palms up and the glove in a basket position. If the outfielder catches the ball near the ground or even if he short hops it, he picks his glove up right away to show the umpire that he has made a catch.

Throwing-Side Fundamental Catch

Purpose. This simple drill reminds the outfielder to catch the ball on his throwing side while moving forward when he knows that he will have to make a throw.

Procedure. Have the outfielders play catch with themselves, throwing the ball in the air and moving into the correct position with momentum going forward. You can also have outfielders perform the drill in pairs so that they can make their throws, using the crow hop to get more power behind the ball.

Three-Man Relay

Purpose. This drill gives the outfielders practice in picking up a ball against the fence and quickly spotting the relay and cutoff man, while the infielders who would normally be receiving the throw work on other drills.

Procedure. In this drill you have an outfielder situated near the fence, another about 90 feet away, and a third 90 feet from the second. The outfielder nearest the fence, maybe 30 feet from it, throws a ball at the fence, runs to pick it up, turns, and throws to the next outfielder, who in turn wheels and throws to the third outfielder. The outfielders should change positions as you go through the drill, and you can have two sets of three competing against each other to be the fastest.

Fence Drill

Purpose. This drill teaches outfielders the correct technique to catch a ball against the fence. Obviously, in the heat of game situations, using proper technique isn't always possible, depending on where the ball is hit, how hard it is hit, and the elevation at which it is hit. Nevertheless, consistent reinforcement of proper technique at each position helps build fundamental footwork and confidence.

Procedure. For this drill put the outfielders 10 to 15 feet from the fence. As they take their ready steps, a coach throws high fly balls either up against the fence or just over it. The outfielder turns and rushes to the fence. He should use his throwing hand for a guide and as a cushion against the fence, keeping his eye on the ball. He is then in position to make the catch leaning against the fence or jumping in front of it.

Backup Drill

Purpose. This drill has the outfielders work on calling off other players when heading for a fly ball or backing up the other fielder.

Procedure. In this drill the outfielders are in two lines, approximately 90 feet apart. A coach using a fungo bat tries to hit a ball between the two outfielders at the head of the lines, who have to communicate as they pursue the ball to avoid running into each other. One outfielder should yell, "I've got it," and the other should respond, "Take it" and then back up the play in case the ball gets through. The coach can hit fly balls or ground balls.

Sun Drill

Purpose. This drill helps players learn how to use their gloves and sunglasses to shield the sun on pop-ups and fly balls.

Procedure. In this drill the coach has his players face the sun and throws fly balls that require them to fight the glare. Even when wearing sunglasses, players may have to use their gloves to provide a shield. Although some technique is involved, most players find that dealing with the sun is only a matter of getting comfortable with the practice of using the glove as a shield or flipping down their sunglasses. Again, practice makes perfect, or at least builds confidence.

Coaches' Keys

1. Defense is essential, and it starts with fundamental fielding skills and the simple act of playing catch, using proper technique when throwing and catching the ball.
2. Good infield skills result from having a stable stance, taking ready steps, and learning to read the big hop, the short hop, and the in-between hop.
3. Outfielders need to remember that they are the last line of defense and that many of their fundamental skills are similar to those required of infielders.
4. Catching is the least coached defensive position and may be the most important.
5. For all positions, coaches can use a variety of drills every day or periodically to enhance skills and performance.

TEACHING DEFENSIVE STRATEGIES

All players love to hit. No part of the game is more fun. But defense is a different story. A coach must convince his players that defense is critical and that they need to work hard on it. After putting this attitude in place, a coach then needs to work his team on the various situations that they must be prepared to defend. The players have to be comfortable and confident that they can defend any situation.

In this chapter, among other things, I will discuss bunt defenses, double-play alignment, and late-inning adjustments. Successful teams are prepared for any situation, and they continue to prepare for those situations at least once or twice a week to maintain their sharpness, physically and mentally.

DEVELOPING EFFECTIVE DEFENSE

When particular defensive situations arise during a game, you must be able to put the proper strategy in place so that your team can make the play. First, you must prepare your team by teaching your players the various situational defenses. After you have those in place you can decide which defensive strategy you want your team to use. In a bunting situation you can use the standard bunt defense or call for a special defense to take away the bunt. When a runner is on third base or when runners are on second and third base with less than two outs, do you bring your infielders in to cut off the runner at the plate or do you keep them back to give them greater range? The inning, the score, and the effectiveness of your pitcher and defense should all contribute to your decision about which strategy to use.

Late in the game with the score tied or when you are down by a run, you will probably want to have your infielders up close to cut off the runner at third and not allow any more runs to score. Late in the game when you are up by two or more runs, you want to keep your infielders back to enhance their range and make sure that you can get an out on a ground ball or keep a ball from getting to the outfield.

The preceding is just one example of knowing and preparing your players to use different strategies to stop your opponent. The defensive team chooses its strategy by determining whether they want to keep their opponent from advancing or scoring the runner, or whether they are far enough up in the score that they just want to get an out and need not be concerned about the runner or runners. These factors should come into play any time the coach considers using a specific strategy.

Basic Defensive Positioning

In baseball, defensive strategy starts with positioning. Proper positioning involves knowing the strengths and weaknesses of both your team and the opposing team. You also need to be absolutely aware of the situation. Knowing how to anticipate what might happen is the key to effective defensive positioning.

Infield Positioning

Your infielders will play their depth according to the outs, inning, score, and capabilities of the hitter. When the game starts with no one on base, you want your shortstop and second baseman to be deep, with their heels on the outfield grass. The third baseman, along with the first baseman, could be up on the infield grass to take away the drag bunt.

With no one on base and the batter not a threat to bunt, you can have all your players deep to give them more range on ground balls. An important note on this positioning is that you do not want your third baseman to play so deep that he is unable to make the throw to first base.

When a runner gets on first base, the infielders can come into double-play depth. The second baseman and shortstop both move up three steps and over four steps toward second base from their normal depth (figure 11.1). The positioning of the first baseman and third baseman will depend on how you

read the situation and your options. As stated in the infield section in chapter 10, the middle infielders have to change their alignment so that they can get to second base and turn a double play. In this same situation with no one out, the third baseman may be up on the infield grass or walking toward home plate, looking for the hitter to bunt.

If a runner is at third and you want to keep him from scoring, you will position all the infielders on the infield grass or even with the base or baseline, similar to the standard positioning.

According to the situation, you can use any combination of these defensive alignments. Have your players know the basics and then make adjustments accordingly.

Outfield Positioning

The outfielders start with a basic positioning and then move to a specific place to take away the batter's hitting tendency. The basic positioning usually starts with the outfielders playing straight up (figure 11.2), which means that the center fielder plays directly in line with second base and home plate. The right and left fielders play at positions equidistant from the center fielder and the foul line on their side. From here, you may shade them toward the power alley, the side of second base that represents the batter's strength, or away from it if the hitter does not have pull power. You can also move the outfielders to a deeper or

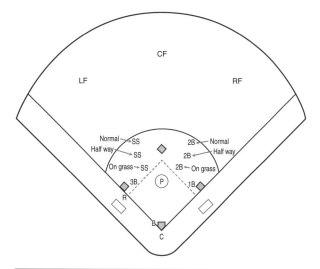

Figure 11.1 Infielder movement from standard, no runners on positioning, to double-play depth.

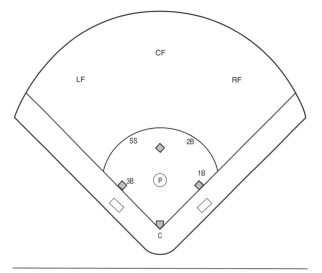

Figure 11.2 Outfielders positioned straight up.

shallower position according to the hitter's power or the importance of preventing the hitter from getting an extra-base hit. Late in a close game with no one on base, you may want to move your outfielders back to prevent the extra-base hit.

A coach on the bench has most of his communication problems with the outfielders. The infielders, of course, are much closer to the dugout and can more easily hear oral commands or spot a coach's hand signal.

Outfielders represent a distant picket line and a challenging communication problem. With this in mind, the head coach should designate one of his assistants to check outfield positioning with each batter. The outfielders, in turn, know which assistant to look for and to look for him with every batter. That coach should be at the end of the dugout farthest from home plate so that he is easier to spot. He should give his direction signals with both arms extended, waving in one direction or another and then putting his hands behind his head to signify to the outfielders they have reached the proper spot. The team must practice this sort of signaling so that it becomes routine during a game.

Defense Versus Opponent

Knowing the hitting tendencies of the opposing hitters is obviously beneficial when setting up a defensive alignment. But coaches can make positioning moves even without a scouting report.

When the coach is operating blind in that regard, the goal is to play the percentages and plug the gaps where most balls are hit. Thus, the first and third basemen should be off the foul lines and shaded toward second base. The shortstop and second baseman should be pinching the middle of the infield, taking away some of that wide area.

In the outfield, a coach should similarly have his left and right fielders shaded toward the gaps, shrinking the left-center field and right-center field alleys. The center fielder can be shaded into either alley, depending on whether the hitter is left-handed or right-handed (figure 11.3a, b). The coach can also position the outfielders deep to protect against a power hitter or to prevent extra-base hits in late innings (figure 11.4). Another available

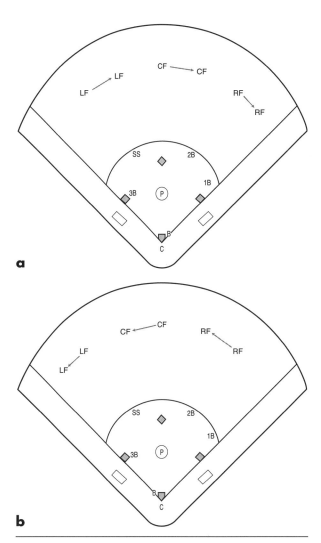

Figure 11.3 Outfielders shaded toward power alley for (a) a left-handed batter, and (b) a right-handed batter.

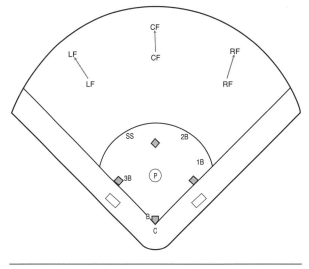

Figure 11.4 Playing deep, outfielders should back up 5-10 steps depending on the hitter's power, but should not be closer than 4 steps to the fence.

outfield move is to have the opposite-field outfielder shaded in to protect against a bloop hit to the opposite field (figure 11.5). In other words, the right fielder would play in, and possibly closer to the line, against a right-handed hitter, and the left fielder would play in, and possibly closer to the line, against a left-landed hitter.

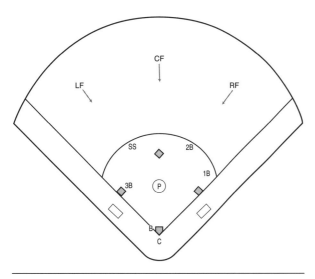

Figure 11.5 When playing shallow, the outfielders should take 3-5 steps up, with the opposite fielder from the batter (right fielder for right-handed batter and left fielder for left-handed batter) playing 5-7 steps up to defend against a bloop.

Another consideration for the coach in aligning his defense is the type of pitcher he has on the mound. If his pitcher throws mostly off-speed stuff, a coach may want his defense to shade every hitter to pull the ball, figuring that they can get the bat around on the off-speed pitches (figure 11.6a). But if the pitcher is a hard thrower, the coach may want to shade his defense the other way in anticipation that hitters will be late with their swings (figure 11.6b).

A coach can also make defensive adjustments as he watches opposing hitters swing during the course of a game. We have an expression at Esperanza that we use as a reminder during every game. We tell our fielders to read the batter's foul balls. When a hitter hits a foul ball, or particularly two in a row, we want our fielders to note the direction of the hit and move a step or two that way. This in-game adjustment can be beneficial.

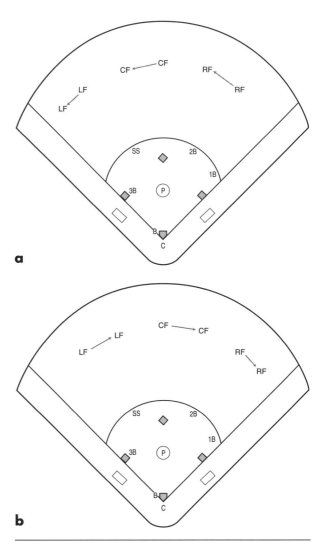

Figure 11.6 (a) For a right-handed batter, shade the outfielders left to protect against pulled hits if the pitcher throws mostly off-speed pitches. (b) For a hard throwing pitcher, shade the outfielders right to protect against late swings.

SITUATIONAL DEFENSIVE STRATEGIES

Each situation in the game offers the defense an opportunity to use a defensive move or strategy to keep the offense from getting runners on and around to score. From the leadoff hitter who can drag bunt to the big hitter who will never bunt, the defense must know where or how to play the hitter.

After a runner gets on base, the coach must decide which defense he wants to employ. The next section will describe the bunt defense with a runner at first or second.

Bunts

When a team sets up to defend the bunt, the coach is trying to get one at least one out. The ideal result is to get the lead runner and thus frustrate the opposition's attempt to advance him. The defensive strategies are designed to give a team a chance to make that play, to retire the lead runner or, at least, to retire the hitter who is bunting.

Sacrifice Bunt

In an obvious sacrifice situation, the offense is prepared to give up an out to advance a runner. The defense must make sure to get at least that one out. In preparing to defend the bunt, you should give your team some options. The most common bunting situation develops with a runner on first and no outs in a scoreless, tied, or close game. In this situation, divide the infield into three parts. The third baseman takes his third of the field on the left side. The pitcher takes the middle of the field, and the first baseman takes the right third of the field. The second baseman must race to cover first base, and the shortstop should be prepared to cover second base (figure 11.7).

So, with the pitcher in his stretch, the third baseman should be on the grass in front of the base, creeping toward the plate. If the hitter squares and shows bunt early, the third baseman crashes hard toward the batter. He is the only one of the three—third baseman, pitcher, and first baseman—who can break early. The

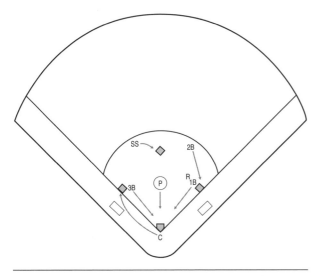

Figure 11.7 Bunt coverage with a runner at first.

pitcher, of course, must wait until he releases the ball to charge the bunt, and the first baseman must hold the runner at first and wait until the pitcher throws to the plate before he charges. If the first baseman leaves early, the runner has an opportunity to get a great jump and steal second.

After the ball is bunted, the players read the bunt—soft or hard—to decide what call to make. The catcher makes this call because he has the field in front of him. If the ball is bunted hard at the third baseman or pitcher, the catcher should call, "Two" to have the fielder throw to second base to force out the runner. If the ball is bunted hard at the first baseman, the catcher must decide according to the first baseman's defensive ability whether to call for the out at second base or to call, "One" to make the out at first.

The infielders need to be able to make several adjustments in this defense. To start, if the ball is bunted to the charging third baseman, the catcher must run down the line to cover third base in case the runner at first sees an opportunity to round second and try for third on the play. Another adjustment is that the shortstop should take all throws to second base on steal attempts after the batter shows bunt. This change frees up the second baseman to go to first base as the first baseman charges. Although this is the most common defense for a bunting situation with a runner at first base only, it is not the only defense.

Instead of charging with three players, some coaches prefer to use just two. When a coach has three infielders play the bunt, he is maximizing his defense. But if the pitcher is a good fielder, the coach can reduce infield movement by keeping his first and second basemen in place. A good-fielding pitcher can cover half the infield. The third baseman charges and takes the area from the foul line to the mound. The pitcher takes the area from the mound to the first-base line. The first baseman does not charge but remains at first. This defense allows the catcher to try to pick off an aggressive runner at first base if the batter misses the bunt attempt or if the batter takes the pitch. The base runner may get too far off the base in anticipation of the bunt, making a pickoff comparatively easy. To run this defense successfully, the pitcher must be a good fielder. He needs to cover half the infield, so he must get off the mound quickly. This defense also allows the second baseman to remain at his position, taking away a hole and eliminating the possibility that a throw will get past him at first if he is late covering when the first baseman charges.

Squeeze Bunts

The squeeze bunt is executed in two ways—the suicide squeeze and the safety squeeze. With both, the offensive goal is to get a run home by giving up an out. To defend this play, the defensive team needs to make the play on the runner at third and put him out before he scores. The defense must first understand what the offense is trying to do and then try to take it away.

If the offense is trying to execute a suicide squeeze, the runner at third base will break full speed as the pitcher prepares to release the ball. If the hitter puts the bunt on the ground, the runner should score easily.

To defend this play, the defensive team can try a pickoff or pitchout in anticipation of the squeeze attempt, which should lead to an easy out on the runner from third because it takes the bat out of the hands of the would-be bunter. Another defensive response is to watch the runner at third base and the hitter. If the runner leaves third base before the pitcher releases the ball, or if the batter shows bunt before the pitcher releases his pitch, the defensive players yell, "Squeeze." This tells the pitcher to throw an automatic pitchout and tells the catcher to be ready for it. The pitcher throws the ball outside the strike zone where the batter cannot bunt it and where the catcher can handle it easily. The catcher can either make a tag on the runner coming home or get him in a rundown. If the pitcher himself sees the runner leaving or the batter squaring early, he makes the automatic pitchout.

Some teams like to throw at the hitter in squeeze situations, but hitting the batter only puts another runner on base, complicating the situation for the pitcher. Moreover, a pitch aimed at the batter is often difficult for the catcher to catch if it misses its target. Furthermore, the umpire can rule that the pitch was intentionally thrown to hit the batter (which it, in fact, was), resulting in ejection of the pitcher and coach.

If the ball is bunted on the squeeze, the pitcher must hope that he can either field the ball in the air for a potential double play or field it quickly off the ground and get it to the catcher for an out. Generally, however, a well-timed squeeze bunt placed on the ground will score the suicide runner from third.

If the offense is running a safety squeeze, the batter may attempt to bunt only on a definite strike and the runner may not break until he sees the bunt on the ground. In this situation the runner is unlikely to give away the squeeze by breaking early. On the other hand, the pitcher has more time to get the ball to the catcher and he may be able to make the throw in time to get the out if the bunt isn't a good one. The pitcher is generally the key defender on a safety squeeze.

Bunt Defense With a Runner at Second Base

The standard defense with a runner at second base is to divide the infield in half (figure 11.8). The pitcher covers from the mound to the third-base line. The first baseman fields bunts from the first-base line to the mound. The third baseman does not charge the bunt unless it is bunted hard past the mound. Obviously, the third baseman needs to stay near the base to prevent the runner at second from stealing third. The third baseman in this situation needs to remind the pitcher that he won't be

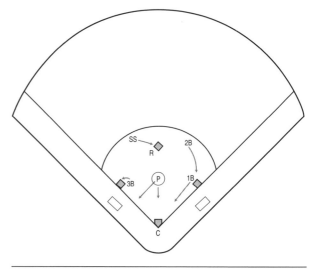

Figure 11.8 Bunt coverage for a sacrifice bunt with a runner on second.

charging and that the pitcher needs to cover to the line. In this setup, the first baseman can charge for the bunt early. If the hitter bunts the ball toward first, the first baseman has an opportunity to throw out the runner at third. To make all this work, the second baseman must again cover first base and the shortstop must cover second. This defense can also be used with runners at both second base and first base.

Another defense in this situation is known as the wheel (figure 11.9). The wheel anticipates that the hitter will try to roll a bunt past the pitcher, forcing the third baseman to charge and field it, making it almost impossible to get the runner going to an undefended third base and requiring a difficult throw to first. In the wheel, the third baseman charges, the shortstop covers third base, and the pitcher takes from the mound to the first-base line.

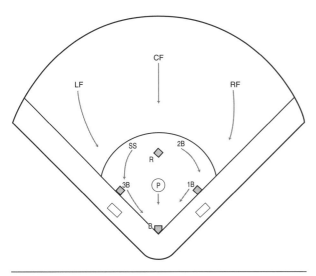

Figure 11.9 The wheel defense.

The pitcher puts this play in motion. When he gets to the set position, the shortstop breaks toward second. He plants his left foot before going all the way to the bag and then sprints to cover third. If the third baseman sees that the runner at second is breaking toward third, trying to beat the shortstop, the third baseman should yell, "Step off" to tell the pitcher to step off the rubber and throw to him at third, usually for an easy out. If the runner stays at second, the third baseman charges,

getting as close to the hitter as possible. The shortstop covers third for a possible force-out or tag play on the runner coming from second. The pitcher, in the wheel defense or any other, needs to check the runner more than once to keep him close to the bag. The second baseman also keeps an eye on the runner and then breaks to first base when he is sure that the runner is not going to take off to third early. The first baseman breaks at the same time that the third baseman does so that both fielders are close to the plate to field the bunt and make the putout at third base.

The wheel defense enhances the possibility of getting the lead runner, but a coach must realize in calling for this bunt coverage that if the hitter takes a full swing or slash, the infield defense is far out of normal alignment. If the wheel works, the coach is a genius. If it fails, he could be open to criticism. Then again, that's baseball.

Double Plays

As mentioned earlier in this chapter, double-play depth refers to the alignment that the shortstop and second baseman use so that they can more easily turn a double play. Often in baseball, you have to give up something to get something, and that's what is at work when the middle infielders are at double-play depth. In this situation, both the shortstop and second baseman cheat closer toward second base so that they can get there quicker on a ground ball when either could be the middle man in a double play. In this alignment, the holes between the shortstop and the third baseman, and between the second baseman and the first baseman, are wider, creating bigger gaps for the hitter. Also, in this alignment, the shortstop and second baseman can't cover as much ground because they are closer to the hitter. But because the double play usually takes the offense right out of the inning, almost all teams align their middle infielders at that depth when the situation dictates. Common double plays have been discussed previously. Figure 11.10 illustrates how to perform a double play on a come-backer to the pitcher with runners at first and second.

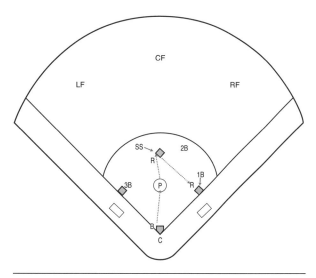

Figure 11.10 Double play on a come-backer to the pitcher.

Guarding the Lines

In a situation late in the game when an extra-base hit down the third-base or first-base line would drive in one or two runs or put the hitter on second or third base with the score tied, the usual strategy is to have the first baseman and third baseman play closer to the foul lines (usually a step off the line) to protect against the extra-base hit.

If a coach has a solid scouting report on the opponent and knows that the hitter seldom pulls the ball, he might choose to keep his corner infielders in their normal alignment or swing them one way or another if the hitter shows a tendency to pull to the left or right side. A coach should play the percentages. But if he doesn't have a scouting report, guarding the lines is the safest bet at crunch time.

Sacrifice Flies

An outfielder defends the sacrifice fly by getting his body in position to catch the ball on the throwing side so that he can quickly release it with a strong throw. He aims for the top of the cutoff man's head. The cutoff man may choose to let the throw go through to the base, ideally on one big hop that will be easy for the fielder at the base to handle. If the throw is head high, the cutoff man can catch the ball and relay it to the base or cut it off and throw it to another base to get an out.

Rundowns

When a runner gets caught between bases, the infielders must execute a rundown to get an out. The rundown involves two fielders who are trying to make a putout on the runner. The infielder with the ball runs at the runner with the ball up in his throwing hand. He runs toward the glove of the fielder at the base. He uses his teammate's glove as the target so that he doesn't throw the ball across the runner, which could cause the throw to hit him and allow him to advance to the next base. The infielder with the ball must accelerate as he moves toward the runner. This action forces the runner to move quickly in the opposite direction, toward the base. The fielder then flips the ball to the fielder at the base and follows his throw to the glove side of that player. He does this so that he is not in the path of the runner without the ball. If contact occurs between a fielder and the runner or the fielder does not have the ball, the umpire will call interference and the runner gets his base. Figure 11.11 diagrams a pickoff to third base and rundown positioning.

After throwing the ball, the fielder goes to the base he threw to. Each subsequent infielder who handles the ball uses the same technique. The ideal rundown results in an out with one throw or without a throw. The more throws the fielders make, the more likely it is that the runner will safely reach base.

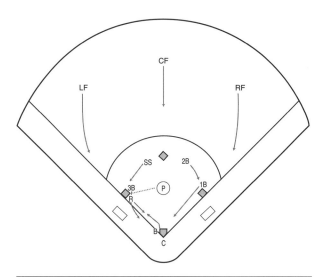

Figure 11.11 Pickoff play to third and rundown positioning.

Relays and Cutoffs

A relay and cutoff man is necessary on any ball hit to the outfield. An outfielder with a strong arm may not need the cutoff man, but a cutoff man should be in position anyway to line him up. With no one on, the infielders should line up a base hit to the outfield. The shortstop becomes the cutoff man to second base on hits to left field and center field, and the second baseman covers the base to take the throw. On a base hit to right field, they reverse roles, with the second baseman becoming the cutoff man and the shortstop covering the base for the throw.

When a runner is on first base, a base hit to the outfield that could move the runner to third will have the shortstop go out as the cutoff man on any hit and the second baseman go to second base.

On a hit to the outfield with a runner at second base, the play is at home plate. On a base hit to left field with a runner at second, the third baseman is the cutoff man to home plate on the throw and the shortstop covers third base. On a hit to center field or right field, the first baseman is the cutoff man. On a ball hit to center field, he positions himself between the mound and second base to line himself up for the cutoff. On a ball hit to right field, he lines himself up between the fielder and the catcher at home plate. He uses his own eyes to line himself up. Figures 11.12*a-c*, 11.13*a-c*, and 11.14*a-c* diagram the cutoff and relay plays for various hits to right, center, and left field with players on first, second, and third base.

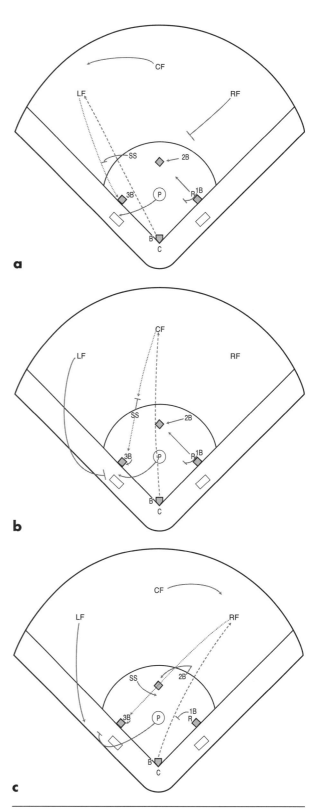

Figure 11.12   Cutoff and relay positioning for a base hit with a runner on first to *(a)* left field, *(b)* center field, and *(c)* right field.

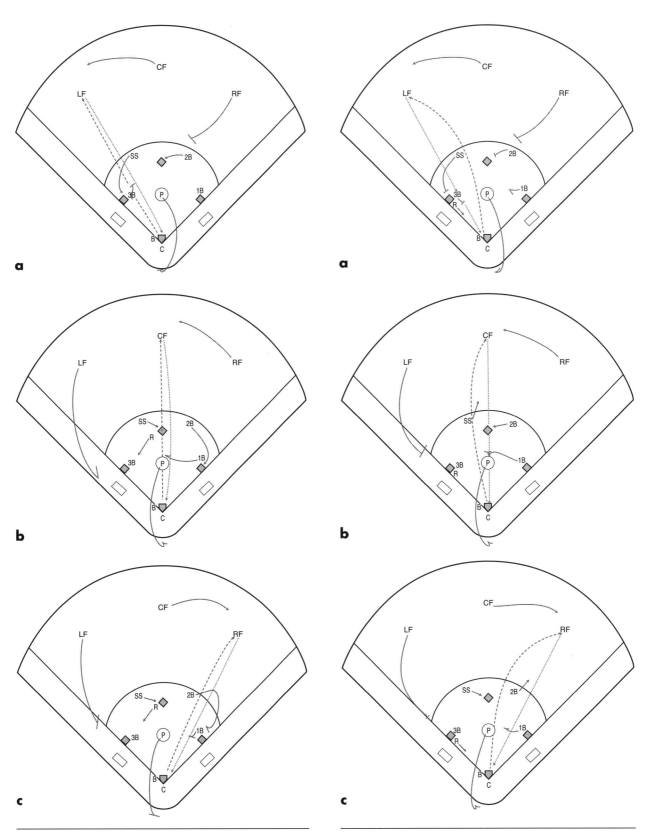

Figure 11.13 Cutoff and relay positioning for a base hit with a runner on second to *(a)* left field, *(b)* center field, and *(c)* right field.

Figure 11.14 Cutoff and relay positioning for a fly ball with a runner on third to *(a)* left field, *(b)* center field, and *(c)* right field.

Coaches' Keys

1. Teaching defensive strategies involves preparing for any situation and practicing it once or twice a week.

2. Bunt defenses should be constructed with the idea of getting at least one out, ideally the lead runner.

3. In double-play depth, the shortstop and second baseman should be three steps in and four steps toward second base.

4. In the late innings of a close game, the first and third basemen should normally move toward the foul lines to protect against the extra-base hit.

5. In defending an opponent, the goal is to take away their strength so that they can't prevail by doing what they do best.

6. Position your players according to the scouting report. If no scouting report is available, shade infielders and outfielders into the gaps and make adjustments as you watch hitters swing during the course of a game.

7. Designate a coach to give outfield direction signals during the game. Remind your outfielders to look for that coach with each hitter.

CHAPTER 12 TEACHING PITCHING

Perhaps the most accurate baseball adage is that pitching is the name of the game. Good pitching almost always dominates, and it stands to reason that pitchers—as the focal point of just about everything that happens on the diamond—must be drilled on the mechanics and skills of their craft, along with much more. A pitcher must learn to cope with every situation that develops, some of his own doing and some not, including walks, hit batsmen, bloop and bad-hop hits, errors, bad calls by umpires, and verbal abuse from the opponent and crowd.

Coaches need to train their pitchers in both the physical and the mental aspects of pitching, as well as work to improve their defense. In this chapter we will cover the skills and drills involved in the important job of teaching pitching.

PITCHING MECHANICS

We talk about technique at the other positions. With pitchers, it's mechanics. The better his mechanics, the better the chance that the pitcher will throw strikes with high velocity and avoid injury.

It all begins for the pitcher when he puts the ball in his glove and holds the glove so that the batter, the base coaches, and the opponent's bench can't see the ball and his grip. He should put his feet a foot to shoulder-width apart on the rubber with his toes just over the front edge of the rubber. Right-handed pitchers should try to work off the right side of the rubber, and left-handers should work off the left. This location presents the batter with the toughest arm angle, although there are exceptions depending on the pitcher's repertoire and the break of his pitches. For example, a right-handed pitcher who relies on a two-seam sinking fastball may be better off using the left side of the rubber to allow more room for his two-seam fastball to work.

The pitcher begins his delivery by taking a short step back or to the side with his opposite foot (right-handers with the left foot and left-handers with the right), maintaining balance with his weight on the balls of his feet (figure 12.1). As he moves through the delivery, his hands can either stretch above his head or remain tucked close to his chest. With a pitcher who prefers to stretch above his head, the extra movement can sometimes prompt an arching of the back. The coach should keep an eye on that and guard against it. A good coaching point is to have the pitcher keep his nose over his front toe, which helps maintain balance and alignment.

Figure 12.1 The pitcher's delivery begins with a short step back or to the side.

Figure 12.2 Having the back leg come alongside the front leg as closely as possible keeps the leg from swinging too far in front.

Now, as the pitcher pivots, his front foot comes off the rubber but remains parallel with it, with the side of his foot in contact with the side of the rubber. At almost the same time as this front foot is pivoting, the back foot rises and the back leg comes alongside the front leg as closely as possible. This action prevents the leg from swinging too far in front and thrusting body weight forward. At this point the pitcher is balanced on one leg with the other leg bent at its side with the front toe of that leg pointing down. This position will help the pitcher land on the ball of his front foot, with the foot at a slight angle toward the plate (figure 12.2). A coach never wants the pitcher to land on his heel.

At this point, the pitcher's glove should be close to his body between the waist and chest. Now the pitcher breaks his hands with the ball coming out and back and his body starting forward. As the pitcher then takes his arm and bent leg forward and prepares to release the ball, with his back foot pushing off the rubber, these are the basic mechanics: Delivery arm and back should be low in the follow-through, and his front foot should be slightly closed as it lands at about a 45-degree angle (figure 12.3).

Figure 12.3 The pitcher's delivery arm should be back and low on the follow-through with the front foot slightly closed as it lands.

By keeping his foot closed he will keep his front side closed into late rotation of his body.

The pitcher's height, wingspan, natural arm slot, and ability to master his mechanics determine the release point. The closer the pitcher can effectively release the baseball to home plate, the less time the hitter has to react to the pitch. Advantage pitcher.

Just before the pitcher gets to his release point, his forearm and wrist will do one of three things: supinate, square up directly behind the baseball, or pronate. When throwing a fastball, the pitcher wants to keep his forearm and wrist directly behind the center of the baseball at release (figure 12.4a). This position will maximize the velocity and accuracy of the pitch. Breaking balls require the pitcher to supinate his forearm and wrist just before he releases the ball (figure 12.4b). Change-ups require the pitcher to pronate his forearm and wrist just before releasing the baseball (figure 12.4c). By off-centering the hand at release, the pitcher can reduce the speed of the pitch and maximize its movement potential.

The pitcher should come down over his front leg, which can be bent but must remain firm. The pitcher's back should be pretty much parallel to the ground at this point, with his delivery arm across his body and the back leg up and bent at the knee. As the pitcher comes through this balance point, the leg will follow through naturally, landing usually across or slightly in front of the other foot so that the pitcher is now balanced again and ready to field the ball if it is hit back at him.

All this changes in some measure when runners are on base and the pitcher works out of a stretch position to hold them close (some pitchers like to work out of a stretch even with the bases empty). The pitcher in the stretch position has his feet parallel to the rubber, looking at the plate sideways, with his back foot against the rubber. His hands are usually set between his belt and letters (figure 12.5). From this point, the pitcher lifts his front leg, tucks his front shoulder and glove in, breaks his hands as he takes his delivery arm back, and gets to the same basics that he uses in throwing from a full windup. In the stretch, the pitcher can more easily keep his weight over his back leg because he starts from a pivoted position and produces less motion.

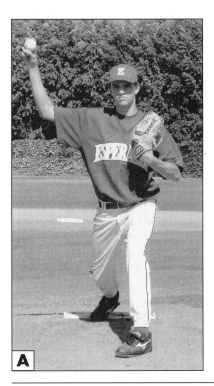 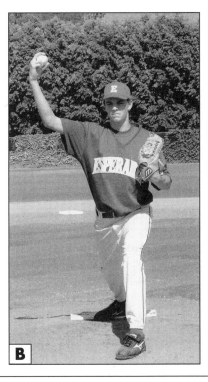 

Figure 12.4 *(a)* The fastball release point, *(b)* breaking ball release point, *(c)* and change-up release point.

Figure 12.5 The stretch position.

Good mechanics in both motions are critical to velocity and control.

ARSENAL OF PITCHES

No pitcher can get by on just one pitch. He needs an arsenal, three or four at the Division I and major league level, and two or three at the high school level. In this section I will discuss the most common pitches and how they are thrown.

Fastball

The fastball can be straight or have movement, depending on the grip and the pitcher's arm angle when releasing the ball. It's the number one pitch in most pitchers' repertoires, and the pitch that most scouts are looking for in young pitchers. No pitch is better than an overpowering fastball, but command of it is essential, and movement can compensate for less velocity.

Four-Seam Fastball

The four-seam fastball has little movement and can be easily controlled because it is generally straight. In the grip, the pitcher has his index and middle fingers on top across the seams and the thumb and ring finger under the bottom, across the two seams (see figure 12.6). Thus, he uses four seams. The four-seamer typically generates more velocity and is easier to locate because it has less movement.

Figure 12.6 The four-seam fastball grip.

Two-Seam Fastball

The other fastball grip is the two-seamer. The pitcher puts his index and middle fingers on the top two seams coming out of the horseshoe-shaped stitching (figure 12.7a). The two-seam grip will make the ball move a lot more than the four-seam grip will. The two-seamer is a difficult pitch to hit when the pitcher gets good movement because it can run in on the hitter's hands. Both fastballs are thrown with the same technique; the pitcher releases the ball out in front of his body. The difference is in the grip and movement. Figure 12.7b diagrams the movement of the two-seam fastball.

a

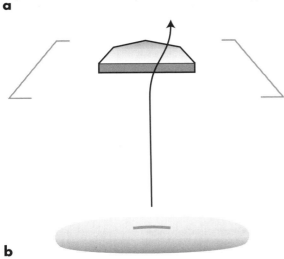

b

Figure 12.7 The two-seam fastball grip *(a)* and its movement *(b)*.

Split-Finger Fastball

To throw a split-finger fastball, the pitcher simply takes the two-seam grip and spreads his middle and index fingers as much as possible. The thumb should split the bottom of the ball in half (figure 12.8*a*). The pitcher throws the pitch just as he would a fastball. The grip should create a tumbling effect with the ball, which drops straight down (figure 12.8*b*).

a

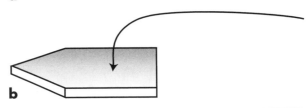

b

Figure 12.8 The split-finger fastball grip *(a)* and its movement *(b)*.

Curveball

The most common curve is the 12 to 6, a reference to the face of a clock and the break of the pitch. The middle finger runs along the top seam so that the pitcher can feel the seam on the outside of his finger. The index finger is right next to the middle finger. The thumb is under the ball and on the inside seam (figure 12.9*a*). The 12 to 6 break (figure 12.9*b*) is most often created by a pitcher who throws over the top rather than with a three-quarter or sidearm delivery. The over-the-top delivery allows the pitcher to get on top of the ball so that the rotation goes straight down—from 12 to 6.

a

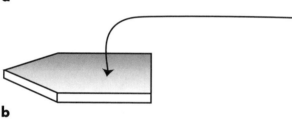

b

Figure 12.9 The curveball grip *(a)* and the 12 to 6 movement *(b)*.

An important coaching point after the pitcher has established the grip is to make sure that he throws the curve with the same arm action as he does the fastball. Arm speed needs to remain constant from pitch to pitch. Maintaining consistent arm speed will help the pitcher keep his arm and elbow up to produce maximum break. If the pitcher drops his elbow, the ball will hang or the break will be shortened, resulting in a pitch that will be much easier to hit. As the pitcher releases the ball and finishes his delivery, he leads with the hand and pulls it straight down to get the tight spin going virtually straight down. The pulling-down action of the arm is essential.

Slider

To throw a slider, the pitcher puts his fingers in a position right between the grip for a curveball and the grip for a two-seam fastball (figure 12.10*a*). Arm action should be like that used for a fastball up until the point of release. At the point of release, the pitcher puts pressure not only behind the ball but also on the outside of the ball. The pitcher will then get the desired hard, late break across the plate (figure 12.10*b*).

a

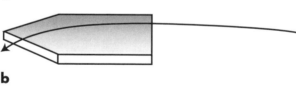

b

Figure 12.10 The slider grip *(a)* and its movement *(b)*.

Slurve

The slurve is something of a combination curve and slider and breaks 2 to 8 on the clock face. The slider break is the movement across the clock face, whereas the curve break is the movement down. To throw the slurve, the pitcher uses the same grip that he uses for the 12 to 6 curveball, but it is a more natural pitch for a pitcher who has a three-quarter-arm release point. The lower arm slot or angle will make the pitch move down and across, which is the ideal slurve movement. The pitcher has the same approach as he does with the curve, but his release and finish point will have his arm going across his lower body and finishing outside his opposite knee. The slurve will be natural for pitchers with the three-quarter-arm release point. Some people believe that this pitch, thrown with proper form and two-way movement, is the hardest breaking ball to hit. Figure 12.11 shows the pitch movement.

Figure 12.12 The change-up grip.

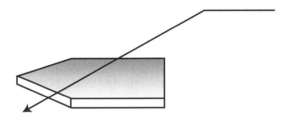

Figure 12.11 The slurve movement.

An important point for coaches is that they should not teach any type of breaking pitch to youngsters under age 12, and maybe even those a few years older, because the pitching action places a lot of stress on the elbow and shoulder. A young pitcher should stick with the fastball and, perhaps, the change-up.

Change-Up

Many people believe that the most effective throw in baseball is the change-up. Thrown correctly, it looks like a fastball when released but comes into the strike zone 10 to 15 miles per hour slower. The most popular grip today is known as the circle change. The pitcher creates this grip by bringing the thumb and index finger together at the fingertips to make a circle on the side of the baseball. The middle and ring finger are on top of the ball, inside the seams (figure 12.12). The pitcher throws the ball as hard as he can with the fastball motion and releases it with his wrist rotating toward the circle. The fingers should turn under the ball to move it down in the strike zone. As the pitcher pronates his arm and releases the ball with full arm speed, he will get movement and a pitch with reduced speed.

The grip and technique required to throw the circle change take time to master, and some pitchers never get comfortable with it. They can use other ways to throw the circle change and the straight change. Many grips are available. The pitcher who finds the grip difficult can split the thumb and index finger so that the tips aren't touching and the circle is an imperfect one. This method will give the pitcher a more relaxed grip, improving his control. The key coaching point is to emphasize that the pitch is thrown with the same arm action as the fastball, creating a similar rotation and the illusion of having the same velocity. Some coaches tell their pitchers to drag the back foot on the follow-through, which can help slow down the ball. Note, however, that a pitcher who employs this technique must retain the same arm speed that he uses for the fastball. Note too that a pitcher who throws predominately four-seam fastballs should use a four-seam change-up as well. The same goes with two-seam fastballs.

The fastball, curve, and change-up are the three most popular pitches today, but there are others, such as the slider, split finger, knuckleball, and screwball, to name just a few. But as a coach, recognize that the success of your pitcher is not related to how many pitches he has but to the effectiveness of each pitch. The best course for a coach working with young pitchers is to tell them to focus on the fastball, curveball, and change-up. They will have time later to expand their repertoires.

DEVISING A PITCHING PLAN

When setting up a pitching plan, start with the basics and work from there. The first concern is the pitcher's ability to throw strikes. A young pitcher who can throw strikes, get ahead in the count, and spot his pitches is far ahead of the game and has a good chance to win. The coach's mantra should be "Throw strikes."

You want your pitchers to attack the hitter. They should be aggressive and pitch inside with the fastball. If a pitcher can make the hitter aware that he is willing to come inside, then he can use any of his other pitches at any time on any part of the plate.

A coach also wants his staff to work the knees, keeping the ball down. If pitchers miss the strike zone, they should miss low. A pitcher is less apt to be hurt with a low pitch over the middle of the plate than a pitch that is belt or letter high. Stress this in bullpen and side sessions, emphasizing to your catchers the need to set up low.

Each pitch that a pitcher throws should have a purpose. A pitcher should follow a few rules each time he delivers the ball.

With the fastball, he should keep it inside or on the outside corner. By getting ahead and throwing strikes, a pitcher has more latitude with what he can throw and where. The pitcher who is ahead in the count, for example, can throw his fastball high and out of the strike zone or off the outside corner as a waste pitch, hoping that the hitter gets himself out by chasing it. But the fastball is the only pitch that should be thrown high in the zone. Hanging a curve or change-up high in the zone, where the hitter has a good look at it, is a good way to give up the big hit.

When the pitcher throws his curveball, he wants to locate it low in the strike zone, avoiding the risk of hanging it high. The curveball can be thrown in the middle of the plate if it's down in the strike zone and has good break.

The plan when throwing the change-up is similar to that of the curve. Neither should be thrown up in the zone. In addition, a pitcher doesn't want to get too fine with the change-up. Being able to hit the corners with it is great, but the key to using the change-up is keeping the hitter off balance velocity wise, resulting in a pop-up or weak grounder. The change-up can be thrown down the middle of the plate. Movement and change of speed can substitute for precise location. Change-ups typically work well when thrown down and away.

Pitching to a scouting report and a hitter's weakness is fine, but the basics of throwing strikes, being aggressive, and changing speeds to keep the hitter off balance are more important than any report and should be the foundation of any pitching plan. Have your pitchers pitch to their strengths first and then to the hitters' weaknesses.

Pitch selection is a combination of what pitches the pitcher can throw effectively and what pitches the hitter cannot hit hard. If the pitcher can throw fastballs inside and the hitter has a long, slow swing, then fastballs inside should be the choice. Watch not only the hitter's swing (swing speed and natural bat path) but also his mannerisms. Most hitters won't hide their aggressiveness, or their patience. Hitters have patterns too! Is he a first-pitch swinger, or does he take until he gets a strike? Can he pick up the off-speed pitch easily out of the pitcher's hand, or does the off-speed pitch fool him? Does the hitter have a slow bat? If so, then stick primarily with the fastball. Does the hitter have a quick bat? If so, use more off-speed pitches. Knowing what the hitter wants makes it much easier to call pitches. Table 12.1 provides an outline that shows which pitches are effective against the various kinds of hitters.

SITUATIONAL PITCHING

Situational pitching refers to the points during a game when because of the score, the number of outs, or the number of runners on base, the pitcher needs to waste a pitch, throw a specific pitch, or pitch a hitter a certain way.

The waste pitch, a pitch intentionally thrown out of the strike zone, is normally used only when the pitcher is ahead in the count and wants to induce the hitter, in a defensive mode because of the count, to swing at a bad pitch

Table 12.1   Pitching to a Hitter's Tendencies and Weaknesses

Hitter's tendency	Hitter's weakness	Pitches
Crowds plate	Cannot get barrel of bat around on ball inside; has less foul territory	Fastball up and inside in the strike zone is the best pitch. Any pitch on the inside corner will be hit weakly or will be hit foul.
Pulls hitter or opens stance	Pulls off the ball Cannot hit outside pitch Trouble with off-speed pitch	Use fastball on outside corner. Use change-up and breaking ball on outside of plate.
Stands away from plate	Cannot cover outside of plate	Use fastball on outside part of home plate. Use change-up and breaking ball on outside corner.
Dives into home plate with his stride	Cannot extend on pitches inside Cannot get hips open in time to pull the bat	Use fastballs inside, especially up and in. Use breaking balls on inside part of plate.

or hit it weakly. Sometimes a pitcher throws a waste pitch simply to show the hitter that he has a certain pitch, thus implanting it in his mind. A pitcher may also use it early in the count to determine the batter's intent, such as whether he is bunting.

An interesting situation that often arises during a game occurs when a runner is at second base or runners are at second and third with first base open. In this situation, with one out or two outs, the pitcher should work carefully. He has the open base to work with, so if he walks the hitter the bases would be loaded, or there would be runners at first and second, increasing the double-play or force-out possibilities. With first base open and not being too concerned about issuing a walk, the pitcher can go after the hitter by attacking the corners or using off-speed pitches. Coaches should consider this situation with first base open as an advantage to their pitcher and try to communicate that thinking.

The pitcher faces another interesting situational development when he has a proficient base stealer on first base. In this situation, most coaches have their pitchers throw primarily fastballs rather than curves or change-ups because the fastball gets to the catcher quicker and gives him more time to make the throw on an attempted steal. A pitcher still has to focus on the hitter, but when the steal is likely, the pitcher should throw the fastball to the outside corner and up so that the catcher can get to it

easily. If the pitch is well outside, it's practically the same as a pitchout.

In an obvious bunting or sacrifice situation, the pitcher should throw hard fastballs. He should never throw a change-up because it is the easiest pitch to bunt. When throwing fastballs in that situation, the pitcher should raise the strike zone and pitch waist high or higher. Pitches in this location are difficult for the hitter to get on top of, thus increasing the possibility that the hitter will pop up the bunt.

The last point in situational pitching concerns dealing with the opposing team's best hitter. You should be able to identify that player and not let him beat you, not let him deliver a big hit in a key situation. If the opponent's lineup has good hitters back to back, you have to pick your poison and pitch to the least dangerous one. The goal, of course, is to keep the hitters who bat ahead of the opponent's strongest hitter off base so that you're not in a situation where you have to pitch to that number one guy. Know your opponent, have a plan, and work on these pitching situations in practice.

PITCHER AS FIELDER

The pitcher who can field his position can be extremely valuable to his team. Many high school pitchers play another position, which enhances their fielding ability when they are on the mound. But even those players need to work on the fielding skills that are unique to the pitcher's position and often require the pitcher to anticipate what he is going to do with the ball if it is hit to him. The pitcher is closer to the hitter than any player other than the catcher, so the ball often gets to him quickly off the bat. He must be in a solid fielding stance after delivering the ball.

The pitcher has to be able to field ground balls, pop flies, bunts, and line drives. He must be able to make pickoff throws, get to first base and field throws from the first baseman on balls hit wide of first, and remember to back up bases when a play may occur there. A coach must have his pitchers ready, both mentally and physically. If he knows that his pitcher simply isn't a good fielder, he must remind his infielders that they have to be ready to cover ground that a good fielding pitcher might otherwise cover.

With the proper drills and fundamental work, however, a pitcher can improve and may one day win a game with his defense.

PICKOFF PLAYS

Pickoff plays are one of the areas that tend to be neglected. Pickoffs, the pitcher's throw to a base to keep a runner close or try to pick him off, are not the same as pickoff plays. A pickoff play is a set play put on by the coach, fielders, or the pitcher himself. A sign given by the fielder, pitcher, catcher, or even the coach triggers the play. A verbal call from any of those people can also put on a pickoff play.

The pitcher and first baseman often use a pickoff play with a runner at first base. Usually, the first baseman calls the name or number of the pitcher. The pitcher then throws over on a pickoff attempt. The first baseman often sees that the runner's lead is too long, so he notifies the pitcher. The first baseman may also hear the first-base coach tell the runner that a steal is on. After hearing this, the first baseman can call for a pickoff throw to stop the steal.

The pickoff play at second base involves the second baseman and shortstop breaking to second base to get the runner to go back. Then, as the runner regains his original lead, the second baseman comes in for the throw

from the pitcher. The timing of this play is crucial. The shortstop breaks to the base after the pitcher looks at the base. Then, as the runner goes back to the base, the shortstop returns to his position and the pitcher turns his head to home plate. The pitcher looks home, lowers his head, and drops his chin. This movement is the key for the second baseman to break to the base. The pitcher lifts his chin, turns, and throws to second base. Figure 12.13 diagrams the pickoff play with a runner at second.

Pickoff plays to third base are usually executed by the third baseman and a right-handed pitcher. A right-handed pitcher usually has a

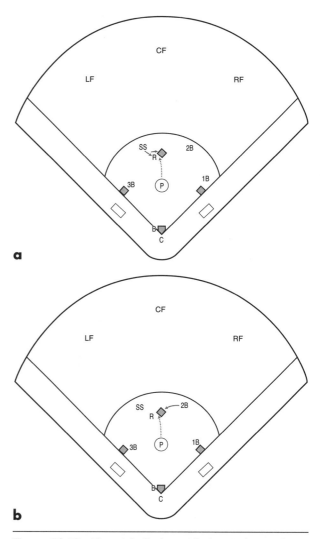

Figure 12.13 The pickoff play with the pitcher and shortstop (*a*) involves the shortstop creeping behind the runner toward second then breaking with his glove out when he sees an opening. The pitcher sees the glove and turns to pick. (*b*) The play works similarly with the pitcher and second baseman executing the pick.

more deceptive pickoff move than a left-handed pitcher, who has his back to third base.

Either the pitcher or the third baseman gives a sign to put on this pickoff play. For instance, the third baseman may get the pitcher's attention and wiggle his glove or put his bare hand across his letters. The pitcher then knows that the pickoff play is on. The pitcher gets set in his stretch position. He lifts his front leg as if to deliver the ball home but instead steps toward third base and releases the ball to the third baseman. The third baseman knows that the ball is coming so he plays his normal position, even with but off the base, and he steps to the base late when the pitcher's front leg starts its downward motion. This method will put the third baseman moving to the base as the pitcher is releasing the ball and will not tip off the runner until the last possible moment.

Practice Made Perfect

In 1991 our Esperanza team was playing Baldwin Hills High in the second round of the playoffs. The game turned into a slugfest, and in the bottom of the seventh inning, with two outs and our team up by only a run, Baldwin Hills had runners at second and third. The batter hit a swinging bunt down the third-base line. We had worked on bunt fielding drills every week. Our pitcher, who was our number two relief pitcher, jumped on the ball, fielded it, took one quick step with his left foot, and threw a strike to first base for the final out. That play was the result of repeated practice, and it enabled us to keep our lead and win the game.

PITCHING DRILLS

Here are some important drills. Understand that at higher levels, your pitchers are more isolated from your position players. At the Little League and travel ball level, most of your pitchers also play the field and are many times your best position players. When you get to the high school level, many pitchers still play a position in addition to pitching. At the college level, few pitchers play another position or hit. With this in mind, you should set up drills that your pitchers can do with or without the supervision of a coach. The following are some drills that you can incorporate into the format.

Warm-Up

Purpose. Your pitchers play catch to warm up and get loose every day. This drill adds discipline to their catch playing and works on their pitching form fundamentals.

Procedure. Pitchers should do this drill daily before they throw off a mound. They start on one knee, a right-hander with his right knee on the ground and a left-hander with his left. They throw the ball to a fellow pitcher, and as they release it, they strive to get the chest to the opposite knee and reach out as far as they can. They make 10 throws in this position before standing and making 20 at long distance (approximately 120 feet) to stretch out their arms further. They then shorten up again to take 20 throws out of their windup and 10 out of their stretch. By playing catch in this structured form every day, they increase their arm strength, loosen the arm for the day's practice, and work on their delivery. You may choose to have your pitchers finish off their warm-up by working from 90 feet apart and throwing change-ups, gaining confidence in the grip and delivery.

Flat Ground, Dry Drills

Purpose. This drill will improve a pitcher's form, and pitchers can do it with the coach's supervision or on their own.

Procedure. Pitchers can do this series of drills with or without a baseball. I like them to do it without a baseball because they can execute it every day, even with a sore or tired arm. In this series of drills the pitchers work together. They start by taking their windup steps. As they lift the leg as they would in their delivery, they hold it there, balanced up with the toe pointing to the ground. They can do just this part of the drill 5 or 10 times. From there they do the same drill but take it a step further. After they balance up, they take their stride toward home plate and freeze as the front foot hits with the arm extended and the ball of the front foot pointing away from home plate. They do this 5 or 10 times, stopping when the front foot hits and making sure that the arm is up and that the ball of the front foot is facing away from the plate. In the last part of these drills the pitchers progress from hitting on the front foot to finishing with the follow-through and reaching with the arm extended as far in front of the body as possible, with the feet balanced in a solid fielding position. By going through these drills for 10 minutes a day without a ball, pitchers can focus on form without taxing their arms.

Pitcher's Fundamental Practice (PFP)

Purpose. This common drill works the plays that pitchers often have to make in a game. The drill involves all your infielders and provides the pitchers with important repetitive work.

Procedure. We use three pitchers at a time with all our infielders. We put one pitcher on the dirt off the mound on the third-base side. The second pitcher is on the rubber on top of the mound. The third pitcher is on the flat dirt off the mound on the first-base side. All three pitchers execute the fundamentals at once. A coach rolls a ball down the third-base line, and the pitcher on the third-base side fields it and throws to the third baseman to simulate fielding a bunt and throwing out the runner going from second to third. The pitcher on the rubber fields batted balls and throws to the shortstop or second baseman covering second base. The pitcher on the first-base side covers first base on a ball hit to the first baseman. Alternatively, the pitcher on the first-base side covers first base, and the first baseman throws the ball to him after fielding the ground ball. The pitchers begin the drill by simultaneously winding up as if they're delivering a pitch, and a coach then hits or rolls the ball for them to make the play. They alternate positions, and the team gets a lot of quality work on three plays that the pitchers will have to make many times. Figure 12.14 illustrates the execution of the drill.

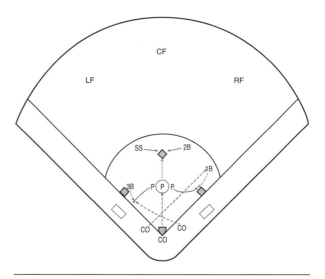

Figure 12.14 Pitcher's Fundamental Practice drill.

Three-Man Pickoff

Purpose. This drill gets your whole pitching staff working on footwork and throwing accurately to each base. They rotate to make pickoffs to first, second, and third base. This drill is a great way to improve your pitchers' pickoff interaction with the various infielders.

Procedure. We use this drill once or twice a week to refine our pitchers' pickoff moves. We put three pitchers at once on the dirt part of the mound. They line up the same way as they did in PFP. The pitcher on the third-base side works with the third baseman on his pickoff to third, the pitcher on the mound works with the second baseman and shortstop on his pickoff to second, and the pitcher on the first-base side works with the first baseman on his pickoff to first. They alternate until each has made 5 to 10 throws to each base. Figure 12.15 illustrates the proper execution.

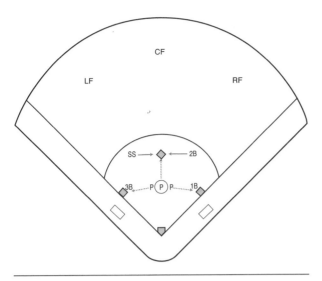

Figure 12.15 Three-Man Pickoff drill.

PITCHER CONDITIONING

Athletes should condition specifically for their sport, and even within their sport for their specific position. Pitchers should adhere to a short-, medium-, and long-distance running program.

- Sprinting to field a bunt, sprinting to back up third or home plate, sprinting to cover home on a wild pitch, and sprinting to cover first base on a ball hit to the right side are all sport-specific conditioning drills. One stone, two birds!

- Performed correctly, forward, side, and reverse lunges can add endurance and muscle strength to pitchers of any age. These exercises are low impact and mimic the muscle movements of a pitcher's mechanics.

- Long-distance conditioning is best reserved for starting pitchers and other pitchers who may be looking to get in better shape physically.

Figure 12.16 on the next page provides a detailed pitcher conditioning program.

Coaches' Keys

1. The pitcher is the most important player on the field. The better your pitchers' mechanics, the more likely they are to throw strikes and avoid injuries.

2. Pitching mechanics involve all the fundamentals of throwing a baseball. Those fundamentals start with the simple act of playing catch.

3. The three pitches that coaches should teach are the fastball (two seam and four seam), curveball, and change-up.

4. A pitching plan should be based on throwing strikes and attacking the hitter by working the inside part of the plate with fastballs.

5. Situational pitching deals with those times when a pitcher needs to waste a pitch, throw a specific pitch, or pitch the hitter a certain way. Situational pitching also means trying to prevent the opponent's best hitter from beating you.

6. A coach needs to prepare his pitchers for the various plays that they will have to make, including fielding ground balls, pop flies, and bunts and making pickoffs at each base.

7. Pitching drills should cover throwing, fielding, and pickoffs. The drills can be used daily or once or twice a week.

8. A dominant pitcher is one thing, but a pitcher who can do more than deliver quality pitches can often be the difference between winning and losing.

Figure 12.16 Pitcher Conditioning Program

Pitchers' Conditioning Program

It is very important that athletes condition for their specific sport and positions within each sport.

- Pitchers should adhere to a short-, medium-, and long-distance running program.
- Sprinting to field a bunt, sprinting to back up third or home plate, sprinting to cover home on a wild pitch, and sprinting to cover first base on a ball hit to the right side are all sport-specific conditioning drills.
- Forward, side, and reverse lunges (when performed correctly) can increase endurance and muscular strength in pitchers of any age. Lunges are low impact and mimic the muscle movements of a pitcher's mechanics.
- Long-distance conditioning is best reserved for starting pitchers as well as any other pitcher who might be looking to get in better physical shape.

Here is an example of a starting pitcher's conditioning routine:

Wednesday: Game (start). Theraband and Jobe exercises, two sets of 10 to 12 repetitions.

Thursday: Two-mile run. Include a hill if possible.

Friday: Sprints (covering first base and fielding bunts), two sets of 10 to 12 repetitions.

Saturday: 30-pitch bullpen. Theraband and Jobe exercises, two sets of 10 to 12 repetitions.

Sunday: Rest.

Monday: 25-pitch bullpen. Theraband and Jobe exercises, one set of 12 repetitions.

    Lunges (one set of each: forward, reverse, and side; one set = 90 feet).

    Medium-distance running (3/4 speed), 8 repetitions at 100 feet.

    Abdominal workout; weight workout.

Tuesday: (day before start). Sprints (backing up third or home plate), three or four repetitions to each base.

Wednesday: Game (start). Theraband and Jobe exercises, two sets of 10 to 12 repetitions.

Here is an example of a reliever's conditioning routine:

Wednesday: Ggame (felief). Theraband and Jobe exercises, two sets of 10 to 12 repetitions.

Thursday: Sprints (back up third or home plate). three or four repetitions to each base.

Friday: Game (relief). Theraband and Jobe exercises: two sets of 10 to 12 repetitions.

Saturday: Lunges (one set of each: forward, reverse, and side; one set = 90 feet.)

    Medium-distance running (3/4 speed), eight repetitions at 100 feet.

    Abdominal workout; weight workout.

Sunday: Rest.

Monday: 25-pitch bullpen. Theraband/jobe exercises, one set of 12 repetitions.

    Lunges (one set of each: forward, reverse, and side; one set = 90 feet.

    Medium distance running (3/4 speed), eight repetitions at 100 feet.

    Abdominal workout; weight workout.

Tuesday: Sprints (covering first base and fielding bunts), two sets of five repetitions.

Part V

COACHING GAMES

CHAPTER 13   PREPARING FOR GAMES

Preparing for games involves more than just filling out a lineup card. The coach must do a number of jobs before his team takes the field. He needs to get his team ready for the opponent, which involves knowing both the opponent and the environment. The coach may need to tell his players that they will be going on a long bus ride or playing at a poorly manicured field or will have to deal with boisterous fans. These intangibles can make it difficult for the players to compete or may catch them off guard and distract them from their goal—to win the game.

The coach should also discuss where the two teams are in the standings to help his players focus on what this specific game means to each of them and the team as a whole.

KNOWING THE OPPOSITION

Knowing an opponent comes from scouting that opponent. In this high-tech era, scouting is easy. With the proliferation of low-cost, lightweight, hand-held video devices, a coach should be able to find someone—a member of his staff, a parent, a kid on campus, or a friend—willing to scout the next opponent. The scout should set up behind the plate with a camera so that the hitter, catcher, and pitcher are in view. Getting every play isn't necessary. The goal is to return

with a tape that the assistant coaches can break down to chart each hitter's strengths and weaknesses, and the type of pitches that he hit and missed. If the coach can scout two or three games, so much the better, because he'll have a more comprehensive view of the opponent's hitters and pitchers. With modern equipment, slow motion can enhance the process.

A coach should also film all his own team's games so that if they play the same team two or three times in league competition, the coach can see how his hitters and pitchers performed against that team, possibly helping him adjust his lineup and make game decisions the next time they meet. In the same context, if a coach is videotaping an opponent for the next game, he may have an opportunity to see two future opponents at once, especially if the game is a league game. Obviously, a video report is far better than a simple written report on an opponent.

Still, in relation to preparing a team for an opponent, the tape can show only so much. Each team has a personality and strength, and even several tapes may not capture it all. But an opponent can only do so many things. If a coach has prepared his team well, worked them on fundamentals from the start of practice, they should be able to handle any development or play. In other words, a coach should be more concerned about his own team than he is about the opposition. Baseball is not like football, which requires a coach to prepare for countless possibilities. If the scouting report shows that an opponent likes to run a certain play offensively or use a particular pickoff play, the coach simply reviews those plays during the week because his team has probably drilled on them previously. The greatest benefit of a scouting report may be that it gives a team's hitters a chance to see what an opponent's pitcher or pitchers like to throw in certain game and count situations. In any case, a basic rule in coaching is leave no stone unturned. By preparing his team for any eventuality from the first day of practice, the coach will see his team reap the benefit of February and March in April and May. Figures 13.1 and 13.2 provide various sample scouting reports for pitchers and hitters.

DESIGNATING ASSISTANTS' RESPONSIBILITIES

As a head coach, you want to use your assistants to make your job easier and help your team win. You may be reluctant to give an inexperienced assistant a crucial task, such as coaching third base or calling pitches or signs. But you can put that same coach in charge of warm-ups and stretching, hitting infield, or supervising the starting pitcher's preparation. Any of these tasks will give your assistant coaches a feeling of ownership and free you up to concentrate on the upcoming game.

You are always responsible for the bottom line, but you can't do it all. Designating responsibility builds knowledge and trust. At Esperanza, where we have established one of the most successful programs in Southern California, I like to let my pitching coach call pitches during games. I stand next to him and may call a pitch now and then, but it's basically his responsibility.

You need to know that your assistants are capable of positioning players on defense, calling pitches, and coaching the base lines. You must also be ready to coach your coaches. When they make mistakes, you need to let them know what they should have done and why. Such corrections are part of their education and will make them more valuable. Knowing when to

approach them in that regard is important. As in the case of that pitching coach, a discussion about a crucial in-game coaching mistake is usually more profitable the next day when things are calmer. No matter the level, a head coach has a lot on his plate. He needs to know that his assistants are capable of easing the burden.

Do You Want to Call the Pitches?

One year, having just hired a new pitching coach, we were playing our fourth game of the season when I saw something about one of their hitters and told my pitching coach that I wanted a specific pitch thrown. He wanted another pitch and called it. The batter hit a shot for a double. I asked my assistant why he didn't call the pitch that I wanted. "Do you want to call pitches?" he barked at me. I understood that in the heat of a game, his temper might have gotten the best of him, so I didn't say anything. The next day, however, I sat him down and told him that I wanted him to call pitches but that when I saw something during a game, I wanted him to listen to me and do as I told him. If I am wrong, it's all on me, as it is anyway. I told him clearly that my way was just the way it was. He understood, and we never had another problem in the five years that he was the pitching coach.

SETTING THE LINEUP

You should establish and set your lineup the night before the game. After practice that day, sit down with your assistant coaches, brainstorm, and put together the lineup for the next day. Some players at certain positions will always be in the lineup because of their ability. Other players may be involved in a revolving situation based on defense, offense, or other factors. Again, you need to involve your assistants and build a consensus, making your staff part of it while retaining the final vote. In addition, an assistant coach may have picked up something about a player in practice that you missed.

Many factors come into play in setting the lineup. You may want to platoon at a position where you have both a left-handed hitter and a right-handed hitter and you want to play the percentages. In that case you would play the

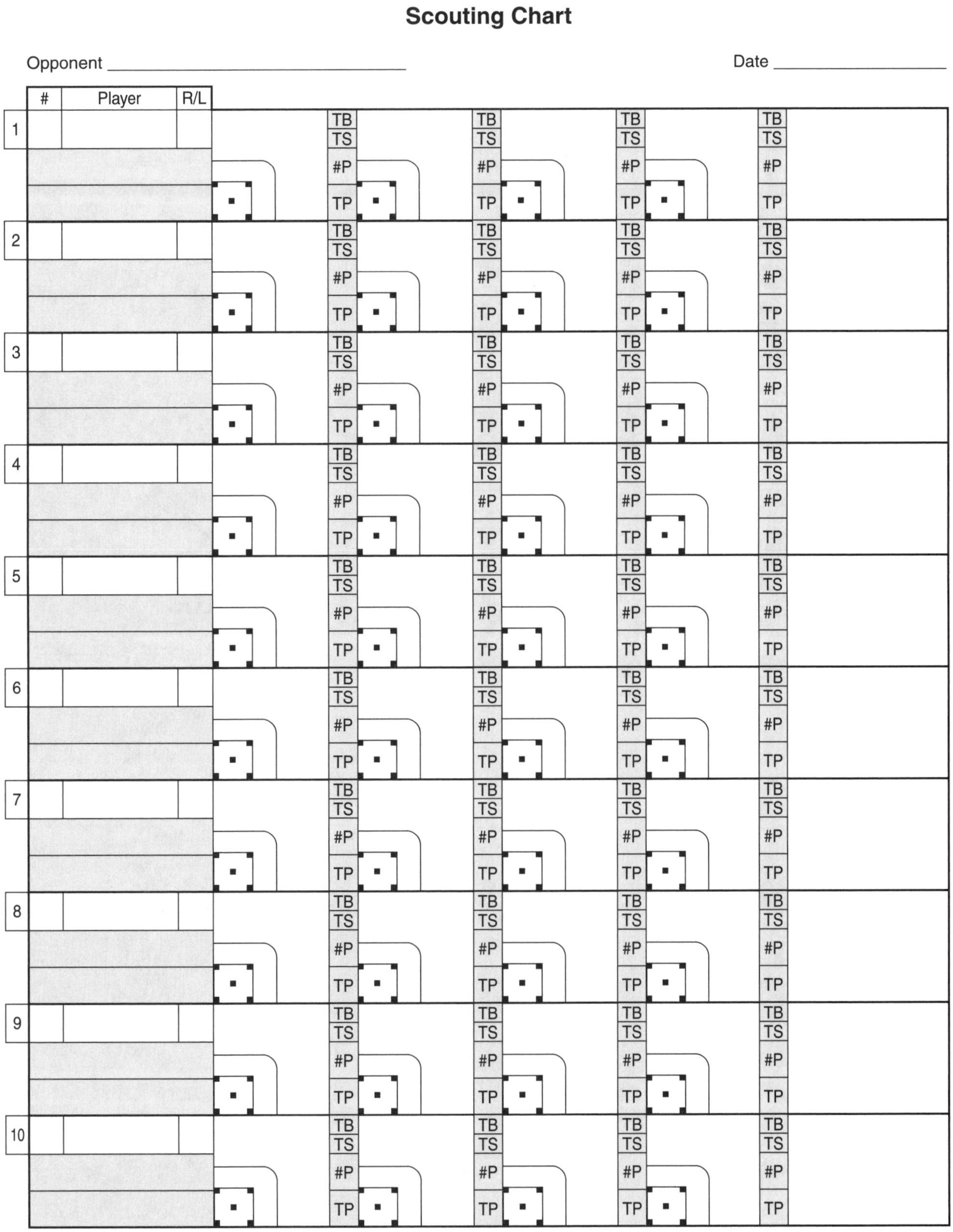

Scouting Chart

Opponent _____   Date _____

	#	Player	R/L									

1
TB / TS / #P / TP (repeated across four batter-box sections)

2
TB / TS / #P / TP

3
TB / TS / #P / TP

4
TB / TS / #P / TP

5
TB / TS / #P / TP

6
TB / TS / #P / TP

7
TB / TS / #P / TP

8
TB / TS / #P / TP

9
TB / TS / #P / TP

10
TB / TS / #P / TP

Figure 13.1   A scouting chart can help coaches track the hitting tendencies of all batters on a team.

From *Coaching Baseball Successfully* by Mike Curran and Ross Newhan, 2007, Champaign, IL: Human Kinetics.

Advance Scouting

Left   Right   Switch
Spot in order: 1 2 3 4 5 6 7 8 9
Speed: ↓Avg.   Avg.   ↑Avg.   ++
Steal: Yes   No   Count(s)-____/____/___s_

Drag: Yes   No
Push: Yes   No

PITCH

Vs. RH	Vs. LH
1st pitch_____	1st pitch_____
Avoid_____	Avoid_____
Primary_____	Primary_____
Secondary_____	Secondary_____
Occasional_____	Occasional_____
Out pitch(s)_____	*Out* pitch(s)_____

POSITIONING CHART

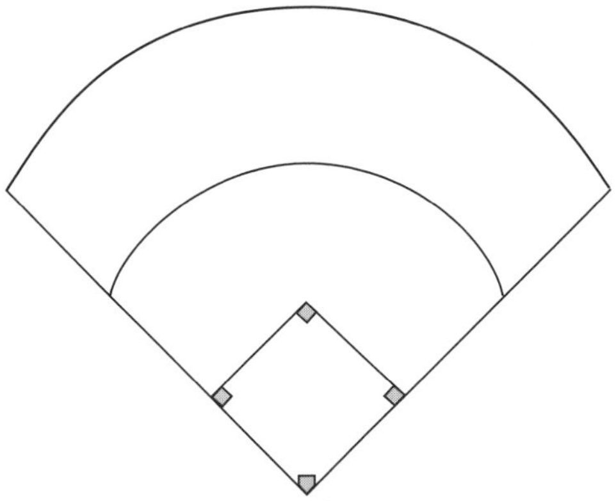

IN-GAME LOG

½		¾	
L/R	L/R	L/R	L/R
0-0		0-0	
0-1		0-1	
1-0		1-0	
0-2		0-2	
1-1		1-1	
2-0		2-0	
1-2		1-2	
2-1		2-1	
2-2		2-2	
3-1		3-1	
3-2		3-2	

SCOUTING LOG

½		¾	
L/R	L/R	L/R	L/R
0-0		0-0	
0-1		0-1	
1-0		1-0	
0-2		0-2	
1-1		1-1	
2-0		2-0	
1-2		1-2	
2-1		2-1	
2-2		2-2	
3-1		3-1	
3-2		3-2	

Name: _____

Figure 13.2   This form can be used to detail all of the useful information about a particular player, including hitting tendencies and pitch selection for pitchers.

From *Coaching Baseball Successfully* by Mike Curran and Ross Newhan, 2007, Champaign, IL: Human Kinetics.

left-handed hitter against right-handed pitching and the right-handed hitter against left-handed pitching. In some situations I have alternated two of my position players even though they both hit from the same side. Both were right-handed, but I wanted to keep them competitive and they were extremely close physically. I would tell them that when one of them caught fire, he would win the job. I've had some years in which my team has gone to the title game with alternating players at a certain position.

At the high school level with the reentry rule that allows a coach to substitute for his starting nine players and then bring the starter back, juggling the lineup is easier. You can start a good defender or good bunter and then bring a better hitter off the bench to pinch hit if the situation warrants it, after which the starter can return. Personally, I don't like to play weak defensive players just to get a bat into the lineup. Pitching and defense win championships, and that's the strength I want to emphasize.

When you and your assistants make out the lineup, you also want to list the players you will use off the bench, including long relief pitchers, short relief pitchers, and the closer. If you play on Tuesday and Friday, a starting pitcher on Friday can often be the closer on Tuesday, pitch an inning or two, and still come back strong as the starter on Friday.

SUBSTITUTIONS

When you set up your substitutes, including pinch runners and pinch hitters, how the game evolves will likely determine when you'll use them. If I'm going to pinch run for one of my players in the third inning, I will not use my fastest or best runner off the bench. I will save him until the late innings when I need a stolen base for the tying or winning run. The same approach applies with my best pinch hitter. I won't use him early but will hold him until late in the game when he can tie or win the game with a hit.

A good way to do this early in the season is to have each of the assistant coaches put together his best lineup. Compare them to see whether you have a consensus. Ideally, you'll have at least the same two-thirds of the lineup on each card. Otherwise, your team probably has many similar parts, which may not be good.

GAME DAY

When the players stretch, play catch, loosen up by running, and do pregame hitting drills, you should designate a coach to ensure that they do each drill or exercise properly. Also, you should never let the starting pitcher go into the bullpen without a coach. The pitcher needs to have a coach watching him to make sure that his preparation for the game is precise. Assign a coach to hit infield to the team before the game, and have a coach organize and supervise pregame exercises.

Field Preparation

At many levels, including youth leagues and high school, preparing for games starts with field preparation such as chalking, watering, and raking the infield. Most high schools have a field man who takes care of the preparation. But if no one has that responsibility, then the coach and his players or his assistant coaches must condition the field.

One of the best ways to prepare is to fill out a sheet designating each player's job if the players are needed to work on the field. The pitching coach should designate which pitchers are to rake and water the field and bullpen mounds. The catcher can rake the home plate area, and the first and third basemen can prepare the area around their bases. An assistant coach can be designated to help certain players drag and then chalk or paint the lines. Many of the jobs involving raking and dragging the field can be done the night or day before the game. Again, the more organized you are, the easier it is for you to keep your mind on the game itself.

Pregame Warm-Up

When preparing for the game, you want to know that when your team ultimately takes the field, all the practice preparation will become execution reality. Give your team time before a game to stretch, warm up, and take batting practice before taking the field for pregame infield.

This pregame routine should start with bringing the players together and having a coach talk to them about the upcoming game and the opponent. I personally have my assistant coach take on this responsibility. The players will hear from me just before we take the field at the start of the game. I want them to hear the message initially from an assistant coach, and I want one of my assistants to have the challenge of doing this job.

From there, the players go into a quick routine of playing catch if they are going to have batting practice. Many of the players play more catch if they are not hitting in the first group. High school programs and the Little Leagues on down do not take batting practice. Usually, only college teams hit before games.

Teams that do not hit before their games usually do some sort of quick running exercise to loosen up the players' legs before they play catch. For this running exercise, most teams work their players in a straight line and have them watch one of the coaches, who acts as a pitcher going through his motion so that the players can work on getting a jump on the pitcher. I personally change this up a little. Instead of having my coach act as a pitcher with the players reading his move to steal a base, I have the coach go out with a baseball. The coach holds the ball out so that all the players in a line can see it. The players are in their base-running stance in a line, just like those teams that are trying to steal on the pitcher. The coach holds the ball and then drops it. The team then takes off to steal a base. This routine has the players focus on one small item—the baseball. In a game you want your players to look at a specific part of the pitcher, his shoulder, feet, knee, or head, to pick up any tendency that will help them get a jump. In this drill the ball is that one thing that they focus on. A coach needs to do the drill only two or three times.

The players then play catch. Following this you must decide what you want your players to do before the teams take their infield. This usually involves some simple hitting drill that the players can do in the outfield. Coaches, or the players themselves, throw Wiffle balls or soft toss, and the players hit the balls into the fence. They can also play pepper in groups of four or five. A hitter has three or four players 5 to 10 yards away. A player throws the ball to the hitter, who works on hitting the ball to the three or four players. The one who fields the

ball throws it to the batter again. They all rotate as the hitter.

The two teams then take their infield. When the other team takes infield, your team should watch them to see how strong each position player's arm is and how good they are defensively. You can use this information in the game. You want to take advantage of the weak-armed players and be aware of the strongest arms. Just before your team is ready to take the field, you want to give your players last-minute instructions and a motivational message to start the game. Your players should then be ready to play.

Nonstarter Roles

For the coach, another important part of game preparation is to designate what the nonstarters are to do during the game. You should make a list and post it next to the lineup. Jobs may include bullpen catcher, scouting the opposing coach's offensive signs, and eyeing the opposing pitching coach to see whether he is calling pitches. You can also designate pinch hitters, pinch runners, relief pitchers, and a toss man to play catch between innings with the right or left fielder. All of this contributes to the overall organization and makes the nonstarters feel part of the team.

The Pitchers

Another part of your game preparation is to make sure that your starting and relief pitchers have a routine in place that they can go right into—knowing when to stretch, play catch, warm up in earnest, and be ready for the start of the game or to be called into it. During the game the coach usually can't go to the bullpen because he's calling pitches or otherwise tied up in what's happening on the field, so he has to set a pattern of how many fastballs, curves, change-ups, and other pitches he want his relievers to throw when warming up. Also, a reliever should know by the coach's instructions before he gets into the bullpen whether he is apt to be used in a situation where he can get loose slowly or if he is more likely to be needed in a hurry and have to warm up quickly.

Team Travel

Travel to away games always creates a situation that can cause your players to lose focus. The longer the ride, the more distracting it can be. You need to make sure that when you arrive at the field, you have plenty of time to get your players ready mentally and physically to play the game. You should know how long the bus ride will be and how much time your players need to do the pregame activities discussed earlier. One thing that you do not want to do as a coach is rush your players. Rushing your players can create anxiety, and you don't want your players in that frame of mind.

Another factor when playing away from home is to make sure that your team knows what to expect at the field. The field may not be in good shape, may not have an outfield fence, or may have a short fence. You want your players to be aware of anything unique before they encounter it, including the possibility of hostile fans. The goal at away games is to make your players as comfortable as you can so that they do not give in to the distractions.

Big-Game Preparation

When you get your team ready for a big game, you want to make sure that they are at their best for the ultimate challenge. When the players come out tight or nervous, they are more likely to make mistakes. An inexperienced coach will often be unable to determine whether his players are nervous. Your infield before the game may offer a clue. If the players are kicking the ball around and having trouble catching and throw-

ing it, you may want to sit them down, tell them to relax, and perhaps tell a joke that will loosen them up. The key thing is to give your players a simple plan by saying things like, "Hey, guys, just go out and play defense" or "Here we go, just throw strikes and we'll be all right." By reducing the big game to something simple, you can help your players relax and play their best.

Coaches' Keys

1. Preparing for a game may involve a number of ancillary jobs, including chalking, watering, and raking the field. Create a list of those jobs and the coaches and players responsible for doing them.

2. The head coach should give each assistant a game-day assignment. The more experienced and knowledgeable an assistant is, the more trust and responsibility he should have. A young assistant who makes a mistake should not be reprimanded until the next day when emotions have cooled. A head coach should not forget his responsibility to coach the coaches as well as the players.

3. To set a lineup, the entire coaching staff should discuss it on the night before the game, with the head coach making the final decision.

4. Scouting is useful in preparing for an opponent. Modern high-tech video options make scouting far easier today than it was in the past, but schooling a team on the fundamentals from the first day of practice to prepare them for any eventuality is the most important kind of preparation.

CHAPTER 14

HANDLING GAME SITUATIONS

After a game begins, the coach should feel confident that he can make offensive and defensive moves to cover any situation. The head coach must decide as he organizes his game-day approach how much control to designate to his staff and players and how much to retain for himself. There is no set rule. Some coaches allow players to call pitches and pickoffs and allow assistants to run the offense. Other coaches maintain control of almost everything. Obviously, the head coach must decide when to use pinch hitters, pinch runners, and defensive replacements and make decisions at critical junctures. It's his team and his responsibility.

CONDUCT

Each team has a personality that reflects how the coaches and players act on and off the field. Their conduct is consistent with the attitude that the coach wants his team to portray, or it may show that the coach doesn't care how his team acts. He may not even care if the team seems to be out of control.

Coaches' Conduct

The way that a coach acts and carries himself will ultimately spill over to his team's behavior. Therefore, the coach needs to establish himself as the role model for his team. In baseball, the head coach is highly visible. Players see him coaching the bases, flashing signs, going out to the mound to talk to his pitcher, or talking with an umpire. The head coach may also designate an assistant to perform those actions or duties while he fills more of a behind-the-scenes role from the dugout.

The head coach should establish a behavior that he wants his assistants and players to follow. He is the example that everyone in the program should look up to. His assistants should know how to act because they have observed him, received instruction from him, and agreed to work under him after going through an interview process in which behavior and conduct should have been key components. When the head coach observes behavior by his assistants contrary to what he deems appropriate, he needs to address it with that assistant or all the assistants in general to make sure that it doesn't happen again.

For instance, some head coaches are extremely vocal. They are always talking to their players in a positive or negative way, often arguing with umpires. The vocal coach may want his assistants to be quiet and low key. If all his assistants are like he is, the dugout can be a madhouse. On the other hand, if the head coach is quiet, he may want one or more assistants to be vocal in dealing with the players and umpires.

The head coach should make sure that both he and his assistants act in the way that he intends the staff to act. The players cannot and should not act in the same way as the head coach does. They need to focus on playing the game, not interacting with the other team, umpires, or fans. At any level of amateur sports, the head coach or a designated assistant should handle disputes with the umpire. The head coach should designate someone to confront the umpires when a dispute involves the players. This not only frees up the players to concentrate on playing the game but also assures the players that the coaching staff is backing them on controversial decisions. The umpires are most often right, and I do not condone umpire baiting from the bench, batter's box, or anywhere else, but at times I will forcefully address an umpire's decision—if for no other reason than to show support for my players.

You'll get the best response if you treat officials and umpires with respect.

Players' Conduct

The way that the players play the game and act on the field is a direct reflection of what the head coach wants his team to look like. If the coach does not control his team, everyone will realize this by their behavior on the field. The positive things—such as a team hustling on and off the field, running out every batted ball, diving for balls hit their way on defense, and encouraging their teammates—all come from the direction of the head coach or coaching staff. At the same time, the team whose players walk on and off the field, go half speed all the time, throw their equipment when they fail, or argue with umpires or with the opposing team or coaches shows a lack of control by the head coach.

With that in mind, the head coach wants to spell out to his players before the season begins exactly how he wants them to react to the various situations that will come up during a game. If they fail to react in the proper way, the coach needs to address that as well. He can do that by calling the player over and talking to him individually, or he can talk about the problem with the whole team so that all the players recognize inappropriate behavior. The coach must confront the problem and the player who created it. If the coach ignores the problem, hoping that it will go away, just the opposite will happen. The problem will fester and spread.

I personally like my players to play up-tempo baseball, always encouraging their teammates. We hustle on and off the field and never question an umpire's call. I take care of the umpires, and I will back my players when I feel that they have been cheated on a call. Of course, the coach does not need to be kicked out of the game or argue on every play, but he does need to stick up for his players and be their mouthpiece when they are subjected to poor umpiring, which can happen, particularly at lower levels.

I also talk to my players about dealing with failure in the game. I remind them that failure occurs more often in baseball than it does in any other sport. They must learn how to handle this. I do not want them throwing their helmets, bats, gloves, or any other equipment when they fail. If a player violates this rule, I confront him and remind him that his actions are not acceptable. If it happens again, I immediately take the offender out of the game. I do not tolerate uncontrolled, undisciplined behavior.

Many teams talk to, yell at, or rag their opponents. Their coaches allow this behavior and in some instances encourage it. I do not want my players talking to the other team, and I especially do not want them saying anything derogatory to their opponent. I feel that teams engage in this behavior only when they are ahead in the score. Teams that are losing become quiet, especially when they are losing by a lot. If you are ragging the other team and then fall behind by four or five runs, your players are likely to go quiet in a hurry. The personality of your team has now changed, and they will probably have a difficult time coming back. And the most important reason not to say derogatory things about the opponent is that a team with that type of behavior simply lacks class.

So with these things in mind, the coach must establish and monitor his players' conduct so that the team plays with the personality that he intends.

GAME PLAN ADJUSTMENTS

When the game begins, the coach should have an idea of what specifically he wants his team to do against the opponent. Each baseball team has a personality and certain abilities, and the coach wants to get in situations where he can play to his team's strengths and take advantage of the other team's weaknesses. If a team has good team speed, the coach obviously wants to get runners on base so that he can turn them loose. If a team excels at bunting, the coach wants to get players on with no outs so that he can use the bunting game to move them around. When the game does not play to a team's strengths, the coach needs to make adjustments. A good coach has the ability to see a weakness and take advantage of it. For instance, when the opponent brings in a relief pitcher, a coach will often turn his runners loose on the bases to shake up the new pitcher. If a defensive player gets hurt, the opposing coach will try to find a way to make his replacement field the ball or make a play, thinking that the replacement may not be as good.

When a team is behind late in the game, the coach needs to instruct his players that they must be conservative on the bases and save their outs. They do not want to run into stupid outs because outs become increasingly precious as the game progresses. Yes, the coach should have a game plan for every game, but as the game progresses he may need to scrap that pregame plan and make adjustments to put his team in the best position to win.

Pitching Changes and Managing the Bullpen

Managing the bullpen starts with a bullpen coach who responds to communication from the head coach about when to get a relief pitcher ready. A relief pitcher may be needed in a number of situations. In some cases the starting pitcher may be on a set inning or pitch count, meaning that the bullpen or pitching coach will get a relief pitcher up when the starter closes in on his limit. More often the bullpen has to respond to a situation that develops in the game. A relief pitcher may be told to get loose and be ready in case a late-inning threat develops. The bullpen coach may tell him to get ready to start the next inning or to warm up quickly in the middle of an inning.

The head coach has to think ahead, and at the high school level teams usually do not have a bullpen coach. In this case either the pitching coach or one of the other assistants must supervise the relief pitcher's preparations. If a relief pitcher is simply warming up to stay loose in case he's needed or is warming up to start the next inning, he can pace himself, working all his pitches out of both a windup and the stretch position. If the relief pitcher is going to start the next inning, he should be given time to go to the dugout, get a drink of water, and relax on the bench for a minute before going to the mound.

If a coach calls for a pitcher to get loose immediately, the pitcher needs to throw his breaking and off-speed pitches as he gets ready so that he will have everything working when he enters the game. If he does not have a chance to get completely warm, he has to accept that. The coach in the bullpen or the pitcher himself can signal to the bench by raising his cap that he has had sufficient time.

A pitching change can be a big turning point in a game, but sometimes a few words can get a pitcher back on track.

In some games, a relief pitcher may have to warm up more than once as situations dictate from inning to inning. As that occurs, the relief pitcher should throw primarily off-speed pitches as he warms up, refraining from throwing the fastball, which can further tire out his arm. If the pitcher is finally called into the game, he usually has time to throw a couple fastballs before leaving the bullpen.

The decision to make a pitching change, of course, can be a huge turning point in the game. The head coach or the pitching coach must keep a pitch count on the starting pitcher. Over the course of the season, pitchers will tend to tire and get in trouble after a certain number of pitches, especially young pitchers at a developing stage. As they reach that point the head coach should get his bullpen ready.

The coach should also know, of course, which of his relievers are rested and ready and what their strengths and weaknesses are. Obviously, if a reliever is not capable of throwing strikes from the start, he should not be used in a bases-loaded situation or any situation that puts extra pressure on him not to walk a hitter. Few starters go the distance in today's game, so a coach

needs to develop his relief pitching. He should feel confident that his bullpen can do the job and know which pitcher is best for each situation.

At the high school level, of course, a coach often doesn't have a lot of options, so the job is difficult. The question that the coach has to ask himself is this: Do I bring in a rested relief pitcher who doesn't have my starter's talent or experience, or do I stay with my tiring starter?

A coach may bring in a relief pitcher because he is capable of throwing to a specific hitter's weakness. For instance, if you're facing a hitter who you know cannot hit a breaking ball and your pitcher on the mound cannot get his curve over, you will want to bring in a relief pitcher capable of throwing a breaking ball for a strike. If your pitcher cannot spot his pitches and you are facing a hitter who has a definite weakness in a specific area, you go to your control pitcher who can attack that area and give you the best chance to retire the batter. It all goes back to knowing whether you have someone in the bullpen who can do those things. If not, you should stay with your horse (your best pitcher) and ride him.

The only time-out in baseball occurs when the coach goes to the mound for a conference with his pitcher. That conference usually occurs when the coach wants to get a point across to the pitcher, when he wants to give a relief pitcher more time to warm up in the bullpen, or when he wants to address something with the infielders, who usually come to the mound when the coach does.

Go With Your Gut

I faced a tough pitching situation in a semifinal playoff game in 1986. We started our number two pitcher, who had been very good all year. We were playing Simi Valley High School, rated number one in the nation at the time. My starter got into trouble early, and we were down 3-0 by the second inning. Our number one pitcher simply couldn't pitch, and we had used only those two pitchers in the playoffs because we had a weak bullpen. Ultimately, as we fell behind 4-1 and the game threatened to get away from us, I decided to stay with my struggling starter. Instincts and feel were part of it, and are always part of it, but basically I couldn't trust my bullpen. On that occasion, it worked out. Our starter battled to keep us in the game, and we won with a late rally. When in doubt, go with your gut.

Pinch Hitting

Pinch hitting is a skill that is not coached. Most coaches at the high school and college levels will respond to a pinch-hitting situation by looking down the bench and sending up the best hitter available. At the high school level the rules allow a coach to substitute for his starting players one time and then reinsert the starter. Therefore, a high school coach can pinch hit for a weak-hitting second baseman and immediately put him back in the game to play defense. The rule paves the way for a coach to use a number of pinch hitters during a game while keeping his best defensive players on the field.

The decision about who to pinch hit and when depends on the situation and the opposition. The coach needs to know his hitters' strengths and weaknesses. In a bases-loaded situation with one out, for instance, a pinch hitter who doesn't run well may hit into an inning-ending double play. The coach doesn't want to pinch hit a player who can't hit a curve when the pitcher is an off-speed pitcher. Another poor matchup would be a batter with a slow bat against a hard-throwing pitcher. The coach should know that these are poor matchups by knowing his players and the opposition. Most often, the percentages win out: left-handed batter against right-handed pitcher and right-handed batter against left-handed pitcher.

Most coaches reserve the team's best pinch hitter for the late innings, when the game is on the line. He may not bat in some games, but it's best to have him available for that crucial at-bat. When the game is decided early and the lead is comfortable, the coach can insert all the pinch hitters to give them an at-bat or two to keep them sharp.

The coach must let his bench players know that they play an important role in the team's success. In that context, with the game on the line, the coach wants to pinch hit with one of his best gamers, a guy who enjoys the pressure and has the best chance of succeeding.

Pinch Running

When choosing a pinch runner, as with any other substitution, the coach needs to know his players' instincts and skills. Speed alone does not mean that a player can steal bases or run the bases well. Among other things, a good base runner must be able to read a pitcher's pickoff move, react to a ball hit into the outfield gap by instinctively knowing how far he can go, and always keep the third-base coach in view so that he can react to his hand signals.

The fastest runner on the bench often does not steal bases or read the pitcher's move well when he is at first base. In that case, a coach should consider using a bunt to get him to second base, where his speed can prove beneficial, producing a run on a base hit. A coach can also insert that fast runner in a key situation at third base, where he may be able to score on a fly ball that might otherwise not produce a run. The coach should recognize, however, that the fast pinch runner with poor base-running skills and instincts can run his team out of an inning by making a mistake on the base path. An average runner with above-average instincts is often better in a pinch and should be saved for that game-on-the-line situation, just as the coach often saves his best pinch hitter.

Defensive Replacements

The defensive replacement is used most often late in the game to help hold a lead. If a team gets the lead after the third inning in a seven-inning high school game or after the seventh inning in a college game, the coach should consider going to his bench and putting in his defensive replacements. High school substitution rules allow a coach to pull his weak-fielding, good-hitting starter when he has the lead and reinsert him to hit if the lead is lost.

One of the most important adages in sports is to be strong up the middle, meaning that a coach should have his best catcher, shortstop, second baseman, and center fielder on the field in a close game, whether ahead or behind, but particularly when ahead. Naturally, if any of the players at those key positions are inept hitters, then keeping a better hitter in the game when trailing is probably preferable. Pitching and defense win games, however, and a good rule to follow is that a team's defensive replacements should have played in every game that the team has won.

CALLING PITCHES

Few high school or college catchers call their own pitches. Most coaches, from high school up, have a pitching coach who calls pitches. This system allows the pitcher to focus strictly on throwing each pitch to the called area. Most pitchers at a formative stage enjoy this because they don't have to think about what to throw or worry about making the right choice.

The head coach or a pitching coach who is calling pitches must do his homework. The coach should have an idea about how he wants his pitchers to throw to each opposing player. The scouting report should provide the strengths and weaknesses of each hitter in the opposing lineup, as well as the reserves, and the coach calls pitches on that basis. If no scouting report is available, then the coach has to adjust as the game progresses, getting a feel for each hitter as he comes to bat.

Pitch calling involves several basics:

- If you don't have a scouting report, don't throw change-ups to hitters at the bottom of the batting order (eight and nine). The change-up, a slower pitch, will speed up a slow bat and help weak hitters.

- When facing a left-handed hitter, don't throw pitches down and inside. Left-handers generally have an easier time dropping the barrel of the bat on a down-and-in pitch, and can hit it hard.

- If no scouting report is available, start all hitters with fastballs and change-ups on the outside half of the strike zone. Adjust as the game progresses. Be more concerned with getting ahead in the count with a first-pitch strike rather than trying to trick the hitters.

- Make an early evaluation of what your pitcher's best pitch is—a pitcher's stuff can vary from game to game—and make that his out pitch.

- No matter what the scouting report says, don't ask your pitcher to throw a curve or a change-up if he can't throw one. The important thing in calling pitches is to call only for what a pitcher is capable of throwing.

All teams should have a shake-off sign that a pitcher uses to shake off the pitch that has been called because he prefers to throw another in that situation. To add to a hitter's confusion, the pitcher should occasionally shake off the pitch that has been called but throw it anyway. Pitching is a matter of timing and movement, of keeping the hitter off balance and creating guesswork for the opposing bench.

COACHING FIRST BASE

Communication is the key for all base coaches. When coaching first base, the coach must immediately get the base runner's mind on the game and the situation. With young players, a hitter may get to first base and have no idea what the score is, how many outs there are, or how many bases are occupied ahead of him. The first-base coach must review all that with the player, and even if the player nods his head to suggest that he understands, the coach should instruct him to use his fingers and let the third-base coach see that he knows how many outs there are. The first-base coach should then point to any runners so that it's clear which bases are occupied.

All these instructions should take place when the runner first gets to the base and is standing on it. When the runner steps off to take his lead, he should focus his eyes only on the pitcher. The last thing that the coach tells the runner before he gets off the base is to look for the ball in the dirt, on which he might be able to advance to second. A coach who has a feel for when the pitcher is going to throw a curve, a pitch that often bounces in front of the plate, can help get the runner to second by reminding him to be heads up on the pitch in the dirt.

When the first baseman is holding the runner on base, the first-base coach should be keeping an eye on both the pitcher and his runner. He shouts, "Back" if the pitcher makes a pickoff throw. If the first baseman isn't holding the runner on base, the coach turns his back to home plate and watches the first baseman in case he breaks back to the bag for a pickoff throw from the pitcher or catcher. If that occurs, the coach alerts the runner to get back to the base. The first-base coach should also remind the runner to use his own eyes to make a decision on whether to advance to third on a hit in front of him, to left field, or to center field. The runner can see the ball in front of him and makes his own decision about whether to advance the extra base, but he should be reminded to pick up the third-base coach's direction on a hit to any other part of the field.

COACHING THIRD BASE

Coaching third base involves getting the runner to third and then getting him home. The third-base coach, often the head coach at the high school or lower levels, must make decisions that directly affect the team's ability to score. In addition, he often has responsibility for flashing signs, putting the offense in motion, and instructing the hitter to take the pitch.

The third-base coach must be aware of where the opposing outfielders are playing and be able to gauge the strength of their arms so that he can make the correct judgment about holding runners at third or sending them home on fly balls and hits to the outfield. He is coaching not only the runner at third but also the runner at second and the runner at first, who may need his help on a hit to right field. The third-base coach often has to give two arm signals back to back on the same hit, sending a runner from second home and then holding a runner from first at second.

Previous chapters have covered the technique that a runner on third uses in taking his lead, what the runner on third does when tagging up on a fly ball, and how a runner on second guards against a pickoff from the pitcher or catcher. The third-base coach is responsible for reminding the runners at those bases about those techniques and others. He has to keep an eye on the runner at second to make sure that the shortstop or second baseman doesn't creep in for a pickoff throw, and he has to make the decision and orally let the runner at third know whether to try to score on a fly ball to the outfield.

The third-base coach, in deciding whether to send a runner home from any base, has to keep in mind the number of outs, where his team is in the batting order, the speed of the runner or runners, and the arm strength of the outfielder. With two outs, he will want to score the runner from second base more often than he will with one out or no outs. If the top of the lineup is coming up, the coach may want to hold the runner or runners and give the hitters a chance to drive in the runs, especially with less than two outs. If the bottom of the order is up next, the coach will want to try to score the runner, especially with two outs. This knowledge of the lineup, the number of outs, and several other factors form a big part of the decision-making process of the third-base coach. He has to have it all in mind before the ball is hit, and he then has to make a call instantaneously.

One helpful technique for the third-base coach in waving a runner from second around third and to the plate is to back up to a position halfway between third base and the plate, so that he has more time to view the overall field situation and make a decision. The runners, however, have to know where he is going to be so that they can pick him up, and working that out in practice is beneficial.

The third-base coach must have good decision-making skills and be able to think and react under pressure. Look for those skills in your staff and put the person who has them in the third-base coaching box. If the head coach possesses those qualities, he should be the third-base coach. The buck stops with him.

POSTGAME PROCEDURES

At the conclusion of every game, teams usually follow the same etiquette with regard to the opponent. The teams usually shake hands before going their own ways. The coaches then talk to players as a group to go over the important points in the game.

The head coach should make sure that his team follows the same procedure, win or lose.

Win or lose you and your team should always show class.

Sometimes a coach or his players will not shake hands with their opponent after a loss. That behavior is not acceptable. The only time that a coach should instruct his players not to shake the opponent's hands is when he feels that doing so could set off some sort of altercation between the players. That circumstance rarely occurs, so in almost every instance the teams should shake hands after a game. If we just lost a close game, we may not feel like congratulating our opponent. Nevertheless, it's the right thing to do and shows class.

During each game, I have a little notebook in my back pocket. When I see something significant during the game, I write it down so that I can go over it with the team afterward. These notes can be about something that we did well or poorly, or something that the other team did. When we meet as a team after the game, I go over these notes with the players. I tell them that reviewing the game is how we learn. Naturally, when we win a game we have more positive things to say. When we are playing at home we do this in our clubhouse away from the parents, so it is just me, my assistants, and the players.

When we are on the road I address the team briefly at the field. We then get on the bus and head home to have a longer meeting in the clubhouse when we get back.

The players know the procedure, and we do it the same way every game. I like it this way because I want to cover these points with just my team, without parents listening in or distracting their sons. A coach should set up a postgame procedure for home and away games and stay with it throughout the year.

Coaches' Keys

1. During the game the head coach wants to feel confident that he can cover any situation. He should use the advice of assistant coaches, but the last decision is his.

2. To call pitches effectively, the coaching staff should have a good scouting report. Know what the pitcher's out pitch is and rely on it. If you don't have a scouting report, a good practice is to start all the hitters with fastballs and change-ups and make adjustments as the game progresses.

3. Count the number of pitches that your starting pitchers throw to judge when they may be getting tired. Bring your relief pitcher into the game in a situation that fits his strength. Use a control pitcher when you can't give up a walk and use a strikeout pitcher when you need a strikeout. Instruct your relief pitchers about the various routines for warming up.

3. Know your rules for pinch hitting and substitutions, and know your pinch hitters' strengths and weaknesses so that you can get the best matchup. Save your best pinch hitter for late in the game.

4. Know your runners' speed and skills. Good speed does not automatically equate to good base-running ability. Use the same rule as you do with your pinch-hitting substitutions: Save your best base runner for late in the game.

5. You can insert defensive replacements into the game early if your team has the lead, but your best defensive players should definitely be on the field if the score is tied or you have a lead late in the game.

6. Communication is the key when coaching first base. The first-base coach must remind the runner how many outs there are, what the score is, and which bases are occupied ahead of him. The first-base coach needs to keep an eye on pickoff throws and remind the runner to be alert on pitches in the dirt, which may allow him to advance.

7. The third-base coach has multiple responsibilities—getting the runners to third, getting them home, and possibly flashing all the signs to hitters and base runners. In deciding whether to try to score a runner on a hit or fly ball, the coach has to be mindful of the number of outs, where his team is in the lineup, the speed of the runner, and the strength of the outfielder's arm.

Part VI

COACHING EVALUATION

CHAPTER 15 EVALUATING YOUR PLAYERS

I believe that coaches must continuously evaluate all aspects of their program. You should evaluate players daily, in practice and games, before the season and after. You measure your assistants in the same way, but it doesn't stop with players and staff. The evaluation at the end of each season should include the way practices are conducted, the improvements needed on the field, the status of equipment, and the effectiveness of off-season fund-raisers, among other aspects.

To keep your program successful and on the cutting edge, you need to be honest with yourself, and that can only happen if you consistently reevaluate all aspects of the program, making improvements where needed and addressing problems in a deliberative and direct way.

EVALUATING YOUR TEAM

We touched on team evaluation in chapter 5, "Planning for the Season," and included approaches to setting season goals. The team evaluation should take place in the fall when you plan practices, develop an overall focus, and list the team's strengths and weaknesses in conjunction with the staff. The evaluation should touch on returning starters and what positions they play, the number of pitchers and their degree of success in the previous year,

potential newcomers, and the level of talent on the lower-level teams. No aspect is more important than any other, but the preseason evaluation should focus on potential weaknesses. Left unrecognized, they can't be corrected.

Tryouts

Tryouts for players at the high school level should be done in two settings. The first is a tryout for returning players. You can do the tryouts over a long period if your school is in a warm-weather state. For instance, in California we have from September until December to do tryouts. We practice with the returning players and the new tryout players during that period, taking advantage of the weather to enter them in a fall league and play games against other schools. During the hour that we have each day to practice, we designate certain days for intrasquad games to help us evaluate all these players. Schools located in cold-weather states, of course, have a much shorter evaluation period.

A crucial part of the tryouts is informing the players who have been in the program previously whether they have made the team. We do this by posting a list of times for each player to come in for an interview. We space these 15 minutes apart so that we can complete the process within two or three days. All members of the varsity staff sit in on the interview, with me in charge. If the player has made the team we tell him immediately, after which we discuss his strengths and weaknesses so that he is aware of the areas that we expect him to work on. If the player has not made the team, I alone explain why and welcome him to try out again next year if he has eligibility left. Cutting players is the head coach's responsibility, not his assistants'. Cutting players is never easy, but we've tried to personalize it rather than simply post a list.

For those trying out for the first time, a good method is to involve as many coaches or former coaches as possible in the evaluation process. In our section of Southern California we are allowed 10 days of tryouts with anyone who has never played baseball at the school. We divide this into two 5-day periods and make a cut after the first period, leaving a smaller, more select group for the final 5 days.

The first step on the first day of the tryouts is to divide the players into groups by position.

Getting cut is never easy, so try to personalize it as much as you can.

The pitchers and catchers are called into the bullpen to throw in front of the pitching coach. We rate our pitchers and players by the following system: 1 for a potential star, 2 for a pitcher or player who will make the team, and 3 for a likely cut. The pitching coach is also involved in rating the skills of the catchers.

Meanwhile, we analyze the outfielders and infielders in both hitting and fielding drills. While one group is fielding, the other is in the batting cage. The group at the batting cage can be divided in two—half hitting and the other half being timed in the 40- and 60-yard dashes. When two or more players are equal in fielding and hitting ability, speed can be the determining factor in a coach's decision. We test the infielders and outfielders on both arm strength and glove work, with each member of the coaching staff applying the same rating system as we do with the pitchers and catchers.

Testing outfield arms can be done by dividing the outfielders into two groups, putting one in left field and the other in right, and having them first throw to a cutoff man about 120 feet away, and then to the plate. An outfielder who can't hit the cutout man on the fly has a below-average arm. An outfielder who can throw to the plate on one hop or on the fly has a strong and potentially great arm.

We test the arms of the infielders by dividing them into two groups, putting one at third base and the other at deep shortstop. We roll balls to their right that they have to cross over to field but don't have to backhand. They then have to straighten up and make the longest throw on the infield, to first base. This test provides us with a good gauge of infield arm strength. The strongest arms, of course, need to be at shortstop and third base. The weaker arms can be at first and second base.

We also have the catchers throw to third base and second base. Here we can judge the strength of each catcher's arm and rate them from strongest to weakest.

To evaluate the glove work of the outfielders, we first give each player a chance to catch a ball that we throw to his glove side but that he has to run and catch. Then we throw a ball to his throwing-hand side that he has to backhand. We repeat this with a coach using a fungo bat to hit fly balls and ground balls to both his glove side and his throwing-hand side. This way the coaches can see how well each outfielder handles the glove.

We do the same thing with the infielders on ground balls. First, we roll a ball to the glove side and then to the backhand side. Then we hit balls a little harder using a fungo bat. Each time the player fields the ball we require him to throw to a base. This requirement makes the glove work more difficult because the player has to finish the play with a throw.

We test the catchers on their glove work in the bullpen when we have our pitchers throw. While we are evaluating our pitchers' arm strength and accuracy, we can also judge how well the catchers handle the glove.

When evaluating all these positions, especially the outfielders and infielders, we are looking for speed and quickness. The players who run fast and are quick to the ball have the qualities that we're looking for in a starter. When we do the total evaluation of these players, we try to find what we consider the five-tool high school player, the player who can run, hit, hit for power, field, and throw. Professional scouts use the same rating system when judging players. Naturally, we seldom, if ever, see a player who excels in all five areas, but when comparing players with one another, it is easy to see which players are the best at these skills. Figure 15.1 is a sample tryout evaluation. Among the things to record are the player's 40- and 60-yard dash times and an overall rank for each day of tryouts. All coaches should use the same ratings and at the end of each tryout day the ratings should be discussed while they are fresh in your mind.

When we judge the pitchers, we also like to stay with the rating qualities that major league scouts use. These areas are fastball velocity, fastball command, and off-speed or breaking ball command. We realize that many of the young pitchers who try out will not have a good off-speed pitch. Some of them may have never thrown a breaking ball. With that in mind we base most of our evaluation on their velocity and command. If a pitcher has never thrown a breaking ball, we don't see that as a problem. We believe that we can teach pitchers the proper way to throw a breaking ball, and many times pitchers have fresher arms

for not having thrown a lot of breaking balls with bad fundamentals at a young age. Figure 15.2 provides a sample of a pitcher evaluation chart. Coaches can record pertinent information of pitchers who are trying out, including any additional comments, such as notes on pitch speed and command, in the "Comments" field.

After the first day we divide the players into teams for daily intrasquad games, with the coaches meeting each day to rate the players again. We tell all players trying out for the first time to put their names on the back of their shirts so that we don't make a mistake in our evaluations. At the end of that first five-day period, we look at the ratings and eliminate the players who are not going to make the team. The surviving group then plays intrasquad games for five additional days, after which we post a list of the players who have made the team.

By employing a daily rating system involving all the coaches, we have conclusive evidence to show any player or parent of a player who was cut that his baseball grades simply weren't good enough. The more coaches involved in the evaluation process, as mentioned previously, the more accurate the evaluation is.

Evaluating Practice

A coaching staff should critique each day's and each week's practice and make any necessary adjustments. The best time to evaluate a practice, of course, is right after it ends, when the staff leaves the field. Did the workout run smoothly? Were the goals accomplished? Did the players show the right attitude and emotion? If postpractice evaluation isn't worked into each day's schedule, the sense of immediacy is lost and the opportunity to make changes the next day may be wasted. I feel strongly about doing an immediate evaluation. The coach who doesn't evaluate from day to day runs a good chance of seeing his program grow stale. You do not need to spend hours evaluating each day's practice, a routine that would be impractical for coaches who teach and have a full work schedule. You can answer the questions that I have proposed with suggestions from your staff to keep your practices

Figure 15.1   Sample tryout evaluation form

Tryout Evaluation Form

Name	Grade	40	60	Day 1	Day 2	Day 3	Day 4	Day 5	Comments

Rating:

1 = Star player

2 = Keeper, will make the team

3 = Will not make team

From *Coaching Baseball Successfully* by Mike Curran and Ross Newhan, 2007, Champaign, IL: Human Kinetics.

Figure 15.2 A pitcher's evaluation chart

Name	IP	BB	K	H	R	ER	Number of pitches	K/BB ratio	LOM	1st Ks	Fines	Comments

Pitcher's Evaluation Chart

From *Coaching Baseball Successfully* by Mike Curran and Ross Newhan, 2007, Champaign, IL: Human Kinetics.

sharp. If you videotape a player or drill, the staff or a specific coach should view that video to provide immediate feedback to the coaching staff, player, or both as a learning device. Video is still new to many programs. The key to daily practice evaluation is for the coaches to give input and make changes when necessary to reinforce the drills and skills and ensure that they progress smoothly.

Selecting Your Starters

When selecting starters at each position, having fixed criteria is important. Some coaches care only about a player's skill at playing the game. Other coaches demand hustle and a consistent work ethic or positive attitude in addition to playing talent. When we set a lineup for our first game, each of our coaches submits his choices. If the staff has been meeting regularly and discussing the players, there should be unanimity at six or seven of the lineup slots. The staff can discuss the remaining positions again, with the head coach making the final decision if a consensus doesn't emerge.

A useful rule in deciding whether to make a change in the starting lineup or pitching rotation is to let the success or failure of the team dictate the decision. If the team is winning, a coach might want to keep the same lineup and rotation even though some players are struggling. The idea here is that the chemistry is good and the team is finding ways to win while not yet click-

The coach should give his players input when necessary to make sure the skills and drills progress smoothly.

ing on all cylinders. On the other hand, a coach might figure that making a couple changes will produce more offense or a better defense, thus keeping the win streak alive.

The staff can offer advice, but the head coach must follow his instincts and make the decision. Over a long season, of course, most coaches are going to want to get all their players into the lineup at some point, keeping them sharp so that they are effective in an emergency or pinch.

Finding Roles for Your Nonstarters

When talking about finding a role, we're talking about the nonstarters. As noted earlier, things can change over the course of a season. Nonstarters can become starters, but communication is always important. The coach and his staff should meet before the season with each player projected to be a nonstarter and inform him what his role is likely to be. At Esperanza we want the player to agree to it so that he can't come back later and say that he was never told that he would be a reserve or is unhappy with his role. All players should want to be starters, but we want the nonstarters to feel that they are filling an important role.

That role might be spot starter, matchup relief pitcher, late-inning defensive replacement, pinch hitter, or pinch runner. The coach can post other game-day roles as well. He can assign a player to chart pitches, keep the scorebook, or eye the opposing coaches to try to steal signs—all jobs that can make a player feel part of the team. Communication should be ongoing.

EVALUATING GAMES

Game evaluation is a twofold job. The first evaluation involves the team's performance as a whole. The second evaluation deals with each player's performance. Just as the practice evaluation should become part of each day's agenda, the game evaluation should be part of each game-day agenda, following the final out or as soon as the staff returns from a road game.

In hiring a varsity assistant I make sure that he understands that I will expect him to stay after each practice and game for a staff meeting. At Esperanza the varsity staff frequently meets for dinner after games so that we can do our evaluations in a relaxed atmosphere, defusing any emotional hangover from the game. We normally have a midweek and a weekend game. After the midweek game the staff goes out for pizza and does the evaluation. After the weekend games (usually on a Friday) the staff and their families go to one of the coach's homes for dinner and to evaluate the game video.

I have found that the staff enjoys the atmosphere of these socially oriented evaluations and accomplishes a lot. As the head coach I continue the evaluation after the staff has left. I go over the scorebook personally to check each player's statistics, and I prepare a stat sheet with a comment about each player that I post in the clubhouse the next day. The comment will be only one or two sentences, which is enough to let the player know what I thought of his performance.

For instance, if our pitcher threw a good game, I might make this comment: "Threw three pitches for strikes, was ahead of hitters all day, a great job." On the same sheet I might criticize a player who struck out chasing pitches out of the strike zone with this comment: "Chases too many pitches out of the strike zone, needs to know strike zone." Although some of the comments will pertain to obvious issues, I want the players to get some feedback from me. In an age when communication is imperative, this method is a succinct way to let each player know what I am thinking. The comments often have particular meaning for the player who only pinch hit or pinch ran. He knows that I recognized what he did. I have posted this comment and statistic sheet after every game since the first game I coached over 30 years ago. I have learned, however, that after a tough loss it is better to sleep on it and wait until the next morning before I make my comments. Nevertheless, one way or another, the players have always responded to the comments.

Coaches' Keys

1. Coaches should continually evaluate their programs—assistants, players, facility, fundraising, and every other aspect.

2. When evaluating your team, list the strengths and weaknesses. Only then can you work to improve and compensate for your weaknesses while maintaining your strengths.

3. When conducting your varsity tryouts, call the players in individually to tell them personally whether or not they made the team. If they made the team, tell them what their role will be. When having tryouts for new incoming players, encourage your coaches to help evaluate and rate the players.

4. Coaches must set the criteria that they will use to determine the starting lineup. Work ethic, attitude, and ability are all part of this. Assistant coaches can provide input, but the head coach should make the final decisions.

5. Every player should know his role before the season and be willing to accept it. For each game create a list with a job for each nonstarter. By having roles, the reserves will stay involved.

6. Evaluate practice each day and make adjustments if necessary before the next practice.

7. Game-day evaluation involves two jobs—evaluating team performance and evaluating each player's performance.

CHAPTER 16 EVALUATING YOUR PROGRAM

Naturally, the best time to perform a total evaluation is at the end of the season. Every coach should plan on doing it, examining the good and the bad. I keep a card file on my desk and make notations during the season on items that we need to change. Often, things go wrong during the season that are too difficult to correct while the season is in progress. I find that if I don't keep notes, I'm too apt to forget those concerns when the season ends. I'd rather not leave it to chance.

I also think that the head coach should lay out his evaluation first and then bring in the assistant coaches for input. The staff should always be involved. The more trust you give the assistant coaches, the greater their contribution is likely to be.

A young coach who is coming off a difficult year may want to go to a respected coach in the area and seek his opinion on troubling issues. An outside perspective or two can be beneficial. No one has all the answers, especially a coach who is just starting out.

Doing Too Much

In 1985 my team had just lost in the second round of the CIF Southern California high school baseball playoffs. I was in my 11th year of coaching, had been to the playoffs in 9 of those years, but had not advanced past the second round. I was

depressed, but I began searching for answers about what I was doing wrong and how I could get my program to that next level and a championship. I went to the California State Junior College Championship game and watched Cerritos Junior College win the title. I saw a coach named Joe Hicks there. He had won a number of junior college state championships. I had met him before, so I went over to say hello. Well, the conversation was baseball, and in the middle of the conversation I told Joe how my teams couldn't get past the second round of the playoffs. I said, "Joe, we work on every little thing, we scout our opponents, we try to cover every minute detail. I'm getting really frustrated and I'm out of answers." Joe looked at me and said, "Maybe that's part of the problem. Maybe you're trying to do too much. You've won all of your league games doing certain things, and then you change for the playoffs. Why?" He went on to elaborate on his practices when he was at Long Beach City College. He talked about how they would prepare for a playoff game by working on the same things that they did all year while trying to cut down on the length of practice to keep their players fresh. The longer they went in the playoffs, the more he tried to keep the practices short and crisp so that his players were always fresh and enthusiastic.

Well, the next year, 1986, we won our league and made the playoffs. I put Hicks' approach into our practices during the playoffs. We didn't worry about our opponent except to be aware of their style of play. We worked on our own game. We did the same things that we had done all year and cut down our practices to keep the players fresh. That year we won the CIF (Southern California high school) Championship, and *USA Today* voted us the number one high school baseball team in the country. We turned it all around in one year. I always attribute the ability to get over the hump to that talk with Joe Hicks. I listened to a coach who gave me good advice. I put his recommendations into place, and the results were dramatic. After that 1986 season we made the CIF Finals again in 1987 and 1988. So a coach who couldn't get out of the second round of the playoffs, a coach who may have been trying to do too much, got into the finals the next three years, winning a national championship by doing less.

DETERMINING GOALS FOR NEXT SEASON

As I discussed earlier, to determine the goals for the next season a coach must look at the strengths and weaknesses of his returning and younger players to establish the areas on which he'll need to focus. Will he need to move a player from a deep position to one where he needs more depth? Will he need to recruit, if allowed? The goals that a coach needs to adjust, fix, or establish for the following season will probably hinge on two critical components—pitching and defense. No team goes anywhere without strength in those areas, and a coach must search for ways to improve his pitching and defense if he faces shortfalls.

The next goal would be related to offense. How you can improve your hitters? Your staff will need to work with individual players to make them better hitters. Improvement in the running game could also help the next year's offense. Achieving that goal will require work on stealing bases and running the bases more aggressively.

Another factor in determining the goals for the next season is to look at each player's approach and personality in relation to the game. You may need to make a point that certain players must change their work habits or other aspects relating to their approach to the game.

You may also want to work with particular players on their interaction with teammates so that they become more positive.

The preceding are some of the elements to consider when setting goals for the next season.

EVALUATING YOUR COACHES

Whether it's been a good year or a disappointing one, the head coach needs to evaluate his assistants at the end of the season, rating their performance on and off the field. He should look at their communication with the players; their knowledge of the game; and their commitment, effort, and promptness at practices and games. How did they interact with parents, administrators, and opposing coaches? Were they willing to participate in fund-raising activities?

After the head coach has made these evaluations, he needs to sit down with each assistant and discuss his performance. The assistant should be told, just as a player is told, where he was strongest and where he came up short. The head coach should be specific when criticizing his assistants and provide a solution at the same time. He should also be complimentary, emphasizing how he wants the assistant to continue using and building on his good qualities.

This occasion is also the appropriate time for the head coach to tell an assistant that he is increasing or changing his responsibility. The head coach might want an assistant to take over calling pitches or become the third-base coach or maybe flash the offensive signs. Good assistants should be rewarded with extra responsibility so that the program benefits from their ability. The head coach should give his assistants something to be excited about over the off-season.

At the same time, the head coach has to be honest and can't worry about hurting someone's feelings. The assistants reflect on the man in charge. If the head coach needs to let an assistant go, it has to be done, and the reasons must be clearly spelled out to the administration, which has to support the decision.

PLACING SENIORS

Senior placement involves trying to place graduating players in a school and program where they can continue playing. A coach who has one Division I player is fortunate; a coach who has more than one is extremely lucky. Most high school players won't be good enough to play at the college level, particularly Division I, and many won't have the desire.

Naturally, the first thing that a coach must do is find out which of his seniors want to continue playing. The time to do this used to be after their final game. I would give each of my seniors a questionnaire that probed their interest in college baseball. Did they have a particular school in mind? Did they want me to make the contact? I would review the questionnaires and then sit down with the players to discuss the reality of their choices and situation. Figure 16.1 provides a sample questionnaire.

The coach has to be honest because a young man's future is involved. All a coach can do is try to measure the player and person he has known and recommend a level that best fits the player's ability. I wrote earlier that I used to do this after the final game of the season. In today's competitive and accelerated recruiting environment, the head coach needs to speed up this process, getting a feel for the player's baseball goal after his junior year. The colleges now use that summer and fall to recruit their early signees. By the time that a player has finished his senior year, many colleges have depleted their scholarship and roster availability. The high school coach should adjust to this environment and be ready to work during the earlier period on the player's behalf. A coach can research schools for his players if they need help with obtaining information on college programs or their requirements. The coach should first go to the player's counselor to learn the player's grade point average and SAT scores and find out whether he has taken and passed the classes that he needs to get into the various schools. The counselor will also be able to provide help in the logistics of getting into the various colleges.

Several books and Web sites can help the coach research this on his own. One of the latest is *High School Athlete's Guide to College Baseball*, which provides useful information for parents and players. Contributions from more than 70 college coaches, pro scouts, and guidance counselors explain how to identify the best school for a child. See the Web site www.worldwidebaseballprospects.com for more information about this publication.

Name_____

Where do you plan to play baseball after high school?

Junior college   **4-year college**

1. _____   1. _____

2. _____   2. _____

3. _____   3. _____

Are there any particular schools or coaches you would like me to contact for you?

1. _____

2. _____

3. _____

Figure 16.1   A sample senior placement questionnaire.

From *Coaching Baseball Successfully* by Mike Curran and Ross Newhan, 2007, Champaign, IL: Human Kinetics.

A coach needs to remind his players continuously throughout their high school careers that even those with tremendous ability will not be able to play college baseball if they don't have the grades. Therefore, players should get their grades to the point that many colleges will accept them so that they can match their playing ability to the best situation. A coach needs to remind his players that life will go on long after baseball ends, and that a college degree is important to success over a lifetime.

It's Only Advice

In my second year of coaching I had a player who wanted to attend and play at Arizona State. He had been a part-time player, and I told him that he wasn't good enough to play at ASU. With his parents' encouragement, he still decided to go there and try out for the team as a walk-on. He was cut and never played again. This sort of thing happens frequently. If the player doesn't overestimate his ability, his parents do.

Of course, sometimes I make mistakes, misjudging a young player's dedication, work ethic, and ability to continue developing, physically and athletically. I had such a player in the early 1990s. He had been a two-time all-league second baseman for me but was neither drafted nor offered a Division I scholarship. He simply refused to take no for an answer. Despite two Division II offers, he told me, "Coach, I'm going to a junior college. I think I'm a Division I player and I'm going to prove it." After one year at a junior college (and they are a great training ground), he received a Division I scholarship to Georgia Tech. He ultimately transferred to Pepperdine on another scholarship, was drafted twice along the way, and has now played in the major leagues for three teams.

EVALUATING RETURNING PLAYERS

When the season ends, the coaching staff needs to sit down with returning players to discuss their future. Coaches also need to do this with lower-level players who have a chance to move up to the varsity. All aspects of the returning player's performance should be discussed—statistics, attitude, future expectations, where he can improve, how he can become a starter if he is not, and what his goals should be on the field and in the weight room. These meetings should always end on a positive note, pumping up the player for the summer and fall, and should occur when everything is still fresh at the end of the season.

EVALUATING YOURSELF AND SETTING FUTURE EXPECTATIONS

Even before conducting the player and staff evaluations, the head coach should evaluate himself, where his program is, and where it has the potential to go. He should step back and take a long look in the mirror. As I have stated previously, it is easy for the head coach to blame every negative development on the assistants, the players, or outside factors. But the buck stops with the head coach, and he should not be immune to the review and evaluation process. He needs to look at his technique, communication skills, practice preparation, game management, and every other aspect of his program, zeroing in on the major problems that developed and how he handled them. The second phase of this self-evaluation is planning for the future, and this task is best done in conjunction with the assistant coaches so that everyone is on the same page and knows what needs to be corrected and what to expect. Maintaining a successful program requires constant review at all levels. As one season folds into another, a program can grow stale if the head coach doesn't stay on top of things and isn't willing to ask himself, "Am I doing everything I can do for my baseball program?"

In the year 2003, my team had a disastrous year, finishing with 10 wins and 14 losses, the worst record of my coaching career. We were bad everywhere—pitching, defense, and offense.

At the end of that season, I sat down and wrote down all the things that I felt I did poorly or must improve on. When I finished with that list I sat down with my assistant coaches. I told them that we were going to evaluate each other's performance as coaches. I also said that at this meeting we were not going to evaluate or criticize the players. We would do that on another day. I wanted to look at myself first and figure out what was wrong with me. I also wanted feedback from my assistant coaches about what they thought I did wrong. Many times I've heard coaches who were coming off a disappointing season talk about how bad their players were, placing all the blame on them. I didn't want to take that approach. That conclusion was too easy and would lead to a band-aid approach to fixing the problem. I was going to look at myself first before I went after my assistants and the players.

We started right away in the summer changing things and making adjustments. The following year we were back in the playoffs and made it to the quarterfinals. Yes, we did change some of the things that the players did the next year, but first I evaluated myself and my assistants.

Coaches' Keys

1. The best time to evaluate a program is at the end of the season when everything is fresh.

2. When evaluating his assistant coaches at the end of the season, the head coach should consider the way in which they communicate with the players and parents; their knowledge of the game; their commitment, effort, and promptness at practices and games; and their willingness to participate in fund-raising and other off-field activities.

3. Senior placement involves trying to place graduating players in a school and program suited to their ability. Amid the accelerated recruiting environment, this process should begin after their junior year.

4. At the end of the season, the entire varsity coaching staff should sit down with the returning players and discuss their performance and future roles in the program, ending those meetings on an upbeat note.

5. Before the head coach reviews his staff and meets with returning players, he should evaluate himself, critically examining the things that went wrong and the problems that developed. He then plots future expectations in conjunction with his assistants.

INDEX

NOTE: The italicized *f* or *t* following page numbers indicate a figure or table will be found on that page. The italicized *ff* following page numbers indicate multiple figures on the page.

ABOUT THE AUTHORS

Mike Curran has coached high school baseball for more than three decades and currently serves as the head coach at Esperanza High School in Anaheim, California. His career record of more than 500 victories makes Curran one of the most recognizable and highly regarded coaches not only in the state of California but in all of the United States. He led Esperanza to win the 1986 national title and California Interscholastic Federation (CIF) titles in 1986, 1993, and 1997 and earned CIF Coach of the Year honors during those three years as well. Curran was named National Coach of the Year in 1998 and served as the District 8 representative for the National High School Baseball Association from 1990 to 1995. He holds a master's degree in education from Azusa Pacific University. Curran, his wife, Lucy, two daughters, Christie and Jamie, and son, Casey, reside in Placentia, California.

Ross Newhan is an award-winning sportswriter who dedicated 40 years of his life to covering baseball in southern California. He began his career in 1961 with the *Long Beach Press Telegram*, covering the Los Angeles Angels. Over the course of his career, Newhan won numerous writing awards, including several from the Orange County and Los Angeles press clubs. He won the Associated Press Sports Editors Award for the top news story of 1997, relating to the sale of the Dodgers, and he won the *Los Angeles Times* Editors Award for sustained excellence the following year. In 2001 Newhan was elected to the writers' wing of the National Baseball Hall of Fame and in 2002 was named the California Sportswriter of the Year. Newhan resides in Corona, California, with his wife, Connie. The couple has a son, David, who plays for the Baltimore Orioles, a daughter, Sara, and four grandchildren.

Build a winning baseball program both on the field and off

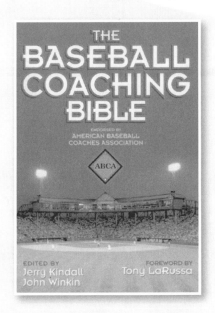

Much more than a book on skills, strategies, or drills, *The Baseball Coaching Bible* represents a landmark work for the sport. 27 of the greatest coaches the game has ever known share their keys to championship baseball, with each coach addressing the subject he knows best. Covering all aspects of coaching, the book's varied and vast amount of information allows you to pick and choose what you implement in your program in any particular season.

384 Pages • ISBN 978-0-7360-0161-8

Some books teach coaches and players what to do; *Baseball Strategies* also explains why. Developed by an all-star cast of coaches, this book is the most comprehensive resource ever written on the tactical aspects of the game. Providing the content are 18 of the game's top strategists, who show how to meet every decision-making challenge, from setting the most effective lineup at the plate and in the field to deciding what play to call and when to call it in tight game situations.

360 Pages • ISBN 978-0-7360-4218-5

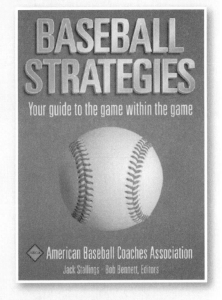

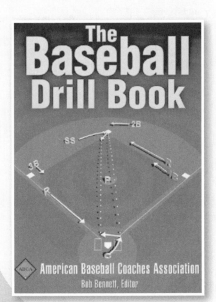

Seventeen of the game's top collegiate coaches have teamed up with the ABCA to bring you an assortment of practice activities in *The Baseball Drill Book*. Featuring 198 drills proven to improve both individual and team performance, coaching greats including Bob Bennett, Ed Cheff, Gordie Gillespie, Gene Stephenson, and Ray Tanner cover all the bases from conditioning and warm-ups to hitting, pitching, baserunning, fielding—and more.

320 Pages • ISBN 978-0-7360-5083-8

To place your order, U.S. customers call
TOLL FREE 1-800-747-4457
In Canada call 1-800-465-7301
In Australia call (08) 8372 0999
In New Zealand call 0064 9 448 1207
In Europe call +44 (0) 113 255 5665
or visit www.HumanKinetics.com

HUMAN KINETICS
The Premier Publisher for Sports & Fitness
P.O. Box 5076, Champaign, IL 61825-5076